# Martin Amis

*Brian Finney*

Routledge
Taylor & Francis Group

LONDON AND NEW YORK

First published 2008
by Routledge
2 Park Square, Milton Park, Abingdon, Oxon OX14 4RN

Simultaneously published in the USA and Canada
by Routledge
270 Madison Ave, New York, NY 10016

*Routledge is an imprint of the Taylor & Francis Group, an informa business*

Typeset in Sabon by Saxon Graphics Ltd, Derby
Printed and bound in Great Britain by
CPI Antony Rowe, Chippenham, Wiltshire

*British Library Cataloguing in Publication Data*
A catalogue record for this book is available from the British Library

*Library of Congress Cataloging in Publication Data*
Finney, Brian.
   Martin Amis / Brian Finney.
      p. cm. — (Routledge guides to literature)
   Includes bibliographical references and index.
   1. Amis, Martin—Criticism and interpretation.
I. Title.
   PR6051.M5Z65 2008
   823'.914—dc22

                                                    2007045137

ISBN10: 0–415–40291–3 (hbk)
ISBN10: 0–415–40292–1 (pbk)

ISBN13: 978–0–415–40291–0 (hbk)
ISBN13: 978–0–415–40292–7 (pbk)

# Contents

# Acknowledgments

The author and publishers thank the Wylie Agency, Hyperion/Talk Miramax Books, the Random House Group Limited, Random House of Canada Limited, and Random House Inc. for permission to quote from the fiction and nonfiction works of Martin Amis.

The author thanks California State University, Long Beach, in particular the Office of University Research, Gerry Riposa, Dean, and Mark Wiley, Associate Dean, of the College of Liberal Arts, and Eileen Klink, Chair of the Department of English, for release time granted to write this book. Thanks also to James Diedrick and Gavin Keulks for personally providing information incorporated in the book.

The publisher and author would like to thank the following for permission to reprint material under copyright:

Excerpted from *Heavy Water and Other Stories* by Martin Amis. Copyright © 1999 by Martin Amis. Reprinted by permission of Knopf Canada. Excerpted from *Heavy Water* by Martin Amis, copyright © 1975 by Martin Amis. Used by permission of Harmony Books, a division of Random House, Inc. Also published by Jonathan Cape and reprinted by permission of The Random House Group Ltd.

Excerpted from *The Information* by Martin Amis. Copyright © 1995 by Martin Amis. Reprinted by permission of Knopf Canada and by permission of Harmony Books, a division of Random House, Inc.

Excerpted from *Night Train* by Martin Amis. Copyright © 1997 by Martin Amis. Reprinted by permission of Knopf Canada and by permission of Harmony Books, a division of Random House, Inc. Also published by Jonathan Cape and reprinted by permission of The Random House Group Ltd.

Excerpted from *Visiting Mrs. Nabokov and Other Excursions* by Martin Amis. Copyright © 1993 by Martin Amis. Reprinted by permission of Knopf Canada and by permission of Harmony Books, a division of Random House, Inc. Also published by Jonathan Cape and reprinted by permission of The Random House Group Ltd.

Excerpted from *House of Meetings* by Martin Amis. Copyright © 2006 by Martin Amis. Reprinted by permission of Knopf Canada and by permission of Alfred A. Knopf, a division of Random House, Inc. Also published by Jonathan Cape and reprinted by permission of The Random House Group Ltd.

Excerpted from *Koba the Dread: Laughter and the Twenty Million* by Martin Amis. Copyright © 2002 by Martin Amis. Reprinted by permission of Knopf Canada. Also published by Jonathan Cape and reprinted by permission of The Random House Group Ltd.

Excerpted from *Yellow Dog* by Martin Amis. Copyright © 2003 by Martin Amis. Reprinted by permission of Knopf Canada. Also published by Jonathan Cape and reprinted by permission of The Random House Group Ltd.

Excerpted from *Dead Babies* by Martin Amis. Copyright © 1975 by Martin Amis. Used by permission of Alfred A. Knopf, a division of Random House, Inc. Also published by Jonathan Cape and reprinted by permission of The Random House Group Ltd.

Excerpted from *Einstein's Monsters* by Martin Amis, copyright © 1987 by Martin Amis. Used by permission of Crown Publishers, a division of Random House, Inc. Also published by Jonathan Cape and reprinted by permission of The Random House Group Ltd.

Excerpted from *London Fields* by Martin Amis, copyright © 1990 by Martin Amis. Used by permission of Harmony Books, a division of Random House, Inc. Also published by Jonathan Cape and reprinted by permission of The Random House Group Ltd.

Excerpted from *The Rachel Papers* by Martin Amis, copyright © 1988 by Martin Amis. Used by permission of Harmony Books, a division of Random House, Inc.

Excerpted from *Success* by Martin Amis, copyright © 1978 by Martin Amis. Used by permission of Harmony Books, a division of Random House, Inc. Also published by Jonathan Cape and reprinted by permission of The Random House Group Ltd.

Excerpted from *Time's Arrow* by Martin Amis, copyright © 1991 by Martin Amis. Used by permission of Harmony Books, a division of Random House, Inc. Also published by Jonathan Cape and reprinted by permission of The Random House Group Ltd.

Excerpted from *Experience, Money: A Suicide Note, The Moronic Inferno and Other Visits to America* and *The War Against Cliché* by Martin Amis, published by Jonathan Cape. Reprinted by permission of The Random House Group Ltd.

Every effort has been made to trace and contact copyright holders. The publishers would be pleased to hear from any copyright holders not acknowledged here, so that this acknowledgement page may be amended at the earliest opportunity.

# Abbreviations and referencing

Throughout the text references to Martin Amis's works are abbreviated as follows:

DB *Dead Babies*. New York: Vintage International, 1991.
E *Experience: A Memoir*. New York: Hyperion/Talk Miramax, 2000.
EM *Einstein's Monsters*. New York: Vintage International, 1990.
HW *Heavy Water and Other Stories*. New York: Vintage International, 2000.
HM *House of Meetings*. New York: Vintage International, 2006.
I *The Information*. New York: Vintage International, 1996
KD *Koba the Dread: Laughter and the Twenty Million*. New York: Vintage International, 2003.
LF *London Fields*. New York: Vintage International, 1991.
M *Money: A Suicide Note*. London and New York: Penguin, 1986.
MI *The Moronic Inferno and Other Visits to America*. London and New York: Penguin, 1987.
NT *Night Train*. New York: Vintage International, 1998.
OP *Other People: A Mystery Story*. New York: Vintage International, 1994.
RP *The Rachel Papers*. New York: Vintage International, 1992.
S *Success*. New York: Vintage International, 1991.
TA *Time's Arrow, or, The Nature of the Offense*. New York: Vintage International, 1992.
VMN *Visiting Mrs. Nabokov and Other Excursions*. New York: Vintage International. 1995.
WAC *The War Against Cliché: Essays and Reviews, 1971–2000*. New York: Vintage International, 2002.
YD *Yellow Dog*. New York: Vintage, 2004.

All references are to page numbers. References to other texts use the Harvard referencing system with full details of items cited given in the Bibliography.

Cross-referencing between sections is a feature of each volume in the Routledge Guides to Literature series. Cross-references appear in brackets and include section titles as well as the relevant page numbers in bold type, e.g. (see Life and Contexts, pp. **14–15**).

# Introduction

This book offers the reader an introduction to Martin Amis's life, work, and the wide range of critical responses to his work. Possibly the most outstanding, and certainly the best-known, novelist of his generation, Amis initially had to compete with his father, Kingsley Amis (1922–95), who was himself a leading novelist of his generation. In carving out his own fictional territory, Amis reacted against his father's realist form of social satire in favor of a self-conscious, ludic mode of fiction that was particularly indebted to Vladimir Nabokov (see Criticism, **p. 89**). This book is divided into three parts. Part 1 places Martin Amis's life in the context of the literary climate, both in Britain and the USA, and of the social, political, and cultural gestalt during his lifetime. As no biography of Amis has yet appeared, this part constitutes the most extensive biographical narrative about him to appear to date. Part 2 consists of a critical introduction to every book he has published so far—eleven novels, two collections of short stories, two autobiographical or semi-autobiographical books, and three collections of his nonfiction reviews, profiles, articles, and essays. These introductions are meant to inform the reader about the basic contents, themes, and formal characteristics of each book. Part 3 offers a more advanced examination of the major critical debates about the nature and value of his work that have appeared since he published his first novel in 1973. These debates range from Amis's rejection of British in favor of American novelistic models and the effect on the reception of his work of his superstar status in Britain, to his portrayal of women and his unique, comic use of language. Where the same book or subject is referred to more than once, cross-references have been provided in bold. The Index offers a full list of page numbers for each of these categories. So, this book is intended to offer students a comprehensive introduction to this author and to summarize and direct them to more specialist or advanced critical studies of individual works as well as of larger collections of works.

# Life and contexts

## The early years, 1949–73

Martin Amis was born on 25 August 1949. Looking back he reflects, "four days later, the Russians successfully tested their first atom bomb, [. . .] the world had taken a turn for the worse" (*EM* 1). As he grew up, Amis came to see himself as representative of a generation that had inherited a world radically different from that in which his father, Kingsley Amis, had lived, one threatened by nuclear annihilation. He concluded that his father's generation "got it hugely wrong," and that, in consequence, his own generation faced a drastically deteriorated stage of modernity, "trapped in the great mistake" (*EM* 13). Frequently Amis depicts his father's generation as the last inhabitants of an Edenic state that they had been responsible for losing: "Post-1945 life is completely different from everything that came before it. We are like no other people in history" (McGrath 1987: 194). So much of Martin Amis's outlook and work has been formed in reaction to the beliefs and writing of his father, Kingsley (see Criticism, p. 86). Martin has called his relationship to his father "a very enjoyable adversarial" one, "argumentative, but close" (Ross 1987: 24). When he came to write his memoir, *Experience*, as he was turning fifty, he significantly chose to organize the material of his own life in parallel to that of his father. The "Envoy" concludes: "I am you and you are me" (*E* 364). But the ways in which he fights off his father as much as he identifies with him are complex and contribute to the originality of the son's fictional writing. A month after Martin's birth Kingsley left Oxford with a BA to take up a position as an assistant lecturer in English at University College, Swansea, South Wales, "Swansea being the last unfilled English post of that year," according to Kingsley (Amis, K. 1991: 120). Apart from a year in the USA (1958–9), the family was to live in Swansea until 1961, when Martin turned twelve.

Martin was the second son of Kingsley Amis and Hilary Bardwell. Whereas Kingsley's father was lower middle class, a mustard manufacturer's clerk, his mother's parents were upper middle class, her father being a civil servant and her mother the daughter of a successful Victorian merchant (*E* 130). In 1946, while an undergraduate, Kingsley had met Hilary, a model, at the Ruskin School of Art. In 1948, she became pregnant, they married, and she gave birth to Philip, Martin's older brother, who was to grow up to become a graphic designer. After moving to Swansea, the family was rescued from living in a series of cramped flats (in one of which Martin slept in a drawer) when Hilary turned twenty-one in 1950 and inherited from her family £5,000 with half of which they bought their first terraced house. In 1954, the year in which their last child, Sally, was born, Kingsley published *Lucky Jim,* a novel that became a bestseller and was turned into a film in 1957. He won the Somerset Maugham Award for it, which required him to spend three months abroad. After much grumbling, he chose to spend the time with his family in Portugal. A comic satire on contemporary campus life in England, the novel propelled Kingsley into the position of a leading spokesman for a new postwar generation of disgruntled writers whom the media dubbed the Angry Young Men (others included John Osborne, Alan Sillitoe, John Braine, and John Wain). Kingsley stood for a rejection of the experimental tradition of modernism in favor of social realism and transparency. Like Charles Lumley, the rebel protagonist of John Wain's *Hurry on Down* (1954), Kingsley's Jim Dixon attacks society not in order to bring it down but in order to obtain a profitable foothold in it. Once Kingsley had done likewise, he exchanged his early left-wing views for a Blimpish reactionary stand in which he was to be joined by his closest friend, Philip Larkin, whom he had met at Oxford and who frequently visited Kingsley in Swansea and acted as Philip's godfather.

When asked in midlife about his childhood, Martin Amis exclaimed, "Childhood? What childhood?" He explained: "When Nabokov said a writer's childhood was his treasure chest, I thought 'Christ, what do I do? I haven't got one'" (Stout 1990: 34). There is little recollection of much of his childhood in *Experience.* Is this because it was so ordinary, which may be true of his years at Swansea up to the age of twelve? Or is it because once he left Swansea he went to some dozen different schools, which offered little narrative continuity? Amis has commented how, with each new school, "having to [re]make your personality [. . .] makes you conscious of how you're going down," which may explain his own later self-conscious approach to writing fiction (Ross 1987: 23). Going to so many schools also made him "quite expert at self-preservation," he has said, which he would need when faced with negative reactions to his work from his father and the press (Bigsby 1992: 169). His peripatetic schooling began when his father was invited to teach creative writing at Princeton for a year (1958–9) when Martin was ten. He recalls: "Soon I had long trousers, a crew cut, and a bike with fat whitewalls and an electric horn" (*MI* ix). The year in New Jersey, where he attended the Valley Road School, made Martin "fully Americanised, for now" (*E* 139). "America excited and frightened me," he recalled in later life, "and has continued to do so" (*MI* ix). His connection to America was destined to resume in his thirties and to play an important role in his development as a novelist with international appeal.

In 1961, Kingsley moved the family to Cambridge where he obtained a fellowship at Peterhouse. Looking back on his years at Swansea, Amis declared that life there was squalid and that he found the Welsh bitter and cruel (Michener 1986: 142). During his two years in Cambridge, where he went to Cambridgeshire High School for Boys, Martin writes that he was "overweight and undersized"—"averagely unhappy for my age" (*E* 102–3). Finding the fellowship too demanding on his writing time, Kingsley resigned in 1963 and took a year's rental on a house in Soller, Majorca, where the family met Robert Graves. But in October of the previous year Kingsley had met Elizabeth Jane Howard (b. 1923), an established novelist, at the Cheltenham Literary Festival, and in summer 1963 he left openly with her for a holiday together. Martin's mother took all three children to the rented villa in Spain and the marriage was at an end. At the time, Martin remembers experiencing "a terrible numbness and incredulity" (Hubbard 1990: 118). One possible effect on him was to implant in him what he later recognized as "an unconscious distrust of love" (E 50). He simultaneously blames the Cuban Missile Crisis of October 1962 for this effect, asserting that he, like all the "children of the nuclear age [. . .] were weakened in their capacity to love" (E 138). Both boys pined for their father. Eventually in November 1963 their mother packed them off on a plane to London and sent Kingsley a telegram that never arrived warning him that they were coming. When they turned up at Kingsley's house at midnight they were met by their father in pajamas and Jane, as Kingsley called her, in a towel bathrobe. Both boys were shocked, and, in their ensuing talks with their father, Philip tearfully called him "a cunt" (E 144–5). Still, Martin quickly grew to like Jane. During their five-day stay with their father they learned of President Kennedy's assassination. Between autumn 1963 and spring 1964, the two boys attended the International School in Palma, Majorca, "full of glamorous foreign girls" (Michener 1986: 142). After moving to the Fulham Road in London with his mother and two siblings and being enrolled in Battersea Grammar School, Martin was offered a part in the film *High Wind in Jamaica* by the director Alexander Mackendrick, a friend of Elizabeth Jane Howard's. Martin, accompanied by his mother, spent two months in the early summer of 1964 in the West Indies shooting the film. On returning to his tough Battersea grammar school in the autumn, he was immediately expelled for chronic truancy. During this period, Martin went through a "mod" phase ("too many scooter crashes") and a hippie phase ("flowered shirt, velvet suit, far more relaxing"). Looked at with hindsight, "it was all a pose," he reflected (Stout 1990: 34). In *Experience* he calls his earlier teenage self "Osric" after the highly pretentious courtier whom Hamlet calls a "water-fly" in Shakespeare's play (see Works, p. 74).

So, Martin's mother enrolled him in a crammer (tutoring school) in Notting Hill, West London, the first of many over the next three years. Instead of studying, he spent his time reading comics, "going to betting shops, smoking dope, and trolling up and down the Kings Road, looking for girls" (Michener 1986: 142). With his earnings from his part in the film he got himself a drumset and a guitar and formed various rock groups that played the youth-club circuit around the Fulham Road. The headmaster of one of the crammers he attended declared that Martin was "unusually unpromising" (Michener 1986: 140). By the time he was seventeen he had managed to pass only three O-Level examinations, one a year. He did manage to lose his virginity at the age of fifteen. When he was sixteen his father bought him and his brother a gross (144) of condoms—"it represented the all-clear," Amis explains in his memoir (E 168). In 1967, he had a six-month affair with a beautiful Jewish teenager a year older than he was. He calls her his "first love" (E 264) and would use her as a model for Rachel, the heroine of his first novel. This is the first of numerous love affairs lasting a matter of months. He was to remain a bachelor for another seventeen years. This could be a result of the model his father provided him, with his reckless philandering (which, Martin writes, "often approached the psychotic" [E 81]), and of the trauma Martin experienced when his parents suddenly separated.

When he failed his A-Level exams, which he took in the early summer of 1965, he and Philip moved into the household his father and Elizabeth Jane Howard had set up in Maida Vale (they were married that June), while his mother would remarry an academic and take Sally with her to Ann Arbor, Michigan, where her new husband was offered a teaching position. Martin and Philip continued to lead a life of truancy, drinking, girls, and dope. The next year, when Kingsley and Jane found drugs in Philip's clothes drawer and tried to ground him, he left home permanently. Martin, a year younger, was not so rebellious. Maybe this was because his stepmother took him in hand. At this time, his reading consisted almost entirely of comics and science fiction. When she asked him what he wanted to be, to her astonishment, Martin answered, "Be a writer." "But you never read anything," she said. When Martin asked her to give him a book to read, she handed him Jane Austen's *Pride and Prejudice* and refused to tell him how it ended (Howard 2003: 358). That's when he got hooked, and she proceeded to feed him books by Evelyn Waugh, Anthony Powell, and Angus Wilson. One could speculate that Martin's acquisition of a well-known novelist as his stepmother allowed him to stop rebelling against the world of literature, which, until then, he had associated primarily with his father. In the autumn of 1967, Jane found a boarding crammer called Sussex Tutors in Brighton which Martin agreed to attend and where he was coached intensively to take the O- and A-Level exams needed to qualify for Oxford University's Entrance Paper. He passed all of them, being the only one at the crammer to obtain an A in English (see Works, p. 35). During his time in Brighton, he acquired a taste for nineteenth-century literature, not just George Eliot and Dickens but also Tolstoy ("bloody good") and Henry James ("Eloquent + rather funny + polished" [*E* 109]). On securing a place at Oxford, he wrote to his stepmother at the beginning of 1968 attributing his success entirely to her influence (*E* 150). Before starting his university life, he worked in his step-uncle's record shop in Rickmansworth and went with his closest boyhood friend, Rob, to Spain, where they ran out of money and then typically waited to be bailed out by their parents. His hippie lifestyle was representative, largely a middle-class phenomenon and rarely self-supporting.

This was the 1960s, the decade of the Beatles, rock, and political activism including the *événements* of May 1968. Amis represents himself as partly the product of this era:

> In 1968 the world seemed to go further left than it had ever gone before and would ever go again. But this left was the New Left: it represented, or turned out to represent, revolution as play [. . .] There were demonstrations, riots, torchings, street battles in England, Germany, Italy, Japan and the USA. And remember the Paris of 1968: barricades, street theater, youth-worship [. . .] The death throes of the New Left took the form of vanguard terrorism (the Red Brigades, the Baader-Meinhof gang, the Weathermen). And its afterlife is anarchistic, opposing itself to the latest mutation of capital: after imperialism, after fascism, it now faces globalization.

(*KD* 11–12)

Amis's account of his later teens in *Experience* show him as an unconscious participant in both the popular culture of the time and, to a lesser extent, the politics of his generation, which set him in conflict with his increasingly reactionary father who had become a vocal defender of the Vietnam War (1964–73). Martin claims that, after he had detached himself from Kingsley's pro-war stance, he and his father argued, often bitterly, about Vietnam for thirty years (*KD* 12–13). Kingsley and Philip Larkin had been inexorably egging each other on to adopt increasingly reactionary right-wing views over the decade. A representative letter from Larkin to Kingsley on April 8, 1969 dismisses Harold Wilson's Labour government: "Fuck the whole lot of them, I say, the decimal-loving, nigger-mad, army-cutting, abortion-promoting, murderer-pardoning, daylight-hating ponces, to hell with them" (quoted in Motion 1993: 409). Subsequently, Martin has asserted, "There are many aspects of the left that I find unappealing, but what I am never going to be is right-wing in my heart" (Morrison 1990: 102). In his first term at Oxford he joined a demonstration against the Russian invasion of Czechoslovakia, affirming his distance from the Communist Party line. Although he says that during this period of his life he was politically "quietist and unaligned" (*KD* 22), his father always considered his son's political views "a lot of dangerous howling nonsense" (Stout 1990: 35).

In the autumn of 1968, Amis went up to Exeter College, Oxford University on an exhibition (financial scholarship). Almost a decade later, he contributed an essay to a book of recollections titled *My Oxford*. In it he claims to have been torn between two antithetical groupings of undergraduates: "'gnome' people" who studied all the time and never left college, and "the 'cool' people [. . .] the aloof, slightly moneyed, London-based, car-driving, party-throwing [. . .] elite" (Amis 1977: 207). He spent the first term in gnome-like isolation reading English classics avidly and preparing for his prelims (exams held at the end of the first year), concentrating on Latin, Old English, and Milton. His tutor was Jonathan Wordsworth whom Amis appears to have liked and learnt from. According to John Walsh, another student of Wordsworth, their tutor "said literary criticism started in establishing whether a piece of writing moved you or didn't, and writing about your personal response" (Walsh 2006: 7). Amis was to use him as the model for Charles Knowd, the English tutor in his first novel, *The Rachel Papers*, who at the end of the book sees right through the protagonist's literary pretensions (see Works and Criticism, pp. 37, 124–5). In his second term he did manage to acquire a girlfriend for a couple of months and passed the prelims. In his second year he began a longer affair with Alexandra Wells ("Gully"), a history fresher whose stepfather was A. J. Ayer, and led more of the life of the "cool" set of students, "[p]unting drunkenly up the Isis [. . .] stealing the odd drug from the trusting, ponderous pushers at Hertford, rather shining in classes with my derivative and journalistic essays" (Amis 1977: 212). He moved out of college, sharing a cottage with Alexandra and three others whose bizarre behavior would provide him with some of the material for his second novel, *Dead Babies* (*E* 270–2) (see Works, p. 39–40).[1]

1 In *Experience* Amis provisionally dates the undated letter referring to this period "[Autumn 1971]". But by then he had left Oxford, while in the letter he refers to it being "Finals Year," that is, 1970–1, which would place this letter in Autumn 1970.

But in his third year (1970–1) he reverted to the life of a gnome to prepare for finals. In the process, he left Alexandra and the cottage they shared to live once again in college. Although he was to continue the relationship with her on and off for several years, he showed a characteristic ambivalence about being "tied down" to her and "wasting the best years of [his] life" (*E* 232). Alexandra said that while he was "very funny, very intense, romantic," the problem was that any minute he would take off, which meant that "while you're with him, you're obsessed" (Shnayerson 1995: 160). His attendance at a series of seminars given by Northrop Frye began his separation from F. R. Leavis's moralistic approach to literature. Frye's definition of literature as "a *disinterested* use of words" (*E* 30) made a big impact on Amis (Wachtel 1996: 53) (see Criticism, p. **138**). In summer 1971 came finals: "The nine three-hour papers came in a heroic blur. I got a formal first, coming in third in that year" (Amis 1977: 213). A formal first is the highest bachelor's degree awarded.

In the autumn of 1971, Amis first planned on staying at Oxford to write a post-graduate thesis on Shakespeare. But when Jonathan Wordsworth, his tutor, challenged him to take a year off to write a novel, he accepted it and left both Oxford and the parental home. He notes in *Experience* that he was now addressing letters home exclusively to Jane, his father having opted out of this parental chore. His comment ("So Dad has dropped out, rather hurtfully in retrospect, now that I know how many letters he wrote to everyone else" [*E* 250]) indicates the extent to which he repressed his sense of rejection at the time. In fact, Kingsley was opting out of all things to do with running the house, parenting his children, or his shared social life with Jane—one cause of her eventual break with him. But his son proved more forgiving. The absent or indifferent parent tends to become by default unusually powerful. Such a figure can leave the child seeking throughout its life to win that parent's love and approval. Martin was no exception. As he told one interviewer, "I suppose we all are trying to please our fathers" (Trueheart 1991: B2). *Experience*, his memoir, is as much about his father as it is about himself: "it feels like a duty to describe our case," he explains as part justification for the book (*E* 7). *Koba the Dread* ends with an "Afterword: Letter to My Father's Ghost." In it, he admits that six years after his father's death he still spends a lot of time in his father's mental company (*KD* 271). This difficult, compelling relationship with his father becomes even more complex once the son has established himself as a novelist of equal or greater stature to that of his father. Near the end of *Experience* he has a dream a year after his father's death in which his father appears to him not as a shade but as a "messenger from my own unconscious, naturally." "But," he continues, "that's all right. Because my mind is his mind and the other way round" (*E* 363). Martin's father alarmingly appears to have entered and become a part of his unconscious.

Amis worked for four months in an art gallery in Mayfair, in the heart of London's West End, and for another three weeks for a Thompson advertising agency that "seemed to be entirely peopled by blocked dramatists, likeably shambling poets, and one-off novelists" (*E* 34n). He happily left the ad agency when Terence Kilmartin, the Literary Editor of the *Observer*, hired him as an untried book reviewer. Kilmartin was impressed with the businesslike letter of application that Martin sent him in which he abstained from presuming on Kilmartin's long acquaintance with Kingsley. When Kilmartin showed Martin's first review around, "[p]eople thought it was the work of someone who'd been reviewing for twenty years" (Michener 1986: 140). From November 1971, Amis reviewed for the *Observer* works of literary criticism and novels by such authors as William Burroughs, C. P. Snow and Alan Sillitoe. In *The War Against Cliché* Amis writes that "[e]njoying being insulting is a youthful corruption of power" for which he has subsequently lost his taste (*WAC* xiv). In these early years, he will dismiss a novel by Iris Murdoch in a scathing sentence: "On the face of it Miss Murdoch seems to be doing little more than guiding the pens of a few Texan thesis-writers" (*WAC* 86). J. G. Ballard's *Crash* is even more economically put down in a brief phrase: "an exercise in vicious whimsy," an opinion he later revised (*WAC* 97).

The reviews of his apprentice period already show the sophisticated wit and linguistic facility that characterize his later writing. For instance, he is unsparing in his treatment of the sixty-seven-year-old C. P. Snow's attempt to portray the younger dissident generation in *The Malcontents* (1972):

> During a party in which LSD is being doled out, one of the boys, Bernard, wanders out of a fifth-floor window. The protagonists spend a lot of time musing about whether someone might have spiked his beer with acid (thus perhaps giving Bernard the impression that he could fly), but finally dismiss the idea as too fantastic to be true. Unless they had spent their university lives entirely behind drawn blinds they'd have dismissed it instantly as far, far too *corny* to be true. If the publicity were anything to go by, you would barely be able to step into the street nowadays without seeing some drug-crazed youngster being hosed off the pavement.
>
> (*WAC* 130)

Here Amis sweeps aside as archaic the older generation of writers, while already displaying his comic penchant for verbal excess that marks his difference from his predecessors. Style is the key to the judgments he makes. After expressing grave doubts about the moral tenor of Angus Wilson's *As If By Magic*, Amis confirms his feeling that the novel is a failure by pillorying what he calls "the scruffiness of much of the writing": "Americans saying 'Noo York' and 'anyways', hippies using 'like' as if they were rustics, the word 'delicious' appearing seven times in as many pages, the whole book riddled with repetitions, unintentional rhymes, jangles, even solecisms" (*WAC* 75). For Amis, style is inseparable from what it conveys (see Works and Criticism, **pp. 82, 147**).

His contributions to the *Observer* included twelve reviews of science fiction between April 1972 and May 1974 under the pseudonym of "Henry Tilney" (a character in Jane Austen's *Northanger Abbey*). This use of pseudonym suggests that from the start of his literary career he was shaping his public persona. It was not until August 1974 that he felt sufficiently confident to allow his own name to be used for a review of science fiction (see Works and Criticism, **pp. 67, 134**). By the summer of 1972, Amis was working full-time as a trainee editorial assistant with the *Times Literary Supplement* (*TLS*), the most prestigious British publication in the field of quality book reviewing. It still published only unsigned reviews (until 1974 and the arrival of John Gross as its new editor). In *The War*

*Against Cliché* Amis confesses to having reviewed that year a book, *Coleridge's Verse: A Selection*, edited by William Empson (one of his heroes) and David Pirie, which he read, then sold, and then reviewed. This led him to criticize the editors for omitting the prose gloss from *The Ancient Mariner* when in fact it had been included as an appendix (see Criticism, **p. 95**). Protected by the anonymity of *TLS* reviewers at that time, Amis was nevertheless compelled to issue an embarrassed apology when Empson wrote a letter of protest. Nevertheless, Amis had the generosity to end his anonymous response with the assertion that "Professor Empson always writes like an angel" (*WAC* 178–81). This early humiliation perhaps contributed to the highly professional standards Amis has adopted as a reviewer ever since. While still in his twenties Amis rose from trainee status to becoming, under the indulgent editorship of Arthur Crook, the Fiction and Poetry Editor of the *TLS*, making him from early on a powerful figure in the London literary world. He was already an established reviewer of stature before his first novel was published.

At this point in his life, Amis is on the one hand still the tearaway young man, using dope and speed, drinking with his rebellious friend Rob, and womanizing. He cannot get himself to live with Alexandra although he continues to see her, while dating other women such as Tamasin, the daughter of the ailing poet Cecil Day Lewis, the latter who died of cancer in Kingsley's house in May 1972. He describes his appearance at this time as "a nightmare of sideburns, flares and dagger-collared flower shirts" (Amis 1992: 18). On the other hand, he has developed the "gnome" side of his personality with which he determinedly forges a career in the literary world. His circle of acquaintances is widening to include many of the up-and-coming literary talents of his generation: Craig Raine, the poet who had tutored him; Julian Barnes who began reviewing for the *TLS* in 1973; Clive James, whom he met at the *Observer* where James was television critic from 1972; and Christopher Hitchens ("the Hitch"), who was to become his lifelong friend, whom he first met in 1973.

He had set his mind on a career as a novelist earlier. While a student at Oxford he had begun trying out his "first paragraphs of fiction (scenes, descriptions)" (*E* 240n). As soon as he left Oxford, he began work on the initial draft of his first novel, *The Rachel Papers*, which he wrote before and after work (even at work occasionally) and during weekends. He based the book on his year spent at crammers in order to get admitted to Oxford. Within a year, the first draft was done. He spent his summer holidays in 1972 rewriting most of it, completing the typescript by November. Near the end of the rewriting period he had a conversation with his father about literary style, in the course of which Kingsley gave him the only literary advice he would offer. In effect, Kingsley insisted that a good writer should not repeat within a short space prefixes or suffixes such as *-ing*, *-ics*, *-tions* and the like. On going back over the typescript, Martin found to his dismay what he called "doggerel"—"It's all 'the cook took a look at the book,'" he told his father—and revised accordingly before sending it to the publisher (*E* 22–3) (see Criticism, **p. 87**). He has said that this novel was the only one that he significantly rewrote on the advice of his female editor at Jonathan Cape. The editor pointed out a formal inconsistency in the typewritten second draft: some chapters failed to return the narrator to the eve of his twentieth birthday. By the time he rewrote this aspect of the novel (1973), he was already well into writing the first draft of his second novel, *Dead Babies* (Reynolds and Noakes 2003: 12–13). Amis used not just the same publisher (Jonathan Cape) as his father but also his father's agent, Pat Kavanagh (who was to marry Julian Barnes). Was the speedy acceptance of his first novel an instance of nepotism as some of the British press were to charge? Amis's response has always been the same: "Any London house would have published my novel out of vulgar curiosity" (*E* 25n). If any nepotism was involved, it was not activated by his indifferent father but by the publishing industry's desire for instant name recognition. Some of the reviewers felt that it must have been particularly difficult for Amis to emerge from behind his father, but Martin claims that on the contrary, "his shadow served as a kind of protection" (*E* 35).

The *Rachel Papers* was published on 15 November 1973 (when Amis was twenty-four) in a very small print run (see Works, p. 35). Given a minute advance, Amis threw his own launch party at the expensive maisonette he was temporarily sharing with Rob and his girlfriend. His father was present to celebrate his son's declaration of fictional independence. *The Rachel Papers* both resembled Kingsley's first novel, *Lucky Jim*, and offered a stark contrast to it (see Criticism, p. 87–8). Like *Lucky Jim*, it was semi-autobiographical, about a young man's coming of age. Yet, it clearly announced its generational difference in its metafictional approach to somewhat similar subject matter. Reviewers were quick to make the comparison. After opening his review for the *TLS* with "Ah, *Lucky Jim* thirty years on, you're meant to feel when you start to read," Blake Morrison goes on to suggest that "only a really clever and obnoxious author would do as Martin Amis does and exorcize it by imitation" (Morrison 1973: 1389). When the novel was published in the USA in April of the following year, American reviewers followed suit. Thus, L. E. Sissman wrote in the *New Yorker* that the novel showed Martin "extending his father's mastery of the comic novel for a second generation" while insisting that the son was "quite his own man" (Sissman 1974: 185) (see Criticism, p. 95).

One way of understanding Amis's fictional oeuvre is to view it as the ambiguous response to his father's work to which he is equally indebted and against which he strongly reacts. *Lucky Jim* is a novel of social and especially cultural protest; the pseudo-estheticism of provincial university culture is seen as the enemy of real life to which Jim escapes at the end of the book. *The Rachel Papers* also satirizes contemporary literary/esthetic pretensions, but these belong not to the establishment but to the book's protagonist. Amis has said that Charles, its protagonist, like a literary critic, is "someone who tries to turn literature to his own advantage" (Haffenden 1985: 10). The irony is not directed at the pretensions of a stratum of society, as it is in *Lucky Jim*; it is used at the narrator/protagonist's expense. Amis was fond of quoting Nabokov's edict that nowadays "you don't punish villains, [. . .] you show them as ridiculous" (McGrath 1987: 191). Kingsley totally rejected the ironic distance that Nabokov cultivated in his fiction, and Martin's use of it was one of the ways in which he distanced his coming-of-age novel from that of his father. So, as James Diedrick points out, *The Rachel Papers* is not just a coming-of-age novel, nor is it simply a parody of that genre; it is also a parody of a specific instance of that genre, *Lucky Jim* (Diedrick 2004: 38). As Amis remarks in *Experience*, "My life looked good on paper where almost all of it was being lived" (*E* 33) (see Criticism, p. 133).

In 1973, at the age of twenty-four Amis had yet to adopt his own stance on domestic and international politics. Yet, his never-more-than-partial adoption of the hippie outlook of the later 1960s and early 1970s was more than a simple pursuit of the hedonistic life. Youth culture merged with the counterculture of the 1960s, so that innovations in styles and fashions came to be identified with innovations in attitudes represented by such loose organizations in Britain as the Campaign for Nuclear Disarmament (CND) (which Amis never joined—his commitment came later) and the New Left. This was the period in which the icons of the counterculture were R. D. Laing, a psychiatrist opposed to traditional psychiatry, and Herbert Marcuse, a radical philosopher who championed a German idealist belief in spiritual freedom. Even rock music, which Amis briefly flirted with, gave voice to a radical break with the postwar ethos. The wide availability of the contraception pill from 1962 onwards caused a major change in sexual attitudes and ideas about the family. If one looks at the range of Amis's reviews up to 1973, it becomes obvious that his interests spread well beyond those of fiction, poetry, and literary criticism. Three reviews show an early fascination with the subjects of sex, strip clubs, and pornography. The review of *The Best of Forum*, a collection of the magazine's articles and letters on sexual behavior, makes fun of its no-nonsense attitude ("If it stirs, the suggestion is, you ought to want to go to bed with it") and concludes in wider terms: "the liberated society tends towards its own brand of triteness" (*WAC* 58). There is a review of David Bowie's "Farewell Gig". He reviews George Steiner's book about the 1972 Fischer–Spassky World Chess Championship with its Cold War resonances. Even his literary reviews focus more widely on one of Leavis's pseudo-sociological disquisitions, *Nor Shall My Sword: Discourses on Pluralism, Compassion and Social Hope*, or on Alan Friedman's *Hermaphrodeity: The Autobiography of a Poet* (back to sexual diversity again). A final instance of his eclectic and original taste is his review of the 1971 *Guinness Book of Records* in which he lightly touches on the enlarged conception of *Homo sapiens* that each volume gives him. For a young man of twenty-four, Amis is already showing a conviction that literature is part of a wider response to contemporary civilization, which is his true subject. Yet, literature can and should use language creatively, a criterion he will apply to every kind of written material with which he comes into contact.

## Emerging from his father's shadow, 1974–84

It is ironic that Amis's first novel, like his father's before him, won him the Somerset Maugham Award for the best literary work by a writer under the age of thirty-five. This is the only literary award Amis was to receive until the next century. The award specified that the recipient should go abroad to spend the money. Unlike his father, who called it "a deportation order" (*E* 4), Amis happily used it to join his mother in Ronda, southern Spain, where she had settled with her third husband, an impoverished Scottish lord (Kilmarnock), Alistair Boyd, and their two-year-old son, Jaime, Amis's half brother. His mother was holding things together by running a bar there. She lived in a house next to a palace with the same name, Mondragón. Amis used a room in the Palacio Mondragón to work on the second draft (a typescript) of *Dead Babies*. Even after he took to a computer, Amis still opted to write the first drafts of his fiction in longhand ("There is something sensual about [it] that has to do with a slightly painterly feel," he says [Richards 2000)). It also enabled him to keep the right-hand page for headings, notes, arrows, and the like. He would type the second draft after which he would do a lot of typed revision.

On his return to London in 1974, Amis quit the *TLS* to become the Deputy Literary Editor under Claire Tomalin of the *New Statesman*, a weekly left-wing periodical for which he had been doing reviews since January 1973. He found himself working with two committed Trotskyists: Christopher Hitchens had already established himself as an iconoclast, stridently attacking Kissinger, the Vietnam War, and the Catholic Church, among other things; James Fenton had joined the *New Statesman* in 1971 and quickly become a political journalist for it while continuing his career as a poet. Under their influence, Amis moved "to the libertarian left of centre," as he put it. By this time, his father had moved much farther in the opposite political direction, and father and son "disagreed on every issue along (approximately) party lines" (*E* 191n). However, Amis never subscribed to his friends' Trotskyist line. As he explained later, "what they were after was to be violent and right at the same time," two positions that Amis, who finds violence "meaningless," considers incompatible (Heawood 2002: 18). Between 1974 and 1978, Amis wrote for the *New Statesman* not just reviews of novels by the likes of Philip Roth, Kurt Vonnegut, Anthony Burgess, and his beloved Vladimir Nabokov; he also produced profiles of John Braine, Peter Parker (in a series on "Captains of Industry"), and the television personality Esther Rantzen, reviewed a number of films including *Emmanuelle*, reported on the 1977 Cannes Film Festival in May as well as the Blackpool Tory Conference in October 1977, and wrote numerous television reviews on a wide range of subjects: programs on cannabis, drinking, the late 1960s in America, *Top of the Pops*, the Royal International Horse Show, and the Rolling Stones in concert at Earls Court. This eclectic range of interests confirms that Amis was both fascinated by and in touch with a wide swathe of popular and high culture in the 1970s.

Early in 1974, Amis moved to a dust-filled bedsit in Earls Court. Despite enjoying his own bachelor pad, he still spent many weekends and Christmas holidays at his father and Jane's house in Hadley Common on the northern outskirts of London where he felt more secure than anywhere else (*E* 53). By 1974, he was entering a series of short-lived relationships with women. During the time that he was dating Julie Kavanagh (half sister to Pat Kavanagh, his agent), who was then the Editor of the trade journal *Women's Wear Daily*, he recounts a party at which he was so strongly attracted by another woman, Lamorna Seale, that he disappeared into the bushes with her to be met on his return by an understandably tearful Julie. Lamorna was married at the time, but the marriage was not going well and was sexless. Three years later (1977), Amis was told by Lamorna that their act of abandon had led to the birth of a daughter, Delilah. The following year Lamorna hanged herself. Her husband, Patrick Seale, remarried and brought Delilah up as his own daughter. Julie Kavanagh found Amis "one of the most wondrous and at the same time cruelest people" she had known: "great affection, but dark moods" (Shnayerson 1995: 161). "Work is his main love," she concluded. "I think, to Martin, women are about equal to a game of Space

Invaders or pinball" (Michener 1986: 140). Next, Amis reconnected with Tina Brown, who was already famous at Oxford where they first met. In the summer of 1974, when he fell in love with her, she was working as a journalist for the London *Sunday Times*. But he quickly fell into the pattern that was to mark his bachelor years of the next decade. His passion diminished, and Tina went on to pursue her incredibly successful career editing *Tatler*, followed by the American *Vanity Fair*, then the *New Yorker*. Tina remarked later that Amis must be emotionally lacking because he had never had his heart broken (*E* 50). They remained friends, and Tina commissioned him to write numerous articles and reviews when she was Editor of the *New Yorker* on subjects from tennis to Philip Larkin and Jane Austen, as well as an important piece on the Los Angeles porn industry for the magazine *Talk* that she co-founded in 1998 and that ran until 2002. This essay was to provide Amis with valuable research material for *Yellow Dog* (see Works and Criticism, **pp. 32, 64, 140**).

Between finishing *Dead Babies* and starting *Success*, Amis began writing a novella that reveals an early penchant for authorial intrusion in his own work. Titled *Me*, its central character was Martin Amis who was going to summon his past fictional characters, such as Charles from *The Rachel Papers* and Andy Adorno from *Dead Babies*, and put things right with them by writing what they asked him to. It was to end by having them kill him. But it quickly proved too difficult to write, and he put it aside (Haffenden 1985: 12; Bellante and Bellante 1992: 4). *Dead Babies* was published in Britain in October 1975 (see Works, **p. 38**). From the start, it elicited strong reactions. This was the first of his books that his father could not get on with or finish. This "was like a blow to the solar plexus," Amis recalled (Brockes 2003: 2) (see Criticism, **p. 89**). The New Fiction Society rejected the novel as a selection for the Arts Council's book club. Its Chairman, Frank Kermode, declared, "I find it almost as unpleasant as the author intended it to be" (Sutherland 2001: 6). Ironically, Amis was a member of the Arts Council's Literature Panel at this time. Some of the reviewers were alienated both by Amis's choice of subject matter and by his vivid physical descriptions. In *Encounter*, James Price characterized Amis's technique as "a kind of literary *tachisme* [action painting], splattering the page with physical and visceral epithets in a furiously excremental manner" (Price 1976: 68). Jerome Charyn claimed that the book "aims to shock and disgust, and it certainly succeeds." But he recognized that it was intended to be a satire "about the nature of civilization, and the world it portrays is quite extraordinarily repulsive" (Charyn 1976: 3). At least one reviewer, John Mellors, drew attention to the epigraph, a quotation from Menippus in which he states that the subject of the satirist "is not tomorrow [. . .] it is today" (Mellors 1976: 582). The novel shows Amis by his midtwenties turning on and exposing for its emptiness the counterculture he had only ever partially belonged to. *Dead Babies* was published in January 1976 in New York and issued as a British paperback in 1977 with a new title, *Dark Secrets* (the original title being thought too morbid to sell well).

Amis's life in the later 1970s was bound up with his life at the *New Statesman* where many of his closest friends worked or for which they were occasional reviewers. Amis had already met Ian McEwan whose first work of fiction, *First Love, Last Rites*, was published the same year as *Dead Babies*. In 1977, Julian Barnes, who had been doing reviews for the *TLS* since 1973 when Craig Raine introduced him to Amis, became the Deputy Literary Editor of the *New Statesman* under Amis, now its Literary Editor. Three years older than Amis and not yet published, he too became a close friend. That year, Christopher Hitchens was responsible for introducing Amis to the work of Saul Bellow who quickly entered the pantheon of Amis's most admired authors. He acted as a balance to Nabokov, countering Nabokov's ironic detachment with his own form of higher autobiography, as Amis thought of it (see Criticism, p. 91). The following year, Hitchens gave a foretaste of his later swing to the right in politics when he left the *New Statesman* for the Tory daily newspaper, the *Daily Express*. Amis ironically recalls how he found himself defending the left against his Trotskyist friend when they fought on the floor of an Irish pub in Piccadilly Circus after Amis had accused Hitchens of "taking the rich man's shilling" (E 259). Their friendship survived this and many other such disagreements.

Amis's third novel, *Success*, was published in April 1978 (see Works, p. 40). It describes the way two stepbrothers, one advantaged, the other suffering from a lack of material success, exchange positions in the course of a year. Its subject centers on the British class system, which might account for the fact that the book was not published in the USA until nine years later, after *Money* had brought his name to prominence there. Kingsley managed to reach the end of this novel, but his verdict was mixed: "The beginning and the end worked, but the middle didn't" (Riviere 1998: 117). As most reviewers recognized, *Success* is another portrait of 1970s Britain. Paul Ableman is representative of British critics when he wrote, "the book is a parable about the decline of the old order in England and the new raj of the yobs" (Ableman 1978: 23). The novel also illustrates a difference between Martin and his father's generation of novelists: Martin preferred to write about working-class and upper-class characters. In his opinion, the middle class about whom his father wrote had been exhausted as a subject. Reviewers of *Success* showed the beginnings of an understanding that, as Nicholas Tredell writes, "here was a writer who was starting to create an oeuvre, a distinctive body of work of his own" (Tredell 2000: 34).

What was becoming evident was that Amis was, as Tom Paulin wrote in his review of *Success*, "deeply sensitive to the mood of the late 1970s" (Paulin 1978: 75). In *Experience* he calls the 1970s "the joke decade" (E 26). *Dead Babies* reveals what Amis has called the "dark underside of hippiedom [. . .] the blood of Sharon Tate on the wall" (Pulver 2001: 14) (see Works, p. 39). With the Oil Crisis in 1973, Britain had witnessed a leap in inflation that set the classes at war. Nineteen seventy-three was the year when the Tory Prime Minister Edward Heath put the country on a three-day week in an unsuccessful attempt to defeat the Miners' Union's strike for higher pay. After the miners had brought down Heath's moderate Conservative government, the Labour governments under Harold Wilson and James Callaghan found themselves at the mercy of the trade unions, which, as Amis has written, "eternally discredited [. . .] both factions of conventional governance" (*WAC* 21). At the time, the country seemed about to fall apart: "everything seemed ready for the terminal lurch [. . .] It was class war" (*WAC* 116) (see Works and Criticism, pp. 42, 106). It was this polarizing political impasse that brought Margaret Thatcher to power in 1979 and ushered in a very different cultural climate. Amis was already disaffected with the hippie ethos, which he saw as responsible for the new age of yuppiedom. Yet, while voting for a Labour government that pledged to transfer wealth from the rich to the working class, Amis continued to argue with Hitchens about Communism: "Rule by yobs. That's what you want," he would shout at him. "Why?" (*KD* 23). Still, in the 1980s, he was to become adamantly opposed to Thatcher's policies and outlook.

Amis's bachelorhood continued along predictable lines: a brief public engagement to Angela Gorgas, a model; a two-year affair with Emma Soames, Winston Churchill's granddaughter, journalist on the *Evening Standard* and then Editor of *Tatler*, whose parents' house and dinners made Amis reflect, "how much stuff there was about class in those days" (*E* 24n); and Mary ("burning fiery") Furness, a writer and editorial assistant on the *New Review* for whom he left Emma and who claimed later that Amis preferred the company of men to women; Victoria Rothschild, daughter of the third Baron Rothschild; Claire Tomalin, literary editor of the *New Statesman* before him—the list could be extended. But his writing career was booming, and his earnings were becoming the cause of envy to his father, who wrote bitterly to Philip Larkin: "Did I tell you Martin is spending a year [1979] abroad as a TAX EXILE? Last year he earned £38,000. Little shit. 29, he is. Little shit" (Amis, K. 2001: 871). Even taking into account the ironic tone, remarks like these reveal the underlying tension between father and son. This tension may account for Amis's toughness, his need to father himself, so to speak, and his competitiveness both in the literary field and when playing friends at tennis or snooker.

In 1979, Amis left his job at the *New Statesman* and turned into a full-time writer. He spent the fiscal year 1979–80 abroad. As his mother had returned to England in 1977, he spent his time primarily in Paris, where in seven months he wrote *Other People* (*E* 250). He returned to London in the spring of 1980. In 1980, *Saturn 3*, a science-fiction film for which he rewrote the screenplay, was released. It bombed, but his experience of being hired to do additional rewrites for Harvey Keitel and Kirk Douglas provided him with source material for his next novel, *Money* (see Works, **p. 47**). He summarized his experience with Hollywood as "head-doctoring and kissing ass, and writing these characters as they [. . .] idealised themselves" (Pulver 2001: 14). That autumn, he wrote an article for the *Observer* in which he charged that the American writer Jacob Epstein had plagiarized *The Rachel Papers* in his first novel, *Wild Oats*. Amis's conclusion was that "Epstein wasn't 'influenced' by 'The Rachel Papers', he had it flattened out by his typewriter." At the same time, Amis generously called Epstein "a genuinely talented writer" (Amis 1980b: 26). When Epstein only removed fourteen of the fifty sizable chunks that Amis claimed he had lifted verbatim, Amis was further infuriated. The account in the *New York Times* of the exchange between the two authors brought Amis's name to the notice of many American readers who had never heard of him before. That October, Jane finally left Kingsley after he refused to agree to join Alcoholics Anonymous. This produced a crisis in the family as Kingsley was thought incapable of looking after himself. Martin and Philip engineered the unconventional but workable arrangement for his mother, her third husband, and their son, who were living in an impoverished state in the Midlands, to move to London and set up house with Kingsley in London. This ménage lasted until Kingsley died. Asked whether he regretted leaving his first wife, Kingsley replied, "Only all the time" (Hawkes 1997: 25).

*Other People* was published in England in March 1981 (see Works, **p. 42**). Because it recounts the reactions of a woman (his first female protagonist) who appears to be suffering from amnesia and who sees everything as if it were for the first time, a number of reviewers labeled this a Martian novel after the school of poetry initiated by Amis's friend, Craig Raine, with his poem "A Martian Sends a Postcard Home" (see Works, **p. 44**). Both writers employ a form of defamiliarization that gives rise to highly original images and perceptions. In a letter to Robert Conquest, Kingsley wrote dismissively that it was "like a novel by Craig Raine, well not quite as fearful as that would be I suppose" (Amis, K. 2001: 916). Kingsley is even more outspoken in a letter to Larkin: "Have you actually tried to *read* Clive Sinclair and Ian MacEwan (mcewan?) and Angela Carter and M\*\*t\*\*m\*\*? Roll on is all I can say boyo. Fucking roll on" (Amis, K. 2001: 950–1) (see Criticism, **pp. 86–7**). Amis subtitled the novel *A Mystery Story*, and the majority of reviewers confessed that the mystery remained one to the end. Subsequently, Amis said that he had to admit failure in this respect, although he went on to explain how the mystery is solved within the book (Haffenden 1985: 17–18) (see Works, **pp. 44–5**). What a few early reviewers like Geoffrey Stakes, Bernard Levin, and Victoria Glendinning came to perceive was that this novel, despite the fact that it continued to echo earlier novelists, especially Nabokov, departed from Amis's earlier oeuvre in important ways. For Levin, it was "a *rara Amis* indeed" (Levin 1981: 43). Glendinning wrote that it was unlike anything else she had read at the time (Glendinning 1981: 320). It is less derivative, less up-to-the-minute, less concerned to shock, and has more of a distinctive narrative voice (see Works, **pp. 42–3**). It also explores the nature of personal identity more subtly and interestingly than do his earlier three novels. At the time he was writing this novel, Amis contributed a short piece to the *New Review* on the current state of literary fiction in Britain. In it he explained that what he was trying to do was to write "a novel that is as tricksy, as alienated and as writerly as those of, say, Robbe-Grillet while also providing the staid satisfactions of pace, plot and humour with which we associate, say, Jane Austen" (Amis 1978: 18). While Amis most often would downplay plot, *Other People* seemed to be taking him in the direction he outlines here—a strange combination of the avant-garde (antirealist) and established literary (realist) traditions.

Amis had already started work on his next novel, *Money*, in November 1980. Before *Money* came out he, published *Invasion of the Space Invaders*, a witty nonfiction book devoted to the obsession with video games that he experienced for a time. During the period he was writing and revising it, he was spending considerable time in America. Hitchens had emigrated there in 1981. Meantime, Amis had met Antonia Phillips, an American from a wealthy, intellectual New England family. She had grown up in Europe, spoke four languages, and was an academic who specialized in esthetics. When Amis met her at the *TLS,* she had been recently widowed by Gareth Evans, a brilliant philosopher whom she had been dating since at least 1977 and whom she married in hospital as he was dying of cancer in 1980. She was a match for Amis intellectually, and he fell for her in a different way from the way he fell for his previous succession of girlfriends. In the early 1980s, he was visiting America to spend time in Antonia's family house on Cape Cod. Simultaneously, he was writing a series of reviews of American fiction (far more than of British fiction) and profiles of prominent Americans for the

*Observer*: Norman Mailer, Véra Nabokov, Diana Trilling, and Steven Spielberg (also Brian de Palma for *Vanity Fair*). The figure who was to have the greatest significance for Amis and whom he interviewed for this series of profiles was Saul Bellow, whom he went to visit in Chicago in October 1983. Amis saw Bellow as the leading exponent of an intensely introspective form of fiction. "Bellow," he wrote in the *Observer*, "has made his experience resonate more memorably than any living writer" (*MI* 200). As he explains in his memoir, Bellow's experience is "of the permanent soul in its modern setting" (*E* 176). Amis was to remain friends with Bellow for the rest of his life (see Criticism, **p. 91**).

This immersion in American culture affects the scope and nature of his fiction from *Money* onwards. *Money: A Suicide Note* was published on September 27, 1984, the same day he married Antonia Phillips who was by then five months pregnant with their first son, Louis (see Works, **p. 46**). According to David Hawkes, the novel "is epic in scale, radically innovative in form and style, and hugely ambitious in its thematic concerns and philosophical implications" (Hawkes 1997: 26). To date, *Money* is one of Amis's finest novels. It reached a far wider readership. Alternating between London and New York, it exposes the extent to which English culture had been permeated by American values. It attempts to catch the spirit of both Thatcher's Britain and Reagan's America. Its voice is assured, and Amis cleverly establishes a double distance between himself, his namesake in the novel, and the pitiful yet sympathetically drawn narrator, John Self. Many of the reviews recognized the importance of this book and praised it as "a highly original and often dazzling piece of work" (Gross 1985: 25). Ian Hamilton ended his long review of it in the *London Review of Books*: "I am already persuaded that *Money* will be thought of for years to come as one of the key books of the decade" (Hamilton 1984: 4). His father, on the other hand, stopped reading the novel as soon as the character Martin Amis put in an appearance and flung the book across the room. "Breaking the rules," he complained, "buggering about with the reader, drawing attention to himself" (Stout 1990: 34–5). As Kingsley confided to Philip Larkin, "I hated its way of constantly remind[ing] me of Nabokov" (Amis, K. 2001: 989). This could well have been a result of professional jealousy. That year, Kingsley compared their Public Lending Right payments and was forced to admit, "Martin Amis is more famous than I am now" (Amis, K. 2001: 969).

Will Self identified the major advance that Amis had made with *Money*. His first four novels were "essentially local satirical dissections of the English class system," Self wrote. With *Money* he "seemed to go global" (Self 1993b: 73). This placed Amis, with Rushdie, as a prime mover in the change that took place in British fiction of the 1980s. Ishiguro summed up the difference between Martin's and Kingsley's generations: The older generation of British novelists asserted "with great authority that British values and British society were de facto of international importance [. . .] The new generation didn't have these assumptions [. . .] Somehow, British culture had become peripheral to the big themes of the time [. . .] The front line was somewhere else" (quoted in Wilson 1995: 100–1). Bill Buford, an American who was British Editor of *Granta*, an influential new literary magazine launched in 1979, was among the first to identify the arrival of this new generation of writers: In the third issue (1980) he drew attention to a new kind of writing "which, freed from the middle-class monologue, is experimentation in the real sense, exploiting traditions and not being wasted by them [. . .] The fiction of today is [. . .] testimony to an invasion of outsiders, using a language much larger than the culture" (Buford 1980: 16). Martin Amis fits this description perfectly. In 1983, the Book Marketing Council published a list of "The Best of Young British Novelists Under 40" which, besides Martin Amis, included Julian Barnes, Kazuo Ishiguro, Ian McEwan, Salman Rushdie, and Graham Swift (there were twenty in all). Buford followed up by publishing in the same year samples of each of their work in the seventh issue of *Granta* (an excerpt from *Money* in Amis's case). In addition, novelists had overnight become newsworthy in the eyes of the British press. The rules of the Booker Prize were altered to turn the announcement of the winner into a media event rivaling *Top of the Pops*. Literary festivals, author appearances and readings, and interviews on television and in papers and magazines turned the new generation of fiction writers into minor celebrities. Becoming a novelist was now seen to be a financially viable lifestyle. The two superstars of the literary scene were to be Rushdie (winner of the Booker Prize in 1981 and the victim of a *fatwa* in 1989) and Amis.

Whereas Rushdie was an immigrant who naturally saw the narrow concerns of Britain in a wider global context, Amis was liberated from the previous generation's insular concerns by his admiration for the amplitude of American fiction and by his repeated incursions into American society. America, he has said, is culturally "the centre of the earth" (Bigsby 1992: 182). He felt that the British were "too closely bound by language and history" to America to isolate themselves from it and from the rest of the world in which it was becoming the dominant superpower (Ross 1987: 23). He called it his second home and explained that the reason he was attracted to it was the stimulus it offered. What he disliked about the English was "the lack of candor between people [. . .] the fact that we reveal so little of ourselves to each other" (Bragg 1989). England, he felt, had evolved into "a modern efficiency state," from which all the earlier "piss and vinegar" (Hitchens' borrowing from Steinbeck) had gone out. America, on the other hand, is "full of conflict, convulsions and extremes" which are precisely what excite him as a writer (Power 2000: 66). Amis offers another reason close to his heart for his involvement in America: Its "appeal is of another vast language center" (Self 1993a: 169). It is the common language that makes him feel closer to America than to western Europe. All these factors—outspokenness, stimulus and linguistic vitality—were vital components of his form of fiction. In *Money*, while borrowing techniques from the American novelists he most admired, he was able to locate the effects of American culture in his uneducated English protagonist, John Self. Self has been raised on a steady diet of popular entertainment, commercials, and porn through his absorption of American values that permeated the British media. From *Money* onwards, all Amis's novels will either contain a scene located in America or bring American characters to England, or both.

## The years of ascendancy, 1985–95

In autumn 1984, Amis and Antonia settled into a house in Notting Hill, and he rented a flat in nearby Westbourne Park where he could go to write. He had already started work on his next novel (*London Fields*), but divided his time over the next two years (1985–7) between the novel and two other books—a collection of essays and reviews and a collection of his short fiction. For his first book of nonfiction, *The Moronic Inferno and Other Visits to America*, he collected most of the American pieces he had written (amounting to about half his published journalism), many as a special writer for the *Observer* (see Works, **p. 77**). This anthology of twenty-seven essays and reviews was published in July 1986. In the introduction, he writes that when he came to collect these pieces from the previous fifteen years he found that he "had already written a book about America—unpremeditated, accidental, and in instalments" (*MI* ix). The main alterations he made were to restore cuts made by editors and to occasionally add comments as postscripts. He says that he got the title phrase, "moronic inferno" from Bellow (his description of Chicago in *Humboldt's Gift*) who got it from Wyndham Lewis. In fact, the year before this book appeared, he had taken part in a late-night television program, a discussion between himself, Michael Ignatieff (the host) and Saul Bellow, titled *Saul Bellow and the Moronic Inferno*. According to Amis, the phrase serves as "a metaphor for human infamy." He insists that it is "not a peculiarly American condition. It is global" (*MI* x). This did not prevent reviewers like Fiona MacCarthy in *The Times* from accusing him of dwelling on the worst side of America. The accusation is particularly inapposite for a writer so identified with things American who claims, "I feel fractionally American myself" (*MI* ix) (see Works, **p. 78**). Many of his reviews of American writers are favorable, especially the two pieces on Bellow with which the book opens and closes. Some of his profiles are extremely barbed, but the form his criticism takes is invariably comic or ironic. His biggest reservation about America, he admits in the introduction, concerns the status of America as a superpower with the power to bring about planetary extinction. This surfaces again in his concluding sentences to a postscript on his piece about President Reagan: "For President Reagan is not just America's keeper: like his opposite number, he is the keeper of the planet, of all life, of the past and the future" (*MI* 96).

Amis writes that he first became interested in nuclear weapons in summer 1984 (*EM* 6). His awakening interest in the nuclear threat is evidenced by his publication in various periodicals of all five stories collected in *Einstein's Monsters* between autumn 1984 and June 1987, and by a piece focusing on the literature of nuclear weapons published in the *Observer* in December 1985 ("Kilotons of Human Blood"). His father's reaction to this piece of journalism, what he called "ban-it bullshit," was to lament (to Conquest) that Martin had "gone all lefty and of the crappiest neutralist kind," all the worse for it happening when he was thirty-seven years old (Amis, K. 2001: 1021–2). *Einstein's Monsters* took the unusual shape of five stories and a polemical introduction ("Thinkability"), all affected by the threat of nuclear apocalypse (see Works, **p. 67**). In "Thinkability," he claims that two events awakened his interest in this subject: the impending birth of his son Louis (born in November 1984—Jacob, his second son, was born in 1986 while he was at work on this book) and his reading Jonathan Schell's 1982 classic study of the likely effects of an outbreak of nuclear war, *The Fate of the Earth*, on which he depends for much of his factual information, as well as "for ideas and for imagery" ("Author's Note," *EM*). Amis claims that fatherhood reawoke the anxiety he had repressed as a child when told to take cover under his school desk during practice nuclear alerts, and that his newly released feelings surfaced in the five stories that he wrote (or rewrote) in succession (E 59–60). The stories reveal Amis's new concerns as a father of young children in the way, as John Lanchester wrote, they are "haunted [. . .] by the imagined deaths of children" (Lanchester 1987: 11).

Simultaneously, in the Introduction, he blames his father and his generation for getting it "hugely wrong," for failing to "see the nature of what they were dealing with." He even goes as far as to suggest, "Perhaps there will be no hope until they are gone" (EM 13). Amis recounts his father's greeting the first time they met after Einstein's Monsters was published in April 1987: "I READ YOUR THING ON NUCLEAR WEAPONS AND IT'S GOT ABSOLUTELY BUGGER-ALL TO SAY ABOUT WHAT WE'RE SUPPOSED TO DO ABOUT THEM" (E 59). In "Thinkability," Amis in effect accepts his father's criticism ("I don't know what to do about them" [EM 16]), while defending his right to protest the futility of Mutual Assured Destruction. In the "Author's Note," he explains that the title refers not to nuclear weapons but to us: "We are Einstein's monsters, not fully human, not for now." Our acceptance of them, he believes, is responsible for "many of the deformations and perversities" of late modernity (EM 7). In an interview at the time he finished this book, Amis says that writing about nuclear weapons helped him realize why he had always taken a jaundiced view of the modern world: In a world threatened by imminent nuclear destruction, "everything tends towards disorder. From an ordered state to a disordered state" (McGrath 1987: 196). Amis never departs from this entropic interpretation of the development of the world since 1945, although his explanation of the reasons for this extend beyond the Cold War confrontation (that at any rate evaporated after 1989) to encompass the Holocaust, Stalin's mass exterminations, environmental pollution, and, more recently, the terrorist attacks of September 11, 2001 (see Works, p. 54).

During the later 1980s Amis spent most summer vacations on Cape Cod at Antonia's father's vacation home. On one occasion, his son fell seriously ill, and, finding that there was no expert medical assistance available in the vicinity, Amis had to drive him all the way to New York. This incident, including the enormous medical bill that followed, brought home to Amis the downside of living in America (McGrath 1987: 187–8). Besides spending time in Spain with his family, Amis also traveled twice to Israel (1986 and 1987), the second time to give a talk on the forthcoming More Die of Heartbreak at a conference on the work of Saul Bellow, who was present. In his talk, Amis compared the work of Bellow to that of Larkin who had died in 1985: "Love was not a possibility for Larkin [. . .] For him, death crowded love out. With Bellow it seems to be the other way around" (E 202). Both writers headed to Jerusalem where they cemented their friendship. Amis visited Bellow in Chicago the following year on his way to cover the Republican Convention in New Orleans and again in 1989 with Hitchens when Hitchens and Bellow got into a bitter argument about the state of Israel with which Bellow identified and which Hitchens criticized. Although Amis's own views of Israel had soured somewhat during his second visit, he was left silent and embarrassed by Hitchens' furious onslaught at Bellow's dinner table. What Amis found most offensive on his second visit to Israel was the arrogance of the orthodox Jews, one of whom, he claims, made

Amis "see in his eyes the assertion that he could do *anything*" to him and his family, "and that this would only validate his rectitude" (*E* 263). Amis carefully balances this impression with a reference to members of the Christian right absurdly attempting to show the Jews that an alternative was on offer. Amis's conclusion points to his own lifelong agnosticism: "Humankind, or I myself, cannot bear very much religion" (*E* 263).

In November 1990, Margaret Thatcher's eleven-and-a-half-year reign as Prime Minister came to an end, although the Conservative Party still held on to power under her more centrist successor, John Major. Under Thatcher, Britain had been radically transformed. Trade-union power, which had brought down Heath's government and dictated economic policy to Callaghan in the 1970s, had been undermined by Thatcher's breaking the miner's strike of 1984 and further reduced by legislation. Keynesianism had been replaced by supply-side economic policies and by denationalization. The long-standing consensual model of politics had been abandoned. Unemployment had risen to as high as 13 percent, and the manufacturing base had shrunk faster and further than had that of other members of the European Community. Stuart Hall offers a convincing explanation of how Thatcher managed to stay in power while pursuing policies that benefited the wealthy and targeted workers. "The aim," Hall wrote, "was to reconstruct social life as a whole around a return to the old values—the philosophies of tradition, Englishness, respectability, patriarchalism, family, and the nation" (Hall 1988: 39). What is remarkable is that Thatcher's appeal to Victorian values was popular among those who suffered most from her legislation. Hall explains that Thatcherism broke down the old barriers of class by appealing to a multiple subject. So, "the liberty-loving citizen is *also* the worried parent, the respectable housewife, the careful manager of the household budget, the solid English citizen 'proud to be British . . .'" (Hall 1988: 49).

Like most of the writers of his generation, Amis was opposed to what Thatcher stood for, to "the boutique squalor of Thatcher's England" (*WAC* 19). He told Mira Stout at the time Thatcher's reign was nearing its end, "I think Thatcher has done a lot of harm. The money age we're living through now is a short-term, futureless kind of prosperity [. . .] you can feel the whole of society deteriorating around you [. . .] Civility, civilization is falling apart" (Stout 1990: 36) (see Criticism, **p. 106**). For Amis, Thatcherism joins those other manifestations of the decline of Western culture. At the same time, it made Britain the perfect subject for a comic writer like Amis. As he told Christopher Bigsby, "we are at the forefront of decline and what happens to a developed nation after its manly noon has passed is uniquely interesting" (Bigsby 1992: 183). Needless to say, Kingsley was a devotee of Thatcher who, after his first meeting with her, pronounced her "bright and tough and nice," adding "and by God she doesn't half hate lefties" (Amis, K. 2001: 840). He even had sexual dreams about her. In 1990, Kingsley was awarded a knighthood for being, according to Martin, "audibly and visibly right-wing, or conservative/monarchist" (*E* 90–1).

Kingsley reported to Robert Conquest at this time, "Martin is getting het up again over greenhouse effect and all that." His father told him that "it was all left-trendy" and asked Conquest for a book with some facts, "or demonstrations that there aren't any facts" (Amis, K. 2001: 1090). Kingsley may be referring to the interviews Martin was giving after the publication of *London Fields* in

September 1989 (see Works, **p. 50**). Set in 1999, the novel, a kind of prequel to *Other People*, portrays a London suffering from the vaguely defined effects of both nuclear fallout and ecological disaster. He was telling journalists that in the brief period since industrialization began, "we turned paradise into a toilet" (Morrison 1990: 102). In the novel, he told Melvyn Bragg, he was "after a kind of millennial unease [. . .] a general unease about the fate of the planet," the "imminent prospect of planetary death" (Bragg 1989) (see Works, **p. 52**). Ironically, the hardback was dedicated to Kingsley Amis. Or maybe not ironically. Father and son were in many ways extraordinarily close. In a dual interview at this time, Kingsley confessed, "I admire Martin. He is the only younger writer I think is any good," while Martin said, "We've always been affectionate. We've always embraced when we meet, without embarrassment, all our lives" (Amis and Amis 1989: 11, 14).

*London Fields* consolidated Amis's reputation as a comic ironist and unique stylist. It is his longest and possibly most ambitious novel to date. Some reviewers felt it was too long. But, in general, it was treated with respect. In a note prefacing the book Amis writes that he thought of calling the novel, among other titles, *The Death of Love* (see Works, **p. 51**). For its central character it has Nicola Six, the novel's murderee (another possible title), who, having come to the end of love, embodies a premise Amis got from a newspaper article he read five years earlier which assumed that "people who are murdered are somehow psychologically predisposed to be murdered" (Stead 1990: 42). Paralleling the planet with its falling skies and rising oceans, Nicola brings about her own destruction. She manipulates both of the major male characters (potential murderers) in the novel by doing advertisements for love with upper-class Guy and by using pornographic videos of herself with lower-class Keith, a reincarnation of John Self in *Money*. In his review of the book, Graham Fuller called the media-driven Keith "the sleaziest excrescence of Thatcherite greed in fiction" (Fuller 1990: 75). The other major character is an American author with writer's block who seizes on Nicola's plan to have herself murdered on her thirty-fifth birthday as a God-given plot for his next book. Both he and one of the two children featured in the novel are suffering from the effects of environmental poisoning. In the *New York Times Book Review*, Bette Pesetsky called *London Fields* "a large book of comic and satirical invention [. . .] a picaresque novel rich in its effects" (Pesetsky 1990: 42). Stephen Amidon caught its unusual tone when he called the novel "a nightmare from which you wake up laughing" (Amidon 1989: 17).

That year, 1990, while his father was receiving recognition with his knighthood, his son was being ostentatiously passed over in the shortlist for the Booker Prize. John Linklater in the *Glasgow Herald* and Jane Ellison in the *Guardian* both asked what the Booker judges had against Amis. Jane Ellison reported that the two women judges on the five-member panel, Maggie Gee and Helen McNeil, insisted upon his exclusion. Ellison raised a minor storm by claiming that "blockbuster porn is currently a genre that is monopolised almost exclusively by women." And in her concluding paragraph, she defended Amis against the charge of pornography: "You may not like the sort of sex that Amis writes about, but it is not pornographic. It is not thrown into *London Fields* at an exact ratio of one paragraph to every five pages, it is not written purely to keep the reader salivating (it is far too nasty for that)" (Ellison 1989: 21). David Lodge, who chaired the judges, expressed his regret that *London Fields* was effectively vetoed by the two women judges on the grounds of its alleged sexism, arguing that it contained "important metafictional and fabulatory elements" that none of the six shortlisted novels possessed" (Lodge 1992: 208) (see Works and Criticism, **pp. 97, 143**). Amis, however, has shown a relative imperviousness to public opinion. He learned a degree of insouciance from his father who, he writes in *Experience*, showed little evidence of being gratified by his knighthood and never talked about it (*E* 90). Looked at another way, as Julian Barnes pointed out, "If his father, whom he loves, dislikes his books, then it really doesn't matter what any critics say" (Stout 1990: 35).

In 1988, Amis started on the first of three drafts written, over the next eighteen months, of what he expected to be his next novel about literary rivalry and middle age (Bellante and Bellante 1992: 16). But in the latter part of 1989, he put aside *The Information* after his friend Robert Jay Lifton, who was on Cape Cod with him that summer, gave Amis his book, *The Nazi Doctors*. The story of the pseudo-medical philosophy of the Nazis, which Lifton recounted, struck Amis as "the only story that would gain meaning backwards" (see Works, **p. 54**). That philosophy justified the idea of killing as a means of healing. Amis felt that as an Aryan the only possible response to this absurd premise was "[d]isgusted laughter" (Trueheart 1991: B2). As Amis later explained, "Nazism was a biomedical vision to excise the cancer of Jewry. To turn it into something that *creates* Jewry is a respectable irony" (Reynolds and Noakes 2003: 20). At first, he thought it was going to be a short story, but it kept growing until he found he had written a short novel. *Time's Arrow, or, The Nature of the Offence* was published in September 1991 (see Works, **p. 54**). The book opens with its protagonist, a Nazi doctor who had escaped to America, at the point of death, producing his double or soul. The soul, which has been repressed from the doctor's consciousness throughout his life, experiences his life in reverse, but its childlike innocence prevents it from interpreting events in their full significance, a task that Amis leaves to the reader.

Most reviewers greeted the novel with admiration. Frank Kermode praised it for its "wit, ingenuity, and an admirably impassioned assurance" (Kermode 1991: 11). More than one critic discerned a new moral seriousness in this work. David Lehman is representative: "The novel's inversions of causality and chronology seem perfectly in keeping with the Nazis' inversion of morality" (Lehman 1991: 15). But a few reviewers obtusely failed to attend to the ironic tone. James Buchan's review in the *Spectator* was the most outrageous example of this tendency, which led to his adopting a wholly inappropriate tone of moral outrage. Accusing Amis of an act of "literary sadism," he claimed that what Amis does in this book is "fabricate an Auschwitz out of literary sources and use it as a setting for an elegant and trivial fiction" (Buchan 1991: 37). Amis made an exception to his usual show of indifference to the opinions of reviewers by writing a letter to the *Spectator*. Where Buchan accused Amis of rearranging Primo Levi "for literary fun and profit," Amis responds bitingly, "All books [. . .] are written 'for profit'. All reviews too—however exalted, however eagerly cynical" (Amis 1990a: 25) (see Criticism, **p. 97**). The widespread respect this book earned in most quarters was reflected by the fact that it was his only novel to be shortlisted for the Booker Prize. When the prize went to Ben Okri, Roger

Scruton wrote to the *TLS* protesting "the slovenly butchering of Martin Amis on grounds of immorality, despite (or maybe because of) the fact that *Time's Arrow* is the first Martin Amis novel to contain the faintest hint of a moral idea" (Scruton 1991: 12). This was a somewhat backhanded compliment, but it shows that even the most qualified readers (the Booker judges) were capable of misreading this ironic book.

In the late autumn of 1991, Amis went on a grueling American tour to promote *Time's Arrow*. The next summer, he was in Hollywood writing the script for another science-fiction movie, *Mars Attacks*. According to Amis, scriptwriting should not be confused with writing fiction. It is all about making concessions. The producer of *Mars Attacks* told Amis that his screenplay was "too hip for the house" (Pulver 2001: 14). When the movie was released in 1996, Amis was not included among the six names appearing under the writing credits. But he used the experience when writing his short story, "Career Move," which anticipated its extended use in *The Information* (see Works, p. 70). In 1992, Amis entered into an extramarital affair with Isabel Fonseca. This was the first indication that he was experiencing a particularly acute midlife crisis. Isabel was born and raised in the West Village. Her father was a Uruguayan sculptor and her mother a Jewish American. Her parents lived in Manhattan and had a large vacation home in East Hampton. Educated at Columbia and Oxford Universities, she had worked as a reader at Bloomsbury Publishing, where she edited the *Soho Square Anthology*, and as an assistant editor at the *TLS*. Like Antonia, Isabel had inherited wealth but was younger. She lived close to Amis in Ladbroke Grove and saw him and Antonia socially. She was at work on a book about Gypsies in eastern Europe at the time they became lovers. Amis described her as "exceptionally kind, and warm, and bighearted" (Shnayerson 1995: 136). In spring 1993, Amis moved out of the family home. Although he went to see Antonia that summer in Cape Cod, they failed to reconcile, and the marriage was at an end. As a child, Amis had been so hurt and disturbed by the breakup of his father's first marriage that he had sworn to himself that he would never do that to his children. So this break with Antonia acted as a double defeat to him. It is ironic that the year in which he followed in his father's footsteps with the breakup of his first marriage coincides with the time when Kingsley added his son to what he called his "Inner Audience" (Amis, K. 2001: 1126). Many friends thought that Amis had been scarred by his father's divorce. In *Experience* he writes that he left Antonia for Isabel "for love," although he stresses that being separated from his two sons caused him a lot of pain: "Divorce: the incredibly violent thing" he comments, reiterating his father's judgment (*E* 256, 7). Amis's midlife crisis did not end with the breakup of his first marriage. In March 1993, the papers broke the news that among the victims of Frederick West's serial murders was Lucy Partington, Amis's cousin, who had disappeared mysteriously twenty years earlier.[2] Reading the news in a taxi from Heathrow, Amis felt "an apprehension of [. . .] obliterating defeat" (*E* 66).

2 In 1994, Frederick West, who lived in Gloucester, was charged with the serial murder of twelve women and his wife Rose with that of ten of them, the first murder dating back to 1973. On January 1, 1995, Frederick West hung himself in his prison cell. His wife was sentenced later that year to life imprisonment.

In October 1993, his collection of occasional journalism, *Visiting Mrs. Nabokov and Other Excursions*, was published (see Works, p. 79). He calls it "an attempt at order and completion" from which "much has been left out" (*VMN* viii, ix). Most of the reviewers saw it as a collection of occasional journalism without much rationale to it, while commenting on Amis's brilliant stylistic feats in some of the pieces. The hard times continued into 1994 when his sister Sally suffered a stroke, and Isabel's brother, Bruno, a painter, died of AIDS. That summer, Amis was suffering from an abscess in his gum. He had lived with acute teeth problems all his adult life. Out of fear, he had not been to a dentist for five years. Determined to put off dealing with his teeth until he finished the final draft of *The Information*, he found himself unusually experiencing severe anxiety about completing it. That autumn, once the novel was more or less done, he began reconstructive surgery on not just his teeth but his lower jaw as well with a New York specialist. In *Experience* Amis describes in graphic detail the series of painful operations (including removing a tumor and rebuilding his chin with cow bone) that he underwent over the next few months. He recovered in between treatments at Isabel's parents' home in New York and for five days in San Juan, Puerto Rico, part of what Bellow called "one huge U.S. recreational slum" (*E* 207). That Christmas Eve, when Isabel's mother passed round the dinner table drawings of Isabel's brother, Bruno, dying, and a photograph of him aged twelve, Amis found that for him the photograph made a disastrous connection: "it encompassed my own sons (in their limbs and lineaments so like the boy in the photograph) and the matter of thwarted parental love, and all the discontinuities and disappearances of 1994" (*E* 199).

His troubles were far from over. Towards the end of 1994, he asked his agent, Pat Kavanagh, Julian Barnes's wife, to negotiate a £500,000 advance on his next book, *The Information*. His long-standing publisher, Cape offered £330,000 for the novel with an additional £70,000 for a collection of his short stories. The best offer Pat Kavanagh could get from an auction was from HarperCollins for £460,000 for the two books. Reluctant to abandon Cape, Amis called in Andrew Wylie, the American agent of Hitchens, Bellow and Isabel, to help Pat persuade Cape that they could afford more than they thought. At this point, the news of these negotiations was leaked to the press, which went to town with it. In the *Independent*, John Walsh accused Amis of acting out of envy of his better-paid friends, Julian Barnes and Ian McEwan. Many newspapers portrayed Wylie as the Jackal, a foreign poacher on English turf. Even Isabel Fonseca was cast in the role of a Lady Macbeth leading her husband to ruin and worse—removal to the USA. It was further alleged that Amis's huge advance would leave first-time authors penniless. The most unlikely attack came from the novelist A. S. Byatt. Speaking to the *Daily Telegraph*, she denounced him for indulging "in a kind of male turkey cocking." "I always earn out my advances," she declared self-righteously, "and I don't see why I should subsidize his greed, simply because he has a divorce to pay for and has just had all his teeth re-done" (Glass 1995: 18). In *Experience*, Amis records that subsequently Byatt offered him an apology, excusing herself by saying that she had a toothache (what irony) when the journalist rang her (*E* 247). At the time, her remarks only added fuel to the flames. Gossip columnists accused Amis of wasting his money on cosmetic surgery to his teeth, of arrogance, of sucking up to America, and so on. When Amis under

Wylie's direction chose HarperCollins, which meant breaking with Pat Kavanagh (just as his father had done in 1976), he received a letter from Julian Barnes angrily breaking off their friendship, causing Amis more "doubts and questions" (*E* 248). Although Amis wrote back to him asking Barnes to stay his friend, Barnes would not relent, and it was not until 2006 that they made up their differences. Amis told one interviewer at the time that the break with Pat and Julian "pushed me up against my limit" (Shnayerson 1995: 162).

The abuse heaped on Amis by even the so-called quality British press during this period turned him into a celebrity, however notorious. He had become the Mick Jagger of the literary world, and for the British press he would remain a name worth invoking (and misrepresenting) in the future. With Rushdie, Amis had inadvertently raised the public profile of the British novelist to a level perhaps last seen in Dickens's day. In the *Guardian*, Charles Glass put things in perspective when he wrote that it was sheer common sense that made Amis request a large advance. His motivation, Glass suggested, "is more understandable than the sanctimonious, petty and ill-informed criticism of him" (Glass 1995: 18). Reporting on the whole affair for the *New Yorker*, Jonathan Wilson observed that it would be hard to imagine that Amis's supposed "crimes" "could cause so much as a ripple in the United States." But, given a xenophobic press, "in England this depressingly cruel assault upon a British literary personality ballooned until it took on the surreal atmosphere of a ritual sacrifice" (Wilson 1995: 102). Amis's friend Ian McEwan discerned in this English resentment of success an anti-intellectual streak (Shnayerson 1995: 162). Amis comments in *Experience*, "this wasn't a story about me. It was a story about England" (*E* 235). England did not emerge well from it. Behind the moral and antimaterialist posturing on the part of the gossip writers lurks the motivation of envy at a writer with so much more ability and financial success than they have. Amis summed up the past two years to Hitchens: "'Breakup, separation from children, health-crisis.' Lucy Partington, Bruno Fonseca, Saul Bellow in the ICU [Bellow nearly died of food poisoning in December 1994]. And a five-year novel, *The Information*, begun in peace and finishing, now, in spasm war" (*E* 269). It is ironic that *The Information*, which started out as a book about literary envy, came to incorporate the literary envy he had experienced first hand during the previous two years (see Criticism, p. 97).

*The Information* was published in March 1995, and its reception in England was similarly skewered by the publicity concerning Amis's private life that had reached a crescendo two months earlier (see Works and Criticism, **pp. 57–8, 97–8**). Amis saw the novel as the last of "a very informal trilogy," the others being *Money* and *London Fields*. What links them is that they are concerned with "the same kinds of things—shifting identities, writer figures [. . .] pornography," and "they all have credulous characters who are affected the wrong way by what they read" (Fuller 1995). In one of the few English reviews that focus exclusively on the book, Adam Mars-Jones prefers to see the three books not as a trilogy but as "a mighty triptych, a love poem to West London from which love is excluded" (Mars-Jones 1995: 19). The novel centers on two novelists, one middlebrow and highly successful, the other avant-garde and unread. The unsuccessful author, filled with envy at the other's undeserved popularity, sets out on a path of revenge but is comically undone at every stage. Both writers turn forty at the beginning of the novel, and the unsuccessful one is afflicted with some of the angst that Amis had been feeling over the last two years of the book's composition, what is called in the novel "a crisis of the middle years" (*I* 43). One of the few English reviewers to concentrate on the novel rather than the novelist was Julian Loose. He drew attention to the repetition of those themes that Amis felt characterized the trilogy of major novels, what Loose listed as "male envy, [. . .] alcohol-fuelled trips to America, [. . .] villains who speak a post-Yardie patois"— the list continues. He goes on, "we may feel that with *The Information* Amis has ended up down a cul-de-sac, but his writing is still fantastically rich" (Loose 1995: 9). Many of the American reviews, unencumbered by the so-called scandals surrounding the book's author, declared the novel "protean" (Bellow 1995: 701), "a perfectly pitched expression of our late 20th-century distopia" (Ward 1996: 561), and a novel that "marks a giant leap forward in Mr. Amis's career" (Kakutani 1995: 17).

## Responding to a changed world, 1995–2007

In spring 1995, Amis returned from his American book tour for *The Information* to find awaiting him a letter from Delilah Seale, his illegitimate daughter. Her stepfather, Patrick Seale, had told her who her true father was when she had reached the age of eighteen. She was now a history student at St. Hugh's College, Oxford, and wanted to meet her father. After conferring with her stepfather, Amis met her with Isabel in the bar of a Knightsbridge hotel. Father and daughter were reconciled, and she became part of his family. Prompted by interviews with Amis, the press chose to publicize this news as an unusual story with a happy ending. While vacationing in the Fonseca holiday house in East Hampton, Amis was reading *noir* fiction and nonfictional books on US criminal justice in preparation for his next novel, *Night Train* (Amis 1997: 18). Within six months of its publication, *The Information* had sold 116,000 hardback copies. Auberon Waugh summed up Amis's new public status in the *Sunday Telegraph*: "Amis is the only superstar in the English literary firmament [. . .] Others may be tempted to feel jealous of him, but he is also their only guarantee that there is a pot of gold at the end of the rainbow, that the literary novel can still bring fame, wealth and beautiful women" (Thomson 1998: 18).

Amis had one more trauma to face. In late summer 1995, his father had a fall while on holiday in Wales. His official biographer, Eric Jacobs, drove him back to London where he was admitted to hospital. The most likely diagnosis was Alzheimer's. Most days Martin visited his father whose moods changed from abusive to bewildered to grateful. Moved to a hospice, Kingsley died there of pneumonia in October 1995. In *Experience*, Amis recalls calling his old friend Rob with the news: "'The King is Dead'" (*E* 358). Amis repeatedly casts himself in the role of Hamlet in his memoir, quoting Claudius's remonstrance to Hamlet: "your father lost a father, / That father lost, lost his" (1.2.89–90). He even records a dream in which his father's ghost visits him and entrusts him with his father's wishes (*E* 363–4). Kingsley's death made Amis feel, "Death is nearer," because now "there is nobody there between you and extinction" (*E* 345). After Rob, the next friend he phoned was the eighty-year-old Saul Bellow. He said to him, "You'll have to be my father now," to which Bellow responded, "Well I love you very much" (*E* 360) (see Criticism, **p. 91**). One way of interpreting the next novel on which Amis was working, *Night Train*, is as a meditation on death in all its manifestations, figural and literal. Amis also records as a postscript to this painful moment in his life the nightmare he was faced with when three days after his father died Eric Jacobs sent him a transcript of notes he had made of Kingsley's last days. He said that *The Times* and the *Daily Mail* were interested in publishing extracts from them. The clumsy and tasteless distortions of his observations caused Amis to "shed tears of pure misery" and temporarily halt their publication (*E* 374). The executors of Kingsley's estate of whom Amis was one declared Jacobs unfit to edit his father's letters and gave the job to Zachary Leader. That may have led Jacobs to give his notes to *The Times* in March 1996 where they were published in three installments to Amis's and his family's dismay. True to form, some of the press offered distorted accounts of the fracas, portraying Amis as ignoring his father's wishes in order to pursue a vendetta against a defenseless biographer and fellow journalist.

Two months after his father's death, Amis bought and, with Isabel, moved into a house on Regent's Park Road, the same street in which his father had spent the last years of his life. Simultaneously abandoning his old writing pad in West London, he converted a shed at the bottom of the garden to act as a workplace. During his summer visits to Isabel's family and vacation home, he usually went to visit Bellow in Vermont. He also participated with Bellow in October 1997 in a Boston television program, *Saul Bellow's Gift*, in which he drew on his most recent review of Bellow's *The Actual* for the *Observer*. In November 1996, Isabel gave birth to a daughter, Fernanda. Amis had long hoped for a daughter, and now he had both Delilah, whom he shared with her stepfather, and his own baby daughter. With his reconstructive dentistry completed, Amis had reached the other side of his crisis and was entering a period of greater inner peace and happiness. By December 1996, he was close enough to fulfilling his much-publicized contract with HarperCollins to sign a four-book contract with his old English publisher, Cape. Two years later, he would sign a US book deal with Miramax, which involved an advance of $850,000 for his next four books and a screenplay of *Northanger Abbey* that got written but has never been produced.

In October 1997, his next short novel, *Night Train*, was published (see Works, **p. 60**). Set in an anonymous American city, this is a police procedural with a difference. For a start, the detective who narrates the story in the first person is a woman. Amis's earlier female characters were neither the narrator nor were they portrayed in the first person. Further, the plot is not so much a who-did-it as a why-do-it, because the dead woman has not been murdered; she has committed suicide. This is not the first time Amis had been drawn to the subject of suicide. In *Success*, Ursula takes her own life in the middle of the novel. *Money* was subtitled *A Suicide Note* and ended with Self's botched attempt at suicide. *London Fields* featured Nicola Six who sets out to have herself murdered on her thirty-fifth birthday and succeeds. Amis seems to have known an unusual number of people who took their life: Claire Tomlinson's secretary, her daughter, Lorna Seale, Amschel Rothschild (whose brains he picked about firearms for *Night Train* three months before Amschel hanged himself), not to mention Hitchens' mother whom he never met and Frederick West, his cousin's murderer. For Amis, "suicide sends you a message from ultimate human collapse" (*E* 196), which is where he drives so many of his characters. *Night Train* concerns a suicide that is inexplicable, but Amis's conclusion in *Experience* is that most suicides are inexplicable to the survivors (see Works, p. 61). A number of influential reviewers, such as John Updike for the *Sunday Times* and Anita Brookner for the *Spectator*, had strong reservations about the novel's alleged post-human lack of soul. But other reviewers on both sides of the Atlantic offered some penetrating observations about it. Both Natasha Walter and Patrick McGrath detected in the novel's use of a female detective a resulting release of emotion unusual in Amis's work to date (Walter 1997: 29). Discerning in *Night Train* a tone of elegiac sadness, Patrick McGrath concluded: "This brilliant, painful short novel is, in fact, so inflected with grief that it achieves in the end a sort of melancholy grandeur" (McGrath 1998: 6) (see Criticism, p. 98).

In July 1998, Amis and Isabel were secretly married in London. The following year, Isabel gave birth to their second daughter, Clio. During this period, Amis was struggling with his next novel, *Yellow Dog*, but put it aside in May 1999 to write two nonfiction books. After all the changes that had occurred in his life, he was not ready to go on as before and plunge into his next major work of fiction. Instead, he prepared a collection of short stories, many already written, which was published in October 1998 as *Heavy Water and Other Stories* (see Works, p. 69). Two of these stories, including the title story, were first published in the 1970s and a third in 1980. The remaining six stories belong to the 1990s. Amis has said that he finds short stories easier to write than novels, which require the writer to carry many more things in his head. At the same time, he has said, the "best short stories are the ones" in which "not a word is wasted and it's the perfect [. . .] *weight* for the perfect cargo" (Richards 2000). The collection consists of some typical black farces: In "Straight Fiction," society has gone gay, and heterosexuals are the oppressed minority, just as in "Career Move" screenwriters are penniless hacks while poets are treated like movie stars and earn millions. But it also contains some stories that reveal the same new depths of feeling that are apparent in *Night Train*; "What Happened to Me on My Holiday" even uses his son Louis's name and is based on his son's loss of his half brother. Other stories comment on late-twentieth-century Western civilization, such as "State of England" and "The Coincidence of the Arts." Russell Celyn Jones, reviewing the collection for *The Times*, discerned maturation between the early and the 1990s stories, one not just in style but also in the compassion found in stories like "State of England" (Jones 1998: 40).

As early as 1995, Amis was half-jokingly contemplating writing an autobiography about the year he had been through (1994–5). At that point, the emphasis was to be on the dental aspect: "It's a good image for everything else," he remarked (Shnayerson 1995: 162). But when his father died later that year, the book that slowly took shape in his mind had to absorb the grieving he underwent for his father over the next few years. Once started, the memoir came fast, he has said, twice as fast as a novel would. It took him eighteen months to write (Richards 2000). *Experience: A Memoir* was published in May 2000 (see Works, p. 71). Its serialization alone in the *Guardian* was reported to have earned him £100,000. It is a highly original instance of the autobiographical genre. By structuring it around themes, he frees himself from any chronological imperative, which in turn offers him at least some of the larger liberties of the novelist. At the same time, his thematic approach allows him to omit material about his private life without explaining why (Richards 2000). In the opening chapter, he states that his motives for writing a memoir were twofold: to commemorate his father and to set the record straight, as the press had created such a distorted portrait of him for his readers, he explained to Linda Richards. Of course some journalists saw the book as Amis's revenge on the press for their treatment of him five years earlier. Others, according to Amis, were "angry that it isn't [his response to them] because it doesn't accord them centrality" (Richards 2000). It is perfectly conceivable that the earlier abusive treatment Amis received from the press was stoked by his indifference to their lies and distortions, an indifference acquired from his father. Most serious reviewers were impressed with *Experience* (see Works, **p. 75**). In the *New York Times*, Michiko Kakutani called it "Amis's most fully realized book yet [. . .] that fuses his humor, intellect and daring with a new gravitas and warmth" (Kakutani 2000: 1). It was the first book to win him a prize since *The Rachel Papers* when it was awarded the James Tait Black Memorial Prize for biography.

Amis's next book was also nonfiction: a collection of his essays and reviews between 1971 and 2000. Compiled with the help of James Diedrick, a leading Amis scholar, it involved much less work for its author. Called *The War Against Cliché*, the book was published in April 2001 and won the 2002 National Book Critics Circle Award for Criticism in America (see Works, **p. 81**). Amis explains the title in its foreword: "To idealize: all writing is a campaign against cliché. Not just clichés of the pen but clichés of the mind and clichés of the heart" (*WAC* xv) (see Works and Criticism, **pp. 82, 148**). The entire book offers many instances of the way in which Amis equates the use of style with the adoption of a moral position. He took the job of reviewing seriously, as he indicated in the introduction to his first collection of nonfiction: "The thousand-word book review seems to me far more clearly an art form (however minor) than any of the excursions of the New Journalism, some of which are as long as *Middlemarch*" (*MI* x). Amis has honed away at this particular art form, as Geoff Dyer attests in the *Guardian*: "Whatever the book, there is no one whose review of it you'd rather read" (Dyer 2001: 10). The book received widespread praise from reviewers who felt that the collection demonstrated Amis's outstanding and unique gifts as a journalist, essayist, and critic. In the *Spectator*, Philip Hensher (inadvertently using a cliché) called the book "detailed, intricate criticism of the highest order" (Hensher 2001: 33). Frank Kermode praised Amis for being "one of the few critics who trouble [. . .] to include some consideration of the fabric of a book, the faults of its texture, its clichés" (Kermode 2001: 27). Amis continues to write essays, profiles and book reviews of a high order for newspapers and periodicals.[3]

Instead of reverting to writing his next novel after completing *Experience*, Amis found himself in 2000 writing a second work of nonfiction, what he called a political memoir. Partly prompted by reading Robert Conquest's *The Harvest of Sorrow* (1986) and *The Great Terror: A Reassessment* (1990), *Koba the*

---

3 See James Diedrick and Hunter Hayes's bibliography which includes Amis's unpublished nonfiction in Gavin Keulks (ed.), *Martin Amis: Postmodernism and Beyond*, London and New York: Palgrave Macmillan, 2006, pp. 211–34.

*Great: Laughter and the Twenty Million*, published July 2002, is about Stalin (whose nickname was Koba) and his extermination of 20 million of his people (see Works, **p. 75**). When Amis was halfway through writing the book his sister Sally died at the age of forty-six. Sally had been an alcoholic and manic-depressive who had been married once for a matter of months and had also had by another man a daughter, Catherine, whom she had allowed to be adopted. Amis incorporated his grief at his sister's death into a book that grieves for the massacre of 20 million members of the USSR. Once again identifying with Hamlet's dejection, he equates grieving with a larger metaphysical angst, musing on his own ultimate demise. He also targeted for criticism his father's early Communist beliefs as well as those of his long-standing friend, Christopher Hitchens. In the last part of the book, he addresses letters to both Hitchens and his father's ghost. His letter to Hitchens asks him whether he admires terror, since an "admiration for Lenin and Trotsky is meaningless without an admiration for terror" (*KD* 250). Hitchens defended himself in the press at length.[4] While exposing weaknesses in Amis's position and knowledge of the subject, he never convincingly refuted Amis's principal accusation that he implicitly condoned Stalin's purges during his earlier allegiance to Communism. Most of the reviewers found Amis's mixture of Soviet history and personal relationships awkward, even embarrassing (see Works, **p. 77**). Michiko Kakutani, who admired *Experience*, is representative. She found that the sections of the book devoted to Sally and other personal asides, "plopped in the midst of what is a historical survey of Soviet crimes against humanity, feel like the narcissistic musings of a spoiled, upper-middle-class litterateur who has never known the real suffering Stalin's victims did" (Kakutani 2002: 9). While this demand that only the victims of a mass crime be allowed to speak of it may be unreasonable, Kakutani's sense of a disparity between the personal and the historical was widely shared.

Amis coped with the grief at his loss of Sally, as he always did, by writing about her. He confessed to one interviewer that while he shared his brother's and sister's weaknesses, such as indecisiveness, the "difference was that I could write," which forced him to act decisively (Shnayerson 1995: 161–2). After Sally's funeral, Amis welcomed her daughter (who had never met her mother) into the family and took her with his own four children to Spain to spend time with his mother who, freed of responsibility for Kingsley, had resettled there. By this time, Amis and Isabel would spend up to three months a year in Montevideo, the capital of Uruguay, near her uncle who was building a house for them in Jose Ignacio on the coast. In his description of one such winter sojourn in *Koba the Dread*, Amis confesses how much he misses being with his sons. In January 2001, the film of *Dead Babies* (for which he did not write the screenplay) was released. Although it was judged a failure by most of the critics, Amis was rumored to have received £250,000 for the rights.

Amis was not in New York when the terrorist attacks on the USA occurred on September 11, 2001. But he regarded New York as his second city: His wife grew up there, and his sister-in-law was downtown when Flight 11 passed over

---

4 See Christopher Hitchens, "Friendship Doesn't Get in the Way of a Feud, and Vice Versa," *Los Angeles Times*, 2 August, 2002, p. 1; "Don't. Be. Silly," *Guardian*, 4 September 2002, pp. G2, 6; and "Lightness at Midnight: Stalinism Without Irony," *Atlantic*, September 2002, pp. 144–53.

her head on its way to crash into the first of the two towers of the World Trade Center. A week later, Amis published in the *Guardian* his first contribution to a series of reports and essays he has written on the geopolitical significance that this event has had on the world. The glint of the second plane aiming itself at the tower "was the worldflash of a coming future," he wrote (or overwrote, as some readers felt). "Weirdly, the world suddenly appears bipolar" (Amis 2001b). At first he concentrated on the manic polarity of Islamic fundamentalism, "convulsed in a late medieval phase of its evolution" (Amis 2001b). Accusing it of misogyny and misology (hatred of reason), he charged that, like all religions, "it is a massive agglutination of stock response, of clichés, of inherited and unexamined formulations" (Amis 2002a: 6). Soon he was portraying the West, especially Bush's America, as reacting like a depressive that finds itself hated by the Islamic world. Terrorism, he argued, undermines rationality and morality. As a result, America is not behaving either rationally or morally. In the aftermath of 9/11, Bush, equally infected by an attachment to religious fundamentalism, is floating in "a sea of illegitimacy" (Muir 2003: 9). Amis reaches the conclusion that our only hope is to abandon identifying ourselves by nationality or religious affiliation and to develop instead what has been called "species consciousness."

The events of 9/11 confirmed Amis's stand as an agnostic. He claims that he had turned atheist at the early age of nine. But, after his life had been turned upside down in the mid-1990s, he decided that atheism was as irrational as religious belief and turned agnostic. As a novelist, he sees himself naturally opposed to what he calls religion's "voice of the lonely crowd" (Northrop Frye's phrase), "a monologue that seeks the validation of a chorus" (Amis 2002a: 5). Amis claims that writers at first felt that 9/11 had made them irrelevant. But slowly their voices reemerged: "they were individual voices, and playfully rational, all espousing the ideology of no ideology" (Amis 2002a: 6). If "September 11 was an attack on words" (Amis 2003b: 29), then it was the task of the writer to absorb the shock and counterattack with words. The day after the terrorist attacks, Amis returned to *Yellow Dog*, which he had put aside two and a half years earlier. Now it was to be "a novel about what it feels like to be living in our current era, which established itself on Sept. 11 [. . .] Everything is qualified now. Everything is contingent" (Curiel 2001: 2). *Yellow Dog* was published in September 2003, his first novel in six years (see Works, p. 62). A comedy, it consists of three major narrative strands and a minor one, each with its own tone and color. There is a writer who gets beaten over the head and changes personality from a devoted husband to a sadist high on testosterone. This strand enables Amis to focus on the phenomenon of male insecurity, which he partly blamed for the actions of Islamic fundamentalists and the counteractions of the West. There is a hack journalist who works for a sleazy paper resembling the British rag, the *Daily Sport*. His obscene articles make him an easy victim of a predatory ex-porn star. There is a royal family subjected to blackmail by the possessor of nude photographs of the teenage princess. And the minor strand concerns a plane crash. The novel is more reliant on plot than most of his novels; it is intended to hook the reader anxious to discover how the various strands connect by the end. The book is also obviously informed by Amis's journalism of the preceding period. In particular, he had written a feature article published in February 2001 in *Talk* magazine on the Los Angeles pornography industry titled "Sex in America," (see Life and Contexts, Works and Criticism, **pp. 12, 64, 140**), and an essay, "The Queen's Heart," for the *New Yorker* in May 2002, in which he reviewed two books about Elizabeth II and the monarchy. To help flesh out his chief gangster figure, he had also read Tony Parker's *Life After Life* as well as all three volumes of the memoirs of Mad Frankie Fraser, two notorious and violent British villains, the latter of whom had spent forty-two years in prison. Amis also incorporated a near brush with death he had on a flight to Malaga when the plane made a crash landing in France after receiving an IRA bomb threat.

The British reviewers and journalists went straight for the gullet with *Yellow Dog*, the journalists possibly annoyed by Amis's barbed portrayal of a gutter journalist in it (see Works, **p. 63**). A fellow novelist, Tibor Fischer, led the pack by releasing a review—more like a diatribe—in the *Daily Telegraph* before the book's release date. "*Yellow Dog* isn't bad as in not very good or slightly disappointing," he wrote. "It's-not-knowing-where-to-look bad" (Fischer 2003: 18). British reviewers largely took their lead from this publicity-seeking example of a review that offers no reasons for its prejudicial judgment. *Yellow Dog* was pronounced "a disaster" in the *Telegraph* (Jones 2001), "a further plummeting in his literary trajectory" in the *Sunday Times* (Kemp 2003), "forced and straining" in *The Times* (Wagner 2003), and, at the least, "a very flawed book" in the *Financial Times* (Hunter-Tilney 2003). Two common refrains were that "Amis has by now done his best work" (Hensher 2003: 37) and that "the novel is a palace of echoes [. . .] all the old Amis riffs are there" (Walden 2003: 48) (see Criticism, **p. 99**). Some American reviewers took a similar line. Even Michiko Kakutani dismissed the novel as "a bunch of unsavory outtakes from an abandoned project" (Kakutani 2003: 1).

How is it, then, that the same book could be simultaneously greeted so differently? Take, for instance, this review: "here is a novel to silence the doubters, because here, as he probes a human world increasingly disconnected from itself, Amis has found a subject to match the tessellated polish of his style" (Douglas-Fairhurst 2003: 15). Opinions about this book differ so radically that it is hard not to think that the early trashing it received from the British press (mostly because it was by Martin Amis) skewed literary judgment. For instance, many reviewers, like Kakutani, felt that the various strands of the plot failed to cohere, that he would have done better to have published three novellas and a short story. Yet, Alan Hollinghurst insists, "Everything Amis writes is highly structured, but *Yellow Dog* gives signs of quite bristling organization" (Hollinghurst 2003: 9). The *Observer* reviewer suggested that "critics [. . .] are condemned to repeat what they fail to understand" (Douglas-Fairhurst 2003: 15). Few reviewers discerned the underlying themes of the book which bind the different episodes to one another in far more interesting ways than does the plot. All the strands of the book are concerned with masculinity, male violence, pornography, and the post-9/11 world. As usual, Amis shrugged aside the brouhaha. He argued that this book, which he considered among his best two or three, continues the trend of ever-widening horizons found in his novels: His first novel was confined to a single consciousness, his second to a peer group, his third to a city, while his tenth novel, *Yellow Dog*, is "about alternate universes. So there is a steady expansion here" (Reynolds and Noakes 2003: 13). This book made it to the long list of the Booker Prize, which is more than Fischer's novel published the same day did, and it was shortlisted for the British Book Awards Literary Fiction Award. It is ironic that it got closer to an award than *Money*, the novel all his detractors in 2003 were citing as his greatest achievement.

In January 2004, Random House published *Vintage Amis*, a selection from his fiction and nonfiction. Between early 2004 and mid-2006 Amis spent most of his time at Jose Ignacio, Uruguay, working on short stories and a new novel. One story, "In the Palace of the End," set in Saddam Hussein's Iraq, was published in March 2004. He found Uruguay provided a counter to the speed of contemporary life. While in South America, he visited Colombia to research a contribution he made to the *Sunday Time Magazine* series, "Authors in the Front Line." In his piece, published in February 2005, Amis reported on gang culture and the violent lives youths live in the major Colombian cities. In April 2005, a year and a half after Amis had published a major essay about Saul Bellow titled "The Supreme American Novelist," Bellow died. In April 2006, Amis published a second story, "The Last Days of Mohammad Atta," which imaginatively reconstructs Atta's life just before he died, flying his plane into the World Trade Center (see Criticism, **p. 109**). He confessed, "I took an enormous liberty in that I made [Atta] an apostate, rather than a religious maniac, which is [. . .] almost certainly what he was" (Jones 2006). Amis also abandoned a short story, "The Unknown Known," in which Muslim terrorists unleash a horde of rapists on "Greeley," Colorado (the locus for the decisive shaping of Islamism in 1949 by Sayyid Qutb).

On his return to England in 2006, Amis published a major essay in the *Observer*, "The Age of Horrorism," on the rise of extreme Islamism (see Criticism, **pp. 109–10**). Amis defended his use of the term "horrorism" by contrasting it to mere acts of terrorism and arguing that "Suicide mass-murder, the act of self-besplattering [. . .] is always horrible" (Amis 2007a). He also distinguishes between Islam, which he respects, and Islamism (Islamic fundamentalism), which represents "a creedal wave that calls for our own elimination," which cannot be respected (Amis 2006a: 4). He sees Islamism as an outbreak of irrationality caused by the "manifest failure" of the Islamic world to compete with the West and its compensatory need to maintain the "suppression of women" (Amis 2006a: 10). Accused of being an Islamophobe, he responded that, rather, he was "an anti-Islamist because a phobia is an irrational fear, and there is nothing irrational about fearing someone who professedly wants to kill you" (Amis 2007a). In an interview he gave in September 2006, Amis also confessed to an irrational urge to want to punish the Muslim community: "Not letting them travel. Deportation—further down the road [. . .] Strip-searching people who look like they're from the Middle East or from Pakistan" (Dougary 2006). Inevitably, the British press ignored the fact that Amis was confessing to an irrational reaction that he rejects in every published pronouncement on the subject of Islamism. More surprising is the attack launched on him in October 2007 by Terry Eagleton in the introduction to the revised edition of his *Ideology: An Introduction* (Byrne 2007). Eagleton incorrectly ascribed Amis's remarks to his essay, "The Age of Horrorism," and, as Amis subsequently pointed out, stripped the prefatory "There is a definite urge—don't you have it?" "I wasn't advocating it," Amis insisted. Eagleton's failure to check the context of Amis's remarks, Amis observed, is a distinctly unscholarly way of arguing a case.

"Moral equivalence is a trap," he thinks, into which the British have particularly fallen (Summerscale 2007). Six years after the event, Amis was still maintaining that "September 11 continues, it goes on, with all its mystery, its instability, and its terrible dynamism" (Amis 2007b).

While in Uruguay, Amis had completed *House of Meetings*, "a story about love" centered on the Soviet labor camp Norlag, which was published in September 2006 (see Works, **p. 65**). This novel represents a fictional revisitation of the Russia treated nonfictionally in *Koba the Dread*. Eschewing comedy for only the second time in his career, Amis has an elderly brother narrate the story of two brothers who fall in love with the same woman and who are both imprisoned in a gulag for eight years. The novel reflects Amis's lifelong fascination with the nature and construction of masculinity and with the violence underlying ideologies—whether Communist, Western, or Islamist. Michiko Kakutani, who savaged *Yellow Dog*, like the majority of reviewers, praised *House of Meetings* for its "powerful, unrelenting and deeply affecting performance" (Kakutani 2007: 1) (see Criticism, **p. 100**). In February 2007, Amis announced that he had accepted an appointment as Professor of Creative Writing at the University of Manchester starting September 2007, conducting two seminars a term for graduates. The number of applicants went up 50 percent on the previous year. He told the *Independent* that the essence of what he would be teaching his students would be' "Don't go with the crowd, don't do anything for the crowd, don't be of the crowd or with the crowd" (Amis, 2007b).

Since completing *House of Meetings*, Amis has been working on two books. *The Second Plane: September 11: Terror and Boredom*, published early in 2008, collects 12 articles and essays on Islamism and the terrorist attacks of 9/11 in the USA and 7/7 in London; it also includes his two stories on this topic, "The Palace of the End" and "The Last Days of Muhammad Atta." The second book is an autobiographically based novel with an Islamic theme modeled on Bellow, who "stares at the real person until he sees the universal" (Dougary 2006). Due to be published in autumn 2008, it will incorporate figures like Bellow, his father, Larkin, Hitchens and Ian Hamilton. His working title is *The Pregnant Widow*. Amis has explained that the title refers to the difficult birth of feminism, adapting the Russian thinker Alexander Herzen's description of the aftermath of revolution, which would leave not a newborn child, but a pregnant widow. Feminism, he believes, "is about halfway through its second trimester" (Amis 2007a). Amis continues to be a controversial public figure in British life and to be seen as a leading, influential writer of his time.

## Further reading

There is no biography of Martin Amis. The best direct source is his memoir, *Experience* (2000). He provides some additional facts about his life in "My Oxford" (1977), *Koba the Dread* (2002), and in the numerous interviews he has given (some available on the Martin Amis website at <http://www.martinamisweb.com>). Some background information is available in Zachary Leader's *The Life of Kingsley Amis*, London: Cape, 2006.

# 2

# Works

## Novels

### The Rachel Papers (1973)

*The Rachel Papers*, Amis's first novel published in 1973 when he was twenty-four years old, signaled the arrival of a formidable new author. The book recounts the last five hours before the narrator, Charles Highway, turns twenty. Each of its twelve chapters starts off moving through these five hours but quickly turns its attention to the morass of papers (autobiographical and biographical, including "the Rachel Papers") that recount or remind Charles of incidents from his past, returning the narrative to the present at the end of each chapter. The plot largely consists of two actions Charles self-consciously undertakes: Firstly, to obtain a place at Oxford (University) by attending a crammer (a school that prepares students for entrance examinations), and, second, to seduce Rachel, a girl whom he met at a party five months earlier. Although she has an American boyfriend with the "preposterous name" of DeForest (*RP* 223), Charles manages to lure Rachel away from him and to seduce her before growing disenchanted and callously breaking off their affair in the final chapter. He also learns in the last chapter that he has been accepted by Oxford. On the second page, Charles claims that he is undertaking the reconstruction of his recent past in order to, as he puts it, " be able to locate my *harmartia* [Greek for "tragic flaw"] and see what kind of grown-up I shall make" (*RP* 4). This sentence alone reveals that Charles is intent on forcing his life and character to conform to a literary template, in this instance an Aristotelian one.

While Charles narrates the novel in the first person, Amis as author attempts to distance himself from his pretentious and egotistical protagonist-cum-narrator. Reviewers and critics have differed as to how successful he has been. One of the sources for this confusion between author and narrator lies in the number of resemblances between Martin Amis and Charles Highway, everything from their getting into Oxford after attending a crammer to the poor state of their teeth (see Life and Contexts, p. 5). Diedrick's balanced opinion is: "In *The Rachel Papers*, it is not always clear where Amis stands in relation to his narrator" (Diedrick 2004: 38). What most critics agree on is that this adolescent coming-of-age novel consciously challenges and interrogates Kingsley Amis's first novel, *Lucky Jim* (1954) (see Keulks 2003: 122–3). Both novelists employ comedy to write a form of *Bildungsroman* (see Criticism, **pp. 87–8**). But Amis explicitly embodies in his novel a form of comedy that differentiates it from the more traditional usage associated with his father's form of comedy. "We," Charles declares, linking himself to Martin's generation of writers, "have got into the habit of going further and further beyond the happy-ever-more promise [found in *Lucky Jim*]: relationships in decay, aftermaths" (*RP* 150). Amis thinks that "comedy is a much looser form than it once was" (Haffenden 1985: 10). Yet, in the same interview, he attempts somewhat unconvincingly to include his father's work in the new form of comedy (Haffenden 1985: 10–11). As Keulks points out, Charles declares that he usually has little time for Fielding's mock-heroic form of comedy to which Kingsley was so indebted in *Lucky Jim*. (*RP* 18; Keulks 2003: 127) (see Criticism, **p. 133**). From the start of his career, Amis saw himself as a comic writer in the contemporary mode, using black comedy to treat potentially dark subject matter.

Kingsley Amis's novel is not the only intertext used in *The Rachel Papers*. Charles is a literary poseur, and the novel makes reference to over 100 authors and works of literature. Charles uses literature to construct a wholly mediated persona for himself. During the obligatory low period of his adolescence, Charles "conscientiously read the literature of nausea, melancholy and absurdity—Sartre, Camus, Joyce" (*RP* 141). He attempts to seduce Rachel by displaying works of high literature in his room. One chapter heading reads "Twenty past: 'Celia shits' (the Dean of St Patrick's)." This reference to Swift's notorious satirical poem, "Cassinus and Peter," in which an undergraduate is horrified to find that Celia, the idealized object of his love, shits, anticipates and offers an indirect judgment on the moment in the chapter when Charles finds a pair of Rachel's panties smeared with "a stripe of suede-brown shit" (*RP* 181). Despite wanting to adopt a mature attitude ("Fair's fair [. . .] They do it too"), Charles ends up performing a teenage sulk, repeating the immature reaction of Swift's student (*RP* 181) (see Criticism, **pp. 140–141**). As Diedrick has observed, Amis's extensive use of intertextuality serves to place a distance between him and his character (Diedrick 2004: 32–3). Even the title of Charles's immature work pretentiously alludes to three classics of fiction, Swift's *The Bickerstaff Papers*, Dickens's *The Pickwick Papers*, and Henry James's *The Aspern Papers*.

Apart from "The Rachel Papers" and *Conquests and Techniques: A Synthesis* (pompously italicized), the other opus on which Charles labors throughout the novel is his "Letter to My Father." This is a poor imitation of Kafka's "Letter to his Father" which ran to forty pages and was also never delivered. Charles, flaunting his knowledge of one of T. S. Eliot's more dubious critical conclusions (about Hamlet's obsession with Gertrude), observes that his father, unlike Kafka's, "constitutes such a puny objective correlative" to his own anger (*RP* 8). This makes his unwarranted Letter another instance of his substitution of literature, especially writing, for life. It might be "lucid," "subtle," "elegant" (*RP* 219), but does it come from the heart? As he resolves, "I will not be placed at the mercy of my spontaneous self" (*RP* 180). So, he constantly sketches out in writing topics he can draw on before talking to a girlfriend or tutor (cf. *RP* 16, 33, 198). Vice versa, he often engages in some action just to provide material for his writing, such as turning "to check on Gloria's face (just for the files)"

(*RP* 21). Writing is, for Charles, the supreme self-indulgence: "I recorded all I saw, felt, thought. I had myself a time" (*RP* 27). He reads others' conversations as if they were themselves writing them. Thus, he characterizes the story Rachel tells him of her life as "dingily enlightened 'sixties fiction" (*RP* 68). Ironically, it turns out that this is exactly what Rachel has done: made up a fictional life for herself. He even speculates about taking his own life and concocts a laughably derivative suicide note, only to dismiss the idea on asking himself, "where would I find a responsible literary executor for the Notebooks?" (*RP* 144).

Chapter 9 contains the bravura description of the occasion when Charles first has genital sex with Rachel (*RP* 157–62), a description that concentrates on the purely physical mechanics of reaching mutual orgasm. Earlier in the chapter, Charles warns the reader: "young poets like myself are forever taunted by subjects which it is no longer possible to write about in this ironic age: evening skies, good looks, dew, anything at all to do with love" (*RP* 152). This is a good example of the ambivalence Diedrick refers to when asserting that Amis is not always clearly detached from Charles. Amis's subsequent fiction similarly categorizes modernity as an "ironic age" and almost always substitutes sex for love (see Criticism, **p. 112**). What distinguishes Charles is the way he confuses the act of sex with that of writing: "Panties. I threw back the top sheet, my head a whirlpool of notes, directives, memos, hints, pointers, random scribblings" (*RP* 158). He even adapts lines from T. S. Eliot's "The Love Song of J. Alfred Prufrock" (too timid to approach a woman) to delay orgasm. It takes the Oxford admissions don, Dr. Knowd, to finally bring Charles to a recognition of the way he has been using literature as a substitute for experience (ironically the title of the subject he chose to write his essay on [*RP* 185]). Knowd tells him, "Literature has a kind of life of its own, you know. You can't just use it [. . .] ruthlessly, for your own ends" (*RP* 215) (see Life and Contexts and Criticism, **pp. 5, 124–5**). The last page of the novel is—whether by design or default—highly ambiguous. After attempting to begin a short story, he decides, "It isn't really convincing." The book ends, "I refill my pen" (*RP* 224). Does this mean that he has finally committed himself to writing only what is "convincing," by which he presumably means "true to his experience"? Or does this imply that he will continue to give his writing priority over his life?

What most reviewers noted was that even in his first novel Amis had a style uniquely his own: witty, punning, and linguistically self-conscious (see Criticism, **p. 95**. He coins or popularizes contemporary terms (like "wrecky" [*RP* 11], or "adolescentiana" [*RP* 173]), draws attention to, by inverting, word combinations ("'How do you do,' I said, hands shaking, shaking hands" [*RP* 49; cf. 71]), makes fun of clichéd expressions ("I'd come up with something to get me down" [*RP* 92]), draws attention to instances of poor language such as Charles's "use of the split-infinitive" (*RP* 95) or Rachel's use of a "low-mimetic remark" (*RP* 150), transfers epithets ("Thus I maintained a tripartite sexual application in contrapuntal patterns" [*RP* 100]), and puns at the expense of his characters ("'Thank you, sir, thank you. Gob less.' 'I'll try,' I said" [*RP* 119]). This is quite an achievement, as Amis is simultaneously manipulating language for his own dark, comic ends and reproducing the language of a character who misuses it; Charles admits at one point, "I seemed incapable of using words without stylizing myself" (*RP* 144). Charles's significance remains problematical. Is he, as Neil Brooks suggests, meant to represent the rise of individualism and narcissism that has caused 1970s society to lose all sense of coherence? Or is he meant to suggest the delusion shared by his generation that he controls the forces that in fact control him? (Brooks 2006: 11, 20).

## Dead Babies (1975)

*Dead Babies*, Amis's second novel, abandons the light comic tone of *The Rachel Papers* for that of comically savage satire. Compared to the first-person focus on one major protagonist, this novel portrays an entire segment of society: the affluent, self-indulgent young generation of the 1970s. Set in Appleseed Rectory in the English countryside, its cast includes six inhabitants of a pseudo-commune led by the lord of this modern manor, the Hon. Quentin Villiers. His wife, Celia ("launched and kept afloat by money" [*DB* 157]), and his friends, Giles (who lives in fear of losing all his teeth), Keith (the "court dwarf"), Andy (filled with "cosmic disgust" [*DB* 182]), and Andy's girlfriend Diana (who spends her time "hating everything" [*DB* 64]): All suffer from abusive upbringing and now indulge in every form of abuse to do with sex, alcohol, drugs, and escalating violence. They are assisted by three American friends of Quentin's whom he has invited for the three-day weekend that constitutes the duration of the novel. Their leader is Marvell Buzhardt, a pseudo-guru of drugs, which, he explains, enable them to "have chemical authority over the psyche," (*DB* 44). He is accompanied by Skip (beaten as a child and violent as an adult), and Roxeanne (whose red-haired pubic bush gets more attention than her hair). "The Americans constituted a 'triad,' a 'troy,' which meant, more or less, that they got to fuck and bugger one another indiscriminately" (*DB* 52). There are also a local young whore, Lucy, down from London; a mysterious trickster, "Johnny;" and the detached yet knowing narrator.

The plot follows the escalating orgy of sex, alcohol, and drugs in which the group indulges over the weekend and which fails to provide anyone with genuine pleasure. "Johnny's" practical jokes also intensify until he reveals himself to be Quentin, the only seemingly civilized character, who in the finale murders Marvell, Celia, and Diana and arranges the deaths of Roxeanne, Skip, Andy, and Giles, as well as shifting the blame for the murders to "the Conceptualists" by planting false evidence ("*the excremental* G" [*DB* 206]), implicating them and freeing him from suspicion. In the last paragraph, Keith is about to walk into the Rectory where Quentin waits to kill him too. Amis's use of Quentin is typical of the way he involves the reader in his nightmare scenario. It is inevitable that readers should want to identify with the only character in the book who retains any semblance of humanist beliefs—what are referred to dismissively as "dead babies" in the book. (He changed the title to *Dark Secrets* for the paperback edition of 1977.) The mysterious narrator even warns the reader not to take Quentin at face value: "Watch Quentin closely. Everyone else does [. . .] it is impossible to meet Quentin without falling a little bit in love" (*DB* 41). In the chapter titled "Quentin" (each of the six Appleseed residents has one chapter devoted to his or her past), the narrator informs us: "Obviously Quentin was an adept at character stylization, a master of pastiche, a connoisseur of verbal self-dramatization" (*DB* 38). The revelation three pages from the end that Quentin is Johnny, who stage manages the deaths of all his friends (thus enabling them to achieve the death wish implicit in their lifestyles), compels readers to acknowledge the fact that by this point they too have been implicated in the narrative. In identifying with Quentin they have desired the destruction of all those characters who saw "love, understanding, compassion" as so many "dead babies" (*DB* 44). As Dern points out, the novel's attempt to draw its readers into the work parallels the way "the supposed audience at 'The Psychologic Review' [Chapter 25] was drawn into the play" (Dern 2000: 67) (see Criticism, **p. 101**).

The curiously detached narrator frequently intervenes with metafictional comments designed to manipulate the reader. Thus, using the first-person plural, the narrator teases the reader with the titillating prospect of having Keith enter into a wide range of possible sexual liaisons: "We could—let's see—we could have Diana take his hand and shoo him off to the woods, have Celia lean over and tenderly unbuckle his thin plastic belt, have Roxeanne shinny beneath him there and then." But, having shown the readers how implicated they are in the mock-pornographic nature of the narrative, the narrator forces them to observe, like him, the logic of his fictional world: "Of course, we can bring this about any time we like—but *Keith* can't, oh no" (*DB* 61). The narrator even apologizes to Keith that he "had to be that way" (*DB* 146). Yet, for many readers, the narrator's hold on the narrative is tenuous at best. Amis has since dismissed this book as "showing off" (Thomson 1998: 4), "a horribly transparent diagram of my early influences, shamelessly in the spirit of Burroughs and Ballard" (Jones 2001). Amis's early reviews of work by Ballard and Burroughs describe the same world found in *Dead Babies*: "the world of spectral rhetoric, drug withdrawal, urban breakdown, rampant vandalism" (*WAC* 301). *Dead Babies* offers a slightly futuristic fantasy of a post-humanist world in which individuals display the same characteristics that Amis discerned in one of Ballard's short-story collections, *Vermilion Sands*, that he reviewed: they are "directionless, soulless, futile with the sullen corruption of boredom and affluence" (Amis 1973b: 23). But Keulks has identified another identifiable influence in Kingsley Amis's 1974 novel, *Ending Up* (Keulks 2003: 133–61), which Martin referred to in a joint interview (Byrne 1974: 219) (see Criticism, **p. 88**).

All these partial borrowings point to the fact that in this novel Amis was intent on dissociating himself from the ethos and lifestyles of a generation which had allowed flower power to go to seed (hence Appleseed Rectory). In one of a number of italicized interventions, the narrator informs us that Appleseed is "*a place of street sadness, night fatigue, and canceled sex*" (*DB* 20). In a later interview given at the time the film of *Dead Babies* was released, Amis talked about the world of the late 1960s and early 1970s that suddenly came to an end in 1973 with the Oil Crisis and the inflation that followed. After 1973, "the wild ideas—political and pharmaceutical—that were going around then had to be dispensed with as leisure-class fripperies." Quentin is representative of "this edge to hippiedom" epitomized by the murders of Charles Manson (Pulver 2001: 14) (see Life and Contexts, **p. 13**). *Experience* recounts the brief period when Amis in his last year at Oxford stayed at the Old Forge in Shilton, Oxfordshire. There, Amis reports on the "interminable dramas" played out by the hippie contemporaries with whom he shared the place which ended with one of them attempting to overdose, being rushed to hospital, and landing up in "the local looney bin," and another being admitted to the London Clinic for an abortion (*E* 270–1) (see Life and Contexts, **p.6**). This episode, combined with his conversion to the political left after leaving Oxford, made Amis a permanent critic of the beat generation with which he had earlier—if partially—identified.

Amis uses a number of intertextual references (to Theodor Adorno, Andy's adopted name, to Diderot's famous eighteenth-century satire that Quentin is reading, to Menippus from whom the epigraph is taken) to indicate the object of his own satire. *Dead Babies* simultaneously satirizes the country-house weekend novel popularized by authors like P. G. Wodehouse and Agatha Christie (see Criticism, **pp. 89, 133**). Like Adorno, Amis is enough of a postmodernist to blame the Enlightenment for the degeneration that an overreliance on reason had produced by the later twentieth century. Thus, Marvell ridicules Andy for insisting that he is solely heterosexual: "why negate yourself into a rationalist one-sex block?" (*DB* 154). Yet, Marvell is himself representative of a more straightforward rationalism, akin to de Sade's. He argues, "sex isn't erotic any more. It's carnal—conceptualized—to do just with geometrics and sensations" (*DB* 154). According to Marvell, "That's what they did. In the seventies [. . .] They separated emotion and sex" (*DB* 122). Sexual liberation meant that "sexual lassitude and disgust seemed to be everywhere among the young, and two-night stands were becoming a rarity" (*DB* 68). Yet, as Celia's father points out to her, "you free libbers [. . .] you thought you'd get free. You didn't get free" (*DB* 158). Instead, their lives have turned into "vanished mornings, lost afternoons, and probable yesterdays" (*DB* 164). Amis is among the early critics of the Beatles generation. Critics continue to dispute whether his satiric fantasy constitutes an achieved work of art or simply a work that "aims to shock and disgust" (Drabble 1976: 2).

## Success (1978)

Unlike *Dead Babies*, Amis's third novel, *Success*, shows tight control of structure and tone. It consists of twelve chapters starting with "January" and ending with "December." Each chapter contains two sections, each a dramatic monologue, the first spoken by Terry, a working-class orphan, and the second by Gregory, his upper-class stepbrother whose family adopted Terry as a nine-year-old after his father had murdered his sister. The plot can be visually represented as an "X" with the successful Greg falling as Terry rises in the world, or as each starting at the top (Terry's being ethical and Gregory's being social) and both sliding to a low of their particular value system. Around the intersection of the "X," Ursula, Gregory's sister, takes her life, a victim of both stepbrothers' manipulation of and indifference to her (see Criticism, **pp. 101–2**). Gregory is a privileged snob who thought that "proper people" didn't need to study to make their way in the world (*S* 183). But, within his lifetime, the world has changed. Now, "the yobs are winning" (*S* 149), "yob" being back slang for "boy," meaning loutish, ignorant and working-class. Terry, a yob in Gregory's eyes, ends up a success in the external sense of being successful financially, sexually, and socially. This exchange of traditional roles may have originated in an exchange of gender roles that Amis used for a short play, *It's Disgusting at Your Age*, which was published in the *New Review*, in September 1976. In it, the two young men spend their time protesting, "We're not just lumps of flesh," while the two young women plot to lure them to bed while complaining that doing so is "too much like hard work" (Amis 1976: 19, 20). Amis's treatment in the novel of the social inversion in 1970s British society is more complex.

Gregory and Terry evolve from Quentin and Keith in *Dead Babies*. In fact, Gregory even calls Terry a "court dwarf" (*S* 93), the exact words used to describe Keith in his cast list of "Main Characters." Gregory, however, lacks the destructive power that Quentin exerts. His reliance on the class system for his initial sense of social superiority and sexual success proves his undoing. Amis skillfully endows him with an affected form of speech, which should warn the reader not to accept his valuation of himself. He uses archaic expressions like "days of yore" (*S* 40), refers to sleep as "an unkind mistress" (*S* 40), and reveals his prejudices when contemptuously dismissing Terry's preferred color schemes as "an absurd motley of nigger primaries and charwoman pastels" (*S* 20). He exaggerates his sinecure of a job at an art gallery, his sexual desirability with men and women, and his cultivated tastes in wine and food. During the first part of the novel, Terry, by comparison, confesses to how he experiences "tramp-dread and street sadness" (*S* 12), cannot get any woman to have sex with him, drinks because, as Amis has him punningly put it, "I'm losing my bottle" (*S* 30), and thinks that Gregory's "life is in some sense a gloating parody of [. . .] his own quotidian dreads" (*S* 48). But the reader is explicitly warned by page 97 that Gregory has a "love of fabrication," while Terry "never could lie." This should have registered already with an alert reader, as Gregory's account of his lavish and prolonged lunch with his sister Ursula at Le Coq d'Or (*S* 69–72) is contradicted by Terry eleven pages later who reports that according to Ursula "they had a very depressing half-hour together in some sandwich bar" (*S* 83). Gregory's lies are exposed in the second half of the narrative. He offers a detailed account of how he stole Jan, the one girl who was about to sleep with Terry, when Terry is called away to deal with Ursula's first attempt to commit suicide. Gregory proudly portrays himself as a handsome, commanding presence who orders Jan to strip and perform fellatio on him before he turns her over and buggers her (*S* 134–6). This near-rape fantasy turns out in fact to have been a sexual fiasco when Jan meets up again with Terry four months later and tells him that Gregory could not perform and broke down in tears "about being queer and broke" (*S* 192).

As in his earlier two novels, Amis is forcing the reader to take an unusually active role in the novel. In his first monologue, Terry, after confessing his envy of Gregory, tells the reader: "My job is to make *you* hate him also," and warns readers to keep their eyes open (but on Gregory? Or Terry?) (*S* 12). Each step-brother addresses his confession to the reader and is unsure whether the other has already told readers what he is recounting (*S* 18, 156). The reader is frequently positioned within the world of the novel, as when Terry early on claims that people pass by him in the street without noticing him, adding, "(you might pass me one of these days; you wouldn't know it. Why should you?)" (*S* 32). And the implied reader is given a masculine gender, for instance when Terry says of Ursula, "You'd fancy her, I reckon" (*S* 54). The reader is not allowed to rest assured once "he" has discovered just how unreliable Gregory's account is. The narrative performs its own reversal partway through when Terry admits to "making everything sound slightly more humiliating and prospectless than it actually is" (*S* 109), while Gregory resolves to "try to tell the truth from now on" (*S* 184). Even their style of speaking is inverted, with Terry beginning to swear less frequently and Gregory deciding to change his style if he is to tell the truth about his life including his "*fucking awful*" job (*S* 181). Further, Terry starts behaving as Gregory was at the start of the book, and vice versa. Terry finally gets to have sex with Jan and reports, "It was okay—with myself in sparkling form, both athletic and pitiless—but nothing special" (*S* 223). This could equally be a highly abbreviated description of Gregory's night with her. The attentive reader also will notice how Amis's description of Terry's seduction of Ursula uses identical language and images as does Gregory's memory of the first time he commits incest with her (cf. *S* 186–7 with 196) (see Criticism, p. 102).

Amis has said that *Success* "is all about the great English disease, Class," which allows "only envy and hatred" (Michener 1986: 38, 40). In reviewing the novel, Graham Fuller wrote that it is "a parody of England's class war, with Gregory and Terry symbolizing the spiritual decay of the landed gentry and the greedy self-betterment of the 'yobs'" (Fuller 1987: 66) (see Life and Contexts and Criticism, **pp. 13, 106**). But Amis seems less interested in offering a satire of English society than in showing how the changing nature of British society was affecting his generation in the 1970s. It is Terry's view at the end of the book that the upper classes "don't belong any more. What they belonged to has disappeared" (*S* 193). At the same time, Terry asks the reader, "Do you still think any of that matters, class and so on? It doesn't. It's crap" (*S* 58–9). But this swing to an imaginary classlessness or to a world where the yobs are in charge, which means that "everyone accepts the fact that they've got to get nastier in order to survive" (*S* 149), turns Terry into the yob he was not earlier, one who declares, "We are getting nastier [. . .] We do as we want now" (*S* 194–5). A victim, he ends up victimizing the hippie tramp whom he feared ending up like. Taking over the reigns of power from Gregory, Terry seems automatically to inherit his arrogance and lack of feeling. By comparison, near the end, Gregory for the first time shows compassion for another suffering fellow human, Damon (*S* 218). What is the reader meant to make of the end of the novel where Terry decides, "I'm going to be all right" (*S* 223), while Gregory is left looking out on the scene of his early sexual fumbling with Ursula feeling that "the lake is trying to warn me—danger in the streets of the trees" (*S* 224). Is Gregory simply a castaway of the new order? Or is he entering, as Neil Powell suggests, "the terrors and the comforts of the rural world that may be bleak but at least they have depth and reality" (Powell 1981: 44)?

## Other People: A Mystery Story (1981)

*Other People*, Amis has said, "is the odd one out among my books" (McGrath 1987: 193) (see Life and Contexts, p. 15). One major departure from his previous novels is the fact that the book is written largely from a female point of view. It concerns a young woman who calls herself Mary Lamb, after hearing someone quote the nursery rhyme, "Mary had a little lamb," who appears to be suffering from amnesia. At the beginning of the novel, she wakes up in the recovery room of a London hospital with no memory of who she is or what her past life consisted of. Her mind is a *tabula rasa*, and she is forced to try to make sense of every new phenomenon and happening. She first joins a group of homeless down-and-outs where she is befriended by an alcoholic, Sharon, and then sexually attacked after Sharon has matched her up with Trev, one of her homeless male friends, in return for some drink money. After hitting Trev with a brick, Mary is briefly picked up by the police and released at the end of Part I. At the start of the long Part II she finds herself in Sharon's home where she is given shelter by Sharon's alcoholic parents and her brother, Gavin, until Trev breaks in one evening and breaks the father's back. From the opening page of the novel, a mysterious young man whose name is later revealed to be John Prince, takes a distant interest in her. When she is forced to leave Sharon's household, Mary goes to an address that Prince has given her, which turns out to be a church-army hostel for young women in trouble. While staying there, she takes a job washing plates at an Italian restaurant. Next, she moves out of the hostel into an organized squat where two of the restaurant's employees live: Alan (a weakly bookkeeper) and Russ (illiterate but full of sexual bravado), a pair who seem to be descended from those earlier pairs, Quentin and Keith, and Gregory and Terry. For a short while, she becomes Alan's lover, and when she breaks off the arrangement he hangs himself.

Meantime, Prince has been prompting her to remember her past life as one Amy Hide, apparently a nasty piece of work. He sends her to meet one of Amy's previous boyfriends, a television journalist, who was so thrown by her rejection of him that he turned gay. At the television studio she meets an assistant, Jamie, who turns out to have a large independent income. He lets her come to stay in his upscale apartment where three past girlfriends are also living. Jamie spends his time drinking, smoking, and reading. Using tears to subdue Jamie, Mary seduces him and then turns into her previous incarnation as Amy Hide, who victimized her men. She has become one of the "other people" of the title. Part III (only twenty pages long) finds Amy living a domestic life with Prince in a suburban house. After Prince has arranged a reunion between Amy and her younger sister, he drives her to a derelict house in London where she learns that she is already dead. After Prince has murdered her a second time, she finds herself, in the last pages, back home as a teenager about to step out of the house and encounter, for a second time, a young Prince waiting across the street to meet her.

So, the design of the narrative is circular. Where Amy Hide moved from a secure position in society to its underlife, Mary reverses this social progression. Yet, both move from innocence to experience, although Mary is given a second chance by being restored to innocence. Amis foregrounds this circularity by using exactly the same wording for the first paragraph of Chapter 1 and for the first paragraph of the final segment of the concluding Chapter 24 (*OP* 13, 222). Similarly, he echoes with significant variations the narrator's words spoken in the Prologue and Epilogue: "I didn't want to have to do it to her," and "she *asked* for it" (*OP* 9) become "I won't do anything to her unless she *asks* for it" in the Epilogue (*OP* 224). In other words, the narrator implies that Amy invited her own destruction by pursuing her self-destructive lifestyle, and that she can avoid

a similar fate the next time round if she acts differently. In both cases, the narrator exclaims, "Oh hell. Let's get it over with" (*OP* 9, 224). The use of "hell" is
not accidental. As reviewers and critics noted, the title of the novel is an allusion
to Jean-Paul Sartre's depiction of hell in *Huis Clos* (1945, translated as *No Exit*
in 1947), in which one of the three characters trapped together in Hell concludes,
"Hell, it's other people." But Mary is in no hell of the afterlife. The circles of Hell
through which she rises are those of contemporary life in London. In Chapter 13,
Prince takes Mary on a guided tour of "the city's abysmal divides and atrocious
energies" (*OP* 119), which culminates in the nightclub where she had been
murdered as Amy Hide. There, she observes a pair of dancers, the man whose
"eyes were quite dead," supported by "a little ruined blonde" who is "hauling
him as if in eternal punishment round the littered floor" (*OP* 123). Mary seems
to evoke Dante's *Inferno* when she thinks to herself, "this was a whole new ledge
on the way down" (*OP* 125). There is a muted assumption in this book (which
will become a major concern in future novels) that something serious "was
wrong with Earth" (*OP* 137), that our world, epitomized by sleazy London, is
turning into its own form of hell.

Another much-cited intertext for this novel is Craig Raine's poem, " A Martian
Sends a Postcard Home," first published in the 1977 Christmas issue of the *New
Statesman*. In it, a Martian visits Earth and encounters everyday objects without
understanding their function. In 1978, James Fenton dubbed the poems of Raine
and Christopher Reid the "Martian School" of poetry. The following year, Amis
published a poem titled "Point of View," which, in Martian style, imagines what
the world looks like from a pervert's eyes. He rendered this poem in prose in this
novel (*OP* 186–7). Several reviewers immediately called the book Martian. Amis
claimed that he began the novel a year before Raine's poem appeared, although
he wrote the novel during his seven-month stay in Paris in 1979–80 (see Life and
Contexts, **p. 15**). More tellingly, he claimed in a television appearance on *The
South Bank Show* that his method differed from Raine's Martian who "described
the world in terms of misconceptions while his heroine did so without preconcep-
tions at all" (Rawson 1981: 22). Whatever the degree of originality, the novel
offers striking effects that compel the reader to see the world anew through
Mary's innocent eyes. In her vision, children become "shrunken, compacted
[people]—mysteriously lessened in some vital respect" (*OP* 16), planes "cruci-
fixes of the sky" (*OP* 18), and television "a window with everything happening
on the other side" (*OP* 53). When Trev forces himself sexually on her, she begins
to understand what he wants: "His two wet red points wanted [. . .] her two
mouths" (*OP* 46). Mary attributes human feelings to animate and inanimate
things alike. "All things are alive, [. . .] she thought" (*OP* 126). Amis is able to
have much verbal fun with this aspect of her perception. Speculating on the way
clothes signify money and sex, Mary reflects, "that wasn't what clothes were in
business to do; that wasn't clothes' line" (*OP* 155). Gradually, Mary's estrangement from everyday life dissipates as she reverts to the manipulative role of Amy
Hide.

What exactly is the relationship between Mary Lamb and Amy Hide? Or
between the narrator and John Prince? Subtitled *A Mystery Story*, the novel had
the unintended effect of mystifying most of its reviewers. A few years later, Amis
admitted that he had failed to communicate the meaning of his mystery to most

of his readers. He explained that the "novel is the girl's death, and her death is a sort of witty parody of her life." So "her life-in-death is one in which she is terrifically well-meaning and causes disaster" (Haffenden 1985: 17). "At the very end of the novel she starts her life again, the idea being that life and death will alternate until she gets it right" (Haffenden 1985: 18) (see Life and Contexts, p. 15). Once given the key, the reader will find all the evidence for this explanation in the text. Thinking about Alan's suicide, Mary is convinced that he "had simply stopped, stopped dead." The narrative continues: "She didn't believe in life after death. She just believed in death" (OP 179). And in the last chapter, Prince tells her, "You are already dead [. . .] but then death is very lifelike" (OP 222). Amy Hide's name alludes to R. L. Stevenson's Dr Jekyll and Mr Hyde (1886), a story of a man who leads two lives—one morally respectable, the other thoroughly evil. In Part II, Mary, the Dr Jekyll figure of this novel, sees Amy, her Mr. Hyde, lurking in her reflection in the mirror. Mary is constantly looking at her reflection in the mirror. "She is afraid that her life has in some crucial sense already run its course, that the life she moves through now is nothing more than another life's reflection, its mirror, its shadow" (OP 97). She has passed through the looking glass of death to confront her life in reverse. But that other life of Amy Hide staring back at her suggests that "there was chaos in there somewhere" (OP 80). At the end of Part II, when Mary is about to become Amy Hide, she looks at her reflection: "She had done it. She had torn through the glass and come back from the other side" (OP 200).

The same act of doubling occurs in the case of the narrator and John Prince. Prince is a Manichean demon-lover, both Prince Charming and the Prince of Darkness (see Criticism, pp. 86, 126). He occupies an ambivalent position in the novel: He is both omniscient, being able to "go anywhere" (OP 123), and yet—like any other character—confined at other times to the dictates of the narrative. In this latter role, he has a minimal history. He complains of what Amy had done to him (OP 106); he has taken a smash (OP 70); he has contemplated suicide (OP 167); and he lies (OP 171). He admits to being both the policeman and the murderer (OP 220, 222). But, for much of the time, the narrator appears to be indistinguishable from the figure of Prince. As narrator, he claims to be in total control of everyone's destiny and can predict future events. So, in a discussion about drunks, he informs the reader: "You'll be running into a few more of them too. But all under my control, of course" (OP 34). This is the first (but not the last) intrusion of the narrator into the narrative in Amis's fiction. Amis has said that in Other People "the narrator is the murderer and the writer and the murderer are equivalent in that each has the power to knock Amy Hide off" (McGrath 1985: 192). Is Amis giving metafictional expression to the sadistic nature of any author figure who gives life to characters in order to subject them to every kind of danger and fear including death (by murder in this case)? Is he also charging his readers with a desire to see the author kill his characters for their sport? Why then does the narrator admit in the Epilogue: "I'm tired. I'm not in control any more" (OP 224)? Prince has reverted to his past role as participant in the narrative. But, at the metafictional level, is this meant to suggest that the narrator inevitably becomes circumscribed by the dictates of his own narration? Only a reformed Amy can release him from his guilt at having ended her life (see Criticism, p. 127).

## Money: A Suicide Note (1984)

Amis has characterized *Money* as a radical departure from the first four novels that were all "well made, balanced, a lot of form, décor." With *Money* he decided not to "worry too much about the form." Instead, his priorities were "shedding restraints," and "a determination to tell the truth and fuck it if it's upsetting, or embarrassing, or in bad taste" (Ungless 1995: 35). The book that resulted was greeted with acclaim by most reviewers (see Life and Contexts, p. 16), and is still considered one of his finest novels, perhaps the definitive novel of the 1980s. The novel features as narrator and protagonist John Self, a thirty-five-year-old British television director of vulgar and popular commercials who has just been offered his first feature film by Fielding Goodney, an American producer. According to Amis, Self is a consumer who "is consumed by consumerism." Having been brought up on a diet of television and pornography, "his life is without sustenance of any kind" (Haffenden 1985: 7). He eats and drinks to excess, drink being in his case, as Amis explained, "more of a painkiller than a quest for a good time" (Haffenden 1985: 13). His addiction to pornography and masturbation illustrates the extent to which his subjectivity has been formed by the mass media. It also dispenses with the need for live women, offering him the satisfactions of solitary gratification. As he sums it up, Self's life consists of "[f]ast food, sex shows, space games, slot machines, video nasties, nude mags, drink, pubs, fighting, television, handjobs" (*M* 67). Yet, for many readers, Amis manages to invoke our sympathy for Self even as he is mocking him for the narrow confines to which his cultural upbringing has condemned him. Take his penchant for handjobs: "*Say what you like about handjobs, slag them off all you want, but they couldn't very well be cheaper or more readily available. In the end you've got to hand it to hand jobs. They're deeply democratic*" (*M* 358). With his usual verbal skill, Amis neutralizes the negativity of "handjobs" by punning positively on "hand" in "hand it to," and then situates this normally private form of self-indulgence within the public sphere of politics.

*Money* is, of course, about money in the money decade of the 1980s. Even the movie that Self is asked to direct in America is called first *Good Money* and then *Bad Money*. References to money appear on most of the pages of this novel. It is what drives Self to behave in the outrageous way he does. "If time is money," Self, a junk-food addict from childhood, reflects with unconscious humor, "then fast food saves both" (*M* 261). His unfaithful English girlfriend, Selina, a pornographer's dream come true in his eyes, sexually excites Self because she "does all this for money" (*M* 39). Money is also associated with death throughout the novel. The entire novel, apart from the final italicized epilogue, takes the form of an extended suicide note. At one point, Self claims, "Money is the only thing we [he and everyone else] have in common. Dollar bills, pound notes, they're suicide notes. *Money* is a suicide note" (*M* 112). The suicide note which acts as a prologue to *Money* is dated September 1981, and the main action of the book appears to occur between June and September 1981 when Self makes his unsuccessful attempt to end his life. The epilogue jumps to late December and ends in early January 1982. The body of the book consists of eight chapters that alternate between New York where it opens and London where it closes.

In the course of these hectic months, Selina in England and Fielding Goodney in America skillfully fool Self. Selina holds him sexually captive until she can land a man who can guarantee her real money. Goodney makes Self believe that he is being paid enormous sums of money to direct a film, when, in fact, Goodney hires actors to impersonate financial backers of the film and has Self sign documents that make him wholly responsible for all the money being lavishly spent on the film. Goodney also hires a writer to produce an unproducible screenplay and impersonates an anonymous caller (Frank the Phone) who taunts Self throughout his stay in New York with accounts of the humiliations he meets there, many arranged by Goodney. Much of the New York part of the novel involves Self's dealings with the film's four main American actors, each displaying an oversized ego. The plot of Self's film is based on his relations to his father and his mistress. After it has been given an American setting and characters, the actors whom Goodney hires attempt to turn it into a vehicle for projecting their own grotesquely aggrandized images of their screen personas. Three of the actors are based on actors with whom Amis came into contact when employed to do rewrites for the screenplay of *Saturn 3* in 1980: Kirk Douglas, Harvey Keitel, and Farah Fawcett (see Life and Contexts, **p. 14**). Thus, Lorne Guyland, the actor modeled on Douglas, turns Barry, Self's publican father (as Self thinks), called Gary in the film, into first Garfield, "a man of some considerable culture" (*M* 171), then Sir Garfield, and finally Lord Garfield, a cultured stud who gives his screen mistress her first orgasm. By the time he has finished turning the script into a vehicle for displaying his virility and social status, the film has lost all its narrative sense and appeal. Of course, Goodney knew that the actors would behave this way, part of the practical joke he is stage-managing at Self's expense.

There are two jokers in the pack (see *M* 345) that prevent Goodney from keeping total control of the fiction in which he enmeshes Self. The first is the presence of a British writer whom Self meets and engages to rewrite the American screenplay so that it will work given the enlarged egos of each of the four principal actors. The writer is named "Martin Amis" and his successful rewrite trumps Goodney's hand. Like Goodney but more so, he stands in for the author "who's duping and buggering him [Self] about the most;" yet, unlike Goodney, he is "very, very fond" of him (Smith 1985: 79) (see Criticism, **p. 127**). The other character who counters Goodney is Martina Twain—a second (twain) female Martin—who, like "Martin Amis," is possessed of the culture lacking in Self, which makes him desire her. She almost succeeds in reforming Self. But his dependence on pornography makes him unable to have sex with her, and their affair comes to a dramatic end when she finds him having sex with his pornographic ex-girlfriend Selina. This time, Self is the victim of Selina's plotting who (with Martina's husband, her lover) arranged for Self and Martina to meet in the first place. As Selina explains to Self, "it can be good fun deceiving people," especially when "they haven't got the talent" for it themselves (*M* 335). As Amis has remarked, Self ultimately "is the victim of all his crimes" (McGrath 1987: 193). Late in the novel, he comes to realize this: "*I was the needing, the hurting artist [. . .] I wanted to believe. I wanted the money so bad*" (*M* 362). Like "Martin Amis," Goodney and Selina, Self is a maker of fictions in this work of fiction; all their lives are shattered by the effect money has on all of them. Money has its revenge on Goodney when his face is kicked in by Self in a climactic fight. In the epilogue, Self is discovered moneyless ("*I feel better now that I haven't got any*" [*M* 361]), having rented out his flat to pay lawyers to fend off all the actions against him, and with a new unglamorous but caring girlfriend, Georgina. Sitting on a bench waiting for her outside the underground station, Self is dressed so shabbily that in the final paragraph he is mistaken for a beggar by a passerby who leaves ten pence in his lap. Amis has said that "the only way John Self is going to get over money [. . .] is to be divested of it. That's probably why it felt like a happy ending to me" (Haffenden 1985: 14).

*Money*, while satirizing the universal pursuit of money that characterized the 1980s, does not attempt to do so from some ascetic norm. Instead, money is comically exposed as the spoiler of quality human life. As in *Success*, money now belongs to a new, mainly lower class of entrepreneurs like John Self, who thinks of himself as "the new kind, the kind who has money but can never use it for anything but ugliness" (*M* 59). His ubiquitous last name makes him representative of a new construction of selfhood in the West: "I'm called John Self. But who isn't?" (*M* 97) (see Criticism, **p. 112**). An Everyman of materialism who describes himself as "so twentieth century" (*M* 308), he is the son of an American mother and an English father and has spent his childhood between the ages of seven and fifteen in the USA. He is truly transatlantic. The 1980s was the decade in which Margaret Thatcher was Prime Minister and Ronald Reagan President. Or, as Self puts it, "they've got an actor, and we've got a chick" (*M* 146). The supply-side economics that both leaders adopted was responsible for an increase in the disparity between rich and poor, a disparity that was part of the root cause of the riots in British cities in 1981 which are alluded to throughout the novel and form the underbelly to the royal wedding of Diana and Prince Charles (see Life and Contexts, **p. 20**). "The talk is all of royalty and riots," Self says alliteratively uniting the two apparently disparate events. But money, which Self idolizes, proves as illusory as the moneymen who turn out to be actors. Incapable of relating sympathetically to others, Self reports, "Selina says I'm incapable of true love. It isn't true. I truly love money" (*M* 221). Amis's clever conversion of adjective to adverb and noun to verb gives linguistic life to Self's perversion of emotions under the corrupting influence of money. Frequently, Self can only express his deeper feelings in financial terms. Faced with a moral dilemma—whether to tell Martina that her husband is cheating on her—he asks, "you chicks out there" whether he should just shut up for her sake: "Well, I don't see the economics in that, quite frankly. I feel I'm owed some kind of kickback on the deal" (*M* 265). By "kickback" he means getting Martina to have sex with him, but the use of the word with its connotations of illegal payment only serves to show the impoverished view of love that money bestows on him (see Criticism, **pp. 112–13**).

"Martin Amis," despite some physical resemblances, is not Martin Amis. He is at once a character in the narrative and its implied author. Seen through the eyes of Self, the unreliable narrator, he is an anachronism, someone who has failed to come to terms with the preeminent need to maximize his income (which Self does for him). He also comes across to Self as an out-of-touch intellectual who rambles on boringly about such abstruse literary matters as the distance between the author and the narrator (*M* 229) and the postmodern assumption that "motivation is pretty well shagged out by now" (*M* 331), "an idea taken from art, [. . .] not from twentieth-century life" (*M* 341) (see Criticism, **p. 112**). On the penultimate page of the novel Self concludes: "*I've settled the motivation question. I supplied it all. The confidence trick would have ended in five minutes if it hadn't been for John Self*" (*M* 362).

Goodney may have imitated Iago's "motiveless malignancy" (Coleridge's term), but, like Othello (to whom there are several allusions throughout the book), Self's self-delusion provides all the motive needed for Goodney and "Martin Amis" to humiliate him. In the last chapter, Self plays "Martin Amis" at chess and is "zugzwanged" by him, that is, as "Amis" explains to him, forced to move and, in moving, to lose. This is precisely what the author has done to his protagonist. Just as Goodney speaking as Frank the Phone tells Self, "I want your life" (*M* 179), so "Martin Amis" deliberately subjects his main character to the series of indignities including a failed suicide attempt that readers looking to be entertained expect of an author. "They [readers] too," "Martin Amis" explains, "have something of the authorial power to create life" (*M* 242).

Self, who says, "Sometimes I think I am controlled by someone" (*M* 305), remembers "Amis" repeatedly saying to him "*I'm so sorry*" (*M* 356). Yet, the last glimpse Self gives us of him is at the pub, where "Martin Amis" asks, "*Hey, what are you doing here [. . .] You are meant to be out of the picture by now*" (*M* 359). Is Amis implying that a character can take on a kind of fictional autonomy, that allows him to escape from an author's absolute control of him? Has the implied author become just another character (like Prince in *Other People*) by this late stage (see Works, **p. 45**)? Amis deliberately adds one more confusing frame to the existing set of frames used to construct his manifestly contrived web of narrative. In *Money*, life becomes art only to escape the orderly schematics of artistic form (just as Self escapes his destined suicide). Self congratulates "Martin Amis" for coming up with a rewrite of *Bad Money* that indulged the four actors' need for self-glorification while showing them to be wanton and weak. This," he adds, "was realism" (*M* 274). But, as Amis told Haffenden, "Realism is a footling consideration" (Haffenden 1985: 8) (see Criticism, **p. 117**). He made this remark while explaining that Self might be "a stupid narrator," but that what he, Amis, writes about his character's thoughts can be expressed with his own unfettered use of language, a purely formal literary device that has little to do with mimetic realism. Amis employs this double perspective to simultaneously display with humor Self's circumscribed responses to life while ironically signifying to the reader the presence of an alternative way of understanding the world. Thus, Self reflects perceptively, "I live like an animal" (*M* 257); but when he describes his attempt to reform his animalistic behavior, for instance exercising by "wiggling my legs in the air like an upended beetle," he is totally unaware of the allusion he is making to Kafka's famous story, *Metamorphosis*, in which a son spurned by his father (like Self) turns into a beetle, any more than when Self describes his attempt to reform himself as "my metamorphosis" *(M* 312). The novel is constructed of such verbal puns, unconsciously spoken intertexts, and situational ironies, all of which contribute to a densely constructed narrative artifact that delights in its fictive world.

## London Fields (1989)

Amis told Will Self that *London Fields* began as a sixty-page novella called "The Murderee" (see Life and Contexts, **p. 21**). It told the story of how the Keith figure and the Nicola figure move towards each other until he murders her. But the novella turned into a novel when he introduced first another potential murderer, Guy, and then turned the narrator (Sam) into a major player (Self 1993a: 149). In effect, Amis resorted to one of his favorite devices—doubling (see Criticism, **p. 101**). Instead of combining opposing moods in one character, he preferred to split the male character into a lustful Keith and a romantic Guy, just as he introduced two children, one monstrous (Marmaduke, Guy's son), the other innocent (Kim, Keith's daughter). *London Fields,* like "The Murderee," opens by casting working-class Keith Talent ("a very bad guy" who "just didn't have the talent" [*LF* 4, 5]) as the murderer and Nicola Six (who not only looks but acts like "a fashion model" who "could do what she liked with you" [*LF* 45]) as the murderee (see titles of the first two chapters). But Chapter 3 is titled "The Foil," and introduces Guy Clinch, "a good guy," who "wanted for nothing," but who is "lifeless" (*LF* 27). In addition, Chapter 1 is preceded by a sub-chapter (Dern's term) in which the reader is introduced to Samson Young, the American narrator of the story. Sam has exchanged apartments with a seemingly successful British author, Mark Asprey (sharing the same initials as the actual author), who is occupying Sam's apartment in New York. Sam has only written two factual books of memoirs and journalism, "praised for their honesty, their truthfulness" (*LF* 39). Unable to invent fiction, Sam is delighted to come across the other three characters in a local pub, the Black Cross, who present him with a murder plot that "hasn't happened yet" (*LF* 1). But he thinks that he knows not only the murderee but also the murderer (he's wrong). All he has to do is "just write it down" (*LF* 1).

Already, Sam's project sounds too simple: "I have the makings of a really snappy little thriller. Original, too, in its way. Not a whodunit. More a whydoit" (*LF* 3). How can Sam know the ending in all its detail (which is described on seven separate occasions) before it has occurred? One could claim that he is anticipating Nicola's description to him of the way she will meet her death on her thirty-fifth birthday, November 6, 1999. Nicola has the gift of clairvoyance, we learn in Chapter 2. But then, Nicola must have misled him about the identity of her murderer. When Sam first meets her in person (she has lured him to her flat by leaving her diaries for him to find and return to her), she reacts to his presence with "physical fear" (*LF* 61). This is because her gift for clairvoyance tells her that Sam is going to turn out to be her actual murderer. Who then is in command of this narrative? Nicola's knowledge of future events puts her on a par with Amis, the author (cf. Diedrick 2004: 119) (see Criticism, **p. 113**). Sam's supposedly superior position as narrator is quickly undermined by his immersion in a narrative that he claims merely to be inscribing from "real" life. Amis recounts Sam's thoughts and actions by using a first-person voice for the sub-chapters in which he features, imbuing Sam with a privileged narrative position that buttresses Sam's deluded claim to be an external reporter of others' lives. Sam narrates the twenty-four chapters (proper) of the book in the third person, frequently employing free indirect discourse, which invites confusion between the voice of the speaker and the narrator, a confusion Amis comically compounds.

As is customary with Amis's fiction, the plot is uncomplicated, more a vehicle for the satire and the verbal play with which the book abounds. Faced with the death of love in her life (and in the contemporary world), Nicola has decided to stage her death (see Life and Contexts, p. 21). After the four principal characters meet, Nicola uses her sexual allure to play Keith and Guy like two fish on lines to bring about her wished-for death on her thirty-fifth birthday. Both men are married, although Keith treats his wife and child as appendages to his consuming interest in darts and pornography (and numerous sexual partners), while Guy tries to be a model husband whose relationship to his wife (Hope) is subverted by their monstrous child, Marmaduke. Nicola gradually succeeds in making both men become obsessed with her, only to manipulate both into breaking up their marriages (though it is hinted that Guy will stage a reconciliation after the end of the novel). This leads Guy to lie in wait to murder Nicola. But Sam persuades Guy to allow him to take his place as murderer in return for Guy's promise to look after Keith's abused daughter, Kim, with whom Sam has become obsessed in the course of the book. Sam finds he is the fourth point of the Black Cross, the pub where all four characters met. Throughout the novel, Sam has been staging his entry into the lives of the other three characters in order to compile his supposedly fact-based work of fiction. In the finale, his formally neat plot is totally negated by Nicola's planned use of him as her murderer. Nicola makes his carefully motivated murderer and foil redundant. "She outwrote me," Sam concludes after killing her and taking a pill that will kill him within the hour. "Her story worked. And mine didn't" (LF 466). Not only is the narrator subsumed into the narrative of the leading female protagonist, but Sam ends the novel writing a letter to Mark Asprey who is left to compile Sam's account of things (now recategorized by him as "a full confession" [LF 468]) in the form that London Fields takes. As Amis explained on BBC Radio 4, "What's happened is that Mark Asprey has come back to the flat, found the novel, and found the intervening material, which is the narrator's little chapters between the chapters, stitched it all together, and brought it out under the name of Martin Amis" (quoted in Diedrick 2004: 263n8). If Nicola outwrites Sam, Asprey is the external narrator or compiler who (like his namesake) becomes the ultimate arbiter of every character's fate. Sam's letter to Asprey ends with a PPS: "You didn't set me up. Did you?" (LF 468). Making that question two sentences shows Sam's dawning realization that Asprey did set him up.

Described in this bare-boned manner, the plot of London Fields sounds as forced as Asprey's romance, Crossbone Waters, which Sam calls "an awful little piece of shit" (LF 389). In fact, the novel is a highly crafted satiric comedy which relies for its effect on characters who are as much representative of end-of-the-century civilization as psychologically individualized personas, a dystopian vision of the state of the world at the turn of the millennium, and a brilliant use of different voices and linguistic devices to draw attention to the literary medium that controls all the characters and events in the narrative. Due to their representative nature, the characters come close to caricature (a few critics claim that they are mere caricatures). Amis, however, does not subscribe to the psychologically realist notion of fiction. Nicola Six (misheard by Keith as "Sex," then "Seeks"

[*LF* 37]) exemplifies his use of characters for his own artistic purposes. Originally, she was an actress. "But then the acting bit of her lost its moorings and drifted out into real life" (*LF* 19). Faced with the death of love in her time, Nicola embarks on a career of "the effortless enslavement of men" (*LF* 71). Her motive is the acquisition of power, which she achieves by employing her sexuality: "she was promiscuous on principle, as a sign of emancipation, of spiritual freedom, freedom from men" (*LF* 68). In pursuing her project—"to get to the end of men" (*LF* 188)—she uses her expertise in pornography to enslave Keith and acts as a sexual tease to appeal to Guy's romantic fantasies. A vehicle for Amis's satire on men's perverted conception of masculinity, she drew widespread criticism from feminist critics, a danger Amis risks by his use of multiple narrative perspectives (see Criticism, **pp. 144–5**).

Keith Talent is a reincarnation of John Self without Self's earlier financial success. Like Self, Keith has been brought up on a diet of television and pornography that "awakened all his finer responses" (*LF* 332). His whole vision of life has been mediated to such an extent that it is "TV that told him what the world was" (*LF* 55). In the same way, his libido is "all tabloid and factoid" (*LF* 202). Amis drew on his research into the world of darts for an essay that he wrote for the *Observer* (cf. *VMN* 223–30) to portray Keith's impoverished conviction that the "whole world [. . .] was definitely a dartboard" (*LF* 396). Shedding tears at the dartboard is "Keith's personal vision of male heroism and transcendence" (*LF* 314). A few critics have also faulted Amis for his portrayal of working-class characters like Keith. But, like Nicola, Keith is representative of his era, just as Guy is representative of the upper-class, outmoded by the end of the century (see Criticism, **pp. 119–20**). Keith displays a "reptile modernity," just as Guy harbors an "archaic heart" (*LF* 192). Upper-class Guy is repeatedly called "The fall guy: fool, foal, foil" (*LF* 240). This is his function in the fiction—to mislead and be misled. He is made foolish by his belief in love, something that the novel claims is dead by this point in time. Sam looks up the definition of *infatuation* in the dictionary and comes up with two meanings: "inspired with extravagant passion" and "made foolish" (*LF* 101). Guy owes his rich lifestyle to his father's tainted accumulation of wealth (cf. *LF* 255). His privileged existence has removed him from the reality of everyday existence and left him vulnerable to Nicola's "little love parodies" (*LF* 348).

In setting the book in the near future, Amis is employing another satiric device. The world is facing what is called the Crisis, which consists of a threat of nuclear war and planetary disaster (see Life and Contexts and Criticism, **pp. 20–1, 106–7**). Amis anticipates the prognostications of the United Nations Intergovernmental Panel on Climate Change (published on February 2, 2007) by depicting as a constant a weather pattern consisting of "gigawatt thunderstorms, multimegaton hurricanes and billion-acre bush fires" (*LF* 276). Guy's son can only be allowed into the contaminated outside air for half an hour at a time. Sam is dying from radiation poisoning. As a child, he was brought up in London Fields (hence the title), where his father worked for the British developing plutonium metallurgy at an establishment called High Explosives Research (*LF* 161). The universe "is heading for heat death" (*LF* 238) (see Criticism, **p. 108**). Each of the major characters is representative of a century turned bad. To torment Guy, Nicola asks him to locate an imaginary friend called Enola Gay (the name of the plane that dropped the atom bomb on Hiroshima) and her son Little Boy (the name given to the bomb) (*LF* 455). With her predilection for life-denying sodomy, she is her own black hole who declares, "*Nothing can escape me*" (*LF* 67). Keith's penchant for cheating as a way of life parallels that of late-twentieth-century civilization where Eastern and Western blocs have "both started cheating as a hedge against the other side doing so" (*LF* 105). Even Mark Asprey turns out to be a cheat, having faked all his awards and the translations of his books (cf. *LF* 434). As for Marmaduke and his "derisory atrocities" (*LF* 142), he is a child of his time, a monster brought to life by a generation that put barbeques before clean air, a symbol, as Diedrick writes, of the death of the myth of childhood innocence (Diedrick 2004: 121). Faced with the extinction of love, each character chooses one of its two opposites—hate or death (cf. *LF* 297).

This is an extremely literary novel in which all the characters resort to writing, or at least to making fiction, at one time or another. In the sub-chapter concluding Chapter 3 Sam observes: "Now here's a pleasing symmetry. All three characters have given me something they've written. Keith's brochure, Nicola's diaries, Guy's fiction" (*LF* 42). The giveaway words are "pleasing symmetry." Later, Sam writes, "Perhaps because of their addiction to form, writers always lag behind the contemporary formlessness" (*LF* 238). For someone whom Nicola calls a "literalist" (*LF* 60), Sam, with his obsession to tell the truth, becomes the butt of "MA's" (Martin Amis's and Mark Asprey's) satire. Believing that he cannot make anything up, he remarks, "Man, am I a reliable narrator" (*LF* 78). But, as Dern sets out to prove, he is far from reliable, for instance reporting on different pages that Guy rang Nicola at six o'clock (*LF* 190) and at seven o'clock (*LF* 156). Writing and life keep on interacting and confusing the boundaries between the two. Sam finds that he "must let things happen at the speed she [Nicola] picks" (*LF* 40). Another time, he describes himself "recuperating from Chapter 5" (*LF* 78). Still later, he admits that he is forced to make things up, by bowdlerizing Marmaduke ("There's some stuff you just cannot put into books" [*LF* 158]), by following "Keith's thoughts where they wouldn't quite go" (*LF* 289), and by ejecting Missy (his ex-girlfriend) from his narrative for "reasons of balance [. . .] She didn't want artistic shape" (*LF* 435). But just as he comes to the realization that art and life can never coincide, Nicola undoes his book, just as she destroyed Asprey's novel, by changing his ending and making him the murderer. The narrator is outnarrated by one of his own characters. Or is he also a victim of MA? On the final page, when he is close to (fictional) death, he admits that he feels "as if someone made me up, for money" (*LF* 470). Although two pages earlier, he made Mark Asprey his literary executor, at the end he acknowledges the shadowy presence of his ultimate author—Martin Amis (see Criticism, **p. 129**).

According to Dern, "*London Fields* is at least two books under one cover": Young's and Asprey's (Dern 2000: 46). Amis makes metafictional fun of the literary conventions he simultaneously employs, playing with the characters, the narrator, and the reader. The book is littered with references to other books. It includes a clever pastiche of the opening of D. H. Lawrence's *The Rainbow* applied to Keith's sordid round of existence (*LF* 114), couples Lawrence's *Women in Love* with *Elle* magazine (*LF* 173), compares Nicola to "Lady Muckbeth" (*LF* 379), and employs comic stream of consciousness to render Keith's thoughts after he has been reading aloud Nicola's literary analysis of

Keats's work (*LF* 356–7). It has many inventive felicities (such as describing how Sam's housekeeper "cleaned the flat and dished the dirt" [*LF* 78]), as well as some of Amis's verbal excesses (such as Chapter 22: Horrorday, with its endless list of horror-thises and horror-thats). Diedrick feels that *London Fields*, with its multiple metafictional layers, "exhibits signs of exhaustion." However, he adds, "In a novel about coming to the end of things, this may be intentional" (Diedrick 2004: 131). The novel continues to elicit such conflicting responses.

## Time's Arrow, Or, The Nature of the Offense (1991)

Amis thought of calling *London Fields*, his novel depicting a world on the brink of planetary death, "Time's Arrow," as "MA" says in the Note at the beginning. Time's arrow points towards death (*LF* 432). Amis sees himself as representative of growing up in the post-World War II world, a world that is radically different from its prewar status. He sees the origins of modernity's self-destructive momentum in the Holocaust, the Soviet gulags and the explosion of the first atomic bomb. Amis considers the Holocaust to be "the central event of the twentieth century" (Bellante and Bellante 1992: 16) (see Life and Contexts, **p. 19**). His attitude to modernity is ambivalent, both ameliorative and pessimistic, and in *Time's Arrow* this double vision finds narrative expression in the two incarnations through which its protagonist/narrator lives his life (see Criticism, **pp. 102–3**). Prompted to write this short novel by reading Robert Jay Lifton's *The Nazi Doctors* (see Life and Contexts, **p. 22**), Amis, aware of the delicacy of writing about the Holocaust as an Aryan, reached for "documentation and technique" (*WAC* 13) (see Criticism, **p. 97**). One technique he employs in this novel is that of temporal reversal. In the Afterword, he acknowledges that he was indebted to the passage in Kurt Vonnegut's *Slaughterhouse Five* (1969) where Billy Pilgrim watches backwards a film of the bombing of Dresden. Amis first tried out this technique of narrative inversion in his short story, "Bujak and the Strong Force or God's Dice" (1985), collected in *Einstein's Monsters* (see Works, **p. 67**). Temporal inversion enabled him to turn a story of unprecedented atrocity into a seemingly philanthropic one. As he has remarked, "Almost any deed, any action, has its morality reversed, if you turn the arrow around" (De Curtis 1991: 147). The other technique Amis employed was also partly inspired by Lifton. This was his division of the protagonist from the narrator, the latter representing the soul or "voice of conscience" (*TA* 47) which his Nazi doctor protagonist repressed during his adult lifetime. Lifton described how the Nazi doctors were psychologically able to break their Hippocratic oath through "the division of the self into two functioning wholes, so that a part self acts as an entire self" (Lifton 2000: 418). The "sharer of his body," the narrator cannot see into Tod's mind (*TA* 55) (see Criticism, **p. 103**).

The novel recounts backwards the life of a Nazi doctor who is at the point of death on an operating table in America to which he escaped after the Nazis were defeated in 1945. His soul, innocent because it had been kept separate from his mind and body throughout his life, relives his life backwards without understanding that this is what is happening. The action is told by what Amis has called "the soul that [Unverdorben] should have had" (De Curtis 1991: 146). Odilo Unverdorben (which is German for "un-corrupt") is his birth name. But in the course of his escape after the war he assumes successive aliases: Hamilton de Souza for his short stay in Portugal, John Young in New York, and finally (that is at the start of the book) Tod (German for "death") Friendly. Amis spends two-thirds of the novel getting Unverdorben back to Auschwitz "to try to familiarize the reader with a backward-time-world" (De Curtis 1991: 146). Amis employs total speech reversal only once in the opening dialogue (*TA* 7) before the narrator learns to translate words back into their conventional order. Once readers have learnt to reverse the sequence of everything, they are rewarded with a truly absurd world in which sustenance issues from the toilet (*TA* 11), the doctor takes candy from babies and money from the church collection bowl (*TA* 12), water rises while smoke falls (*TA* 42), trash trucks litter the streets (*TA* 43), and John Kennedy is "flung together by the doctors' knives and the sniper's bullets and introduced onto the streets of Dallas and a hero's welcome" (*TA* 81). Unverdorben has a succession of affairs. Ironically, the narrator comments on how, unlike most conversations, "with this man-woman stuff, you could run them any way you liked—and still get no further forward" (*TA* 51). This is because Unverdorben's affairs end where they began—in estrangement.

The novel consists of eight chapters divided into three parts. Part I covers Tod Friendly's life in a typical town in the American Northeast (Chapters 1 and 2) and John Young's life in New York (Chapter 3) which he is forced to flee when his past threatens to catch up with him. Part II has four chapters. Chapter 4 covers his stay in Portugal where he had fled from Germany, assuming the first of his aliases, Hamilton de Souza. It opens with his reverse boat trip from New York to Lisbon in which "we leave no mark in the ocean, as if we are successfully covering our tracks" (*TA* 99), which is precisely what the protagonist is doing in the reverse direction. Chapter 5 recounts Odilo Unverdorben's stay at Auschwitz where he helped the notorious Dr. Josef Mengele ("Uncle Pepi") in the extermination of the Jews, although in inverted time this becomes the creation of the Jews. Chapter 6 recounts his earlier service at Schloss Hartheim where the physically "impaired" were put to death and his period spent with the Nazi SS forcing the Jews into ghettos. Chapter 7 covers Unverdorben's days at medical school and with the Reserve Medical Corps. With this chapter, he and his dreams revert to innocence: He is "innocent, emotional, popular, and stupid" (*TA* 150). Part III consists of Chapter 8, a mere eight pages in which Unverdorben reverts to his childhood in Solingen, the birthplace of Adolf Eichmann. At the end (1916), he enters his mother's body and waits for death from his father's body at the moment of conception (*TA* 164).

The chapter devoted to Auschwitz provides the justification for both techniques—temporal inversion and doubling. When everything in the book is viewed backwards in time, "the only thing that makes sense in that world is Auschwitz," Amis explains, "which is a sort of tribute to its perverted perfection—100 percent wrong" (Bellante and Bellante 1992: 16). When he was a doctor in New York, John Young bewildered his uncomprehending alter ego by doing his patients harm. A man comes into the emergency room with a bandage which is removed, has a rusty nail driven into his head, and is led back to the waiting room to holler with pain (*TA* 76). But at Auschwitz, the reverse takes place. "Our preternatural purpose?" asks the narrator. "To dream a race" (*TA* 120). With time's arrow flying backwards, Unverdorben reverses his role in the gassing of the Jews: "It was I, orben, who personally removed the pellets of Zyklon B and entrusted harmacist" (*TA* 121). Further ironies abound: "to prevent needless dental work was usually completed while the patients were not yet 1). Just as the gruesome task of extracting gassed victims' teeth for their gold is recast as a humanitarian act (the gold is donated by the Reichsbank and thieving officials like Unverdorben), so the rounding up and incarceration of the Jews becomes a reuniting of families who are returned to their homes. As Richard Menke puts it, the narrator has "recast genocide as genesis" (Menke 1998: 964). The narrator's delusion may embody a contemporary nostalgia for a return to an Edenic prewar state, when the pursuit of reason had not yet been contaminated by the Nazis' ruthless application of a perverted rationality that brought the Age of Reason to an abrupt end.

Amis's reversal of not just chronology but causality parallels the Nazis doctors' reversal of morality. As he points out, "the entire medical profession in Germany [went] from healing to killing in the name of healing" (Trueheart 1991: 2). The Hippocratic oath that all doctors take (part of which is quoted in the novel) makes them swear to "wield the special power" they are given (*TA* 81) "to help the sick" (*TA* 25), not kill the healthy. Power forms one of the novel's recurrent motifs, associated with not just doctors but also sex. The first (i.e., last) time that Tod (as well as the narrator) has sex with Irene, as he "loomed above her," he is "flooded by thoughts and feelings I've never had before. To do with power" (*TA* 37). Like surgery, sex offers "[i]nstant invasion and lordship" (*TA* 51). The lust for power that Unverdorben shares with his fellow Nazis (epitomized by Uncle Pepi) also characterizes his earlier (later) relations with his wife, Herta, who becomes "his chimpanzee required to do the housework naked, on all fours" (*TA* 151). His inadequacies make him turn all his women into subordinated recipients of his perverted will to power. It is ironic that as soon as he acquires power rounding up Jews for the Waffen-SS unit he joins he becomes sexually impotent. The power he acquires renders him powerless: "I am omnipotent. Also impotent" (*TA* 140). Chapter 6 begins, "Multiply zero by zero and you still get zero" (*TA* 137). Unverdorben has added political to sexual power and ultimately ends up impotent in both areas.

Amis's use of an unreliable narrator is an essential part of his narrative strategy. In *Experience* he writes, "If the trick is to work, the unreliable narrator must in fact be very unreliable indeed: reliably partial" (*E* 380). Early on, the narrator concludes, "I am generally rather slow on the uptake. Possibly even subnormal, or mildly autistic" (*TA* 29). He keeps on "expecting the world to make sense. It doesn't" (*TA* 82). Confronted with two selves, each of which is in its own form of self-denial, the implied reader is constantly required to supply the truth about the historical events that the protagonist wants to repress and that the narrator misinterprets. As Amis explained, "the reader has to become a kind of soul or conscience and has to do the moral reordering from his chair" (Wachtel 1996: 47). This is a risky strategy seeing that the younger generation, on Amis's own testimony, either do not know the facts about the Holocaust or see it as a myth.[1]

---

1 Amis visited Auschwitz in 1995, where his guide told him, "We now have people coming here [. . .] who think that all this has been constructed to deceive them. Not just from Germany. From Holland, from Scandinavia. They believe that nothing happened here and the Holocaust is a myth" (*E* 369).

For those readers who discern the irony, the effect is contradictory: They simultaneously get pleasure from the conceits produced by the reversal of history and, forced to recollect the atrocities that actually occurred, recast the comedy as dark satire. Amis calls this book "a sort of anti-comedy," adding, "Irony and indirection and humour are still the only things you have to work with" (Bigsby 1992: 172–3). In *Experience* Amis asserts, "style is morality" (*E* 122). His use of irony compels a reader, in reversing the events and the narrator's interpretation of them, to enter the novel as a participant. Unverdorben's successive aliases are another instance of how Amis uses language to make a moral point. The book traces the progress of the protagonist from death (the meaning of "Tod") to childish innocence (the meaning of "Unverdorben"). But the pervading use of irony compels the reader to reverse this progression and read it as a journey from innocent childhood to deathly maturity (see Criticism, **pp. 151–2**). How, then, is the reader to understand the final paragraph in which the narrator sees "an arrow fly—but wrongly. Point first" (*TA* 165)? Is the narrator destined to relive his life in reverse—i.e., historical—time when he will be made to experience his life in real time? Or will he again become separated from the intellectual self that shies away from the consequences of its actions? Does he embody the wishful fantasy that it is still possible to reverse the deleterious history of the world since World War II? Or is he condemned to once more be excluded from Unverdorben's consciousness and, Sisyphus-like, relive the same nightmare again?

## The Information (1995)

Amis begins to find fictional expression for his own powerful midlife crisis in *London Fields* where Sam observes, "Like middle age [. . .] death is packed with information [. . .] When middle age comes, you think you're dying all the time" (*LF* 432). The title, *The Information*, primarily refers to the realization that when you reach midlife the inevitability of death becomes your reality (see Life and Contexts, **pp. 23–5**). Amis refers to this book as his "death-awareness novel" (Trueheart 1991: 2). "Nothing," he has explained, "is the void we come from and return to. You're dead for a lot longer than you're alive." But he also insists that the midlife crisis is "an over-reaction" that "does end" (Laurence and McGee 1995). Afterwards, he claims, "[l]ife seems sort of clearer. Diminished, but clearer" (Fuller 1995) (see Criticism, **p. 104**). At the same time, Amis has said elsewhere that the title, apart from referring to "the knowledge that you're going to die," "refers to about half a dozen things: the information *on* someone, the dirt on someone; the information revolution; one character informing another, like a succubus" (Wachtel 1996: 48). Ostensibly a narrative about literary envy, the book satirizes the extent to which the contemporary novel has become one more product which is not just sold through media hype but which creates star authors and makes money out of sending them on book tours and (mis)quoting them whenever the media needs free copy (see Criticism, **p. 97**). Ironically, this is just what happened to Amis after he had finished writing the novel (see Life and Contexts, **pp. 24–5**). As a result, the British reception of the book was largely distorted by the extensive press coverage accorded Amis's large book advance, change of agent, expensive dental work, and the breakup of his marriage (see

Life and Contexts, **pp. 23–5**). The novel proved unusually hard to write. He worked on it over five years (with a year's interruption to write *Time's Arrow*), writing three drafts of it (see Life and Contexts, **p. 22**). Amis has said that while the portrayal of the main protagonist's, Richard's, midlife crisis makes the novel "very personal" in that "a lot of emotion that I was feeling went into it," the "book isn't autobiographical" (Moss 1998: 22).

The plot centers on the revenge that one writer attempts to exact on another (see Criticism, **p. 103**). Richard Tull is a writer of three virtually unreadable highbrow novels (the last called *Untitled*) who is described as "a marooned modernist" (*I* 124). As Fiction and Poetry Editor of the Tantalus Press he ekes out a living writing book reviews (and everything else in the case of the *Little Magazine*, which "stood for not paying people" [*I* 117]) and publishing books as unreadable as his own. He sees the Tantalus Press as a form of prostitution because its writers pay it to be published. About to turn forty when the novel opens, Richard cannot believe that his old friend, Gwyn Barry, also forty, has become a wildly successful novelist with the recent publication of *Amelior*, an anemic novel about the establishment of a utopian community. Richard despises it for "its cuteness, its blandness, its naively pompous semicolons, its freedom from humor and incident, its hand-me-down imagery" (*I* 28). Suffering from "the tiredness of time lived" (*I* 4), Richard becomes "a revenger, in what was probably intended to be a comedy" (*I* 96). He wants "an I for an I" (*I* 64) (see Criticism, **pp. 137–8**). Where Gwyn's fiction is all content, Richard's is all style: "the thought of getting a character out of the house and across town to somewhere else made him go vague with exhaustion" (*I* 125). As Richard Menke remarks, given Richard's aversion to literary realism, "it should come as no surprise that his own plotting, his attempts at literary revenge, all end in failure" (Menke 2006: 150–1).

The plot consists of Richard planning one revenge plot after another, each redounding on the perpetrator. The book is divided into four parts. In Part I, Richard decides to use Gwyn's narcissism against him. He sends a copy of Sunday's *Los Angeles Times* to Gwyn, confident that Gwyn will spend days searching in vain for his name in print buried in it somewhere. The joke plays out with Gwyn almost instantly locating a brief request from a reader for a first edition of his first novel, leaving Richard to spend days finding the reference to Gwyn that he had missed when choosing the paper. In Part II, Richard turns from literary to physical revenge and pays a local hooligan, Steve, to rough Gwyn up. But, again, Richard meets the fate he planned for Gwyn for whom he is mistaken by the incompetent villain Steve uses. Next, Richard resorts to an attempt to seduce Gwyn's wife Demi, gets invited to her father's house, and gets so drunk that he injures himself after having been abused by her father who ironically mistakes him for his hated son-in-law—Gwyn. Part III, covers Gwyn's American book tour on which Richard accompanies him in order to write a commissioned profile of him. While Gwyn is adulated by packed audiences and the media, Richard, whose *Untitled* has also just been published, attracts a token multicultural audience of four. Apart from humiliating Richard, Part III allows Amis to satirize a world in which hype replaces substance, in which literature was "getting heavier and heavier, until it was all over and you arrived at paperwork. You arrived at *Amelior*" (*I* 141). Part IV brings four of Richard's ongoing revenge plots to their unintended conclusion: To have an underage nymphomaniac, Belladonna, seduce Gwyn and then expose him; to write a savagely negative profile of Gwyn; to concoct an original work and then accuse Gwyn of plagiarizing it in his novel; and to have him badly beaten up by Steve's gang. Gwyn not only escapes these traps but also turns the table on Richard by turning out to have been having weekly sex with Richard's wife, Gina, whom he paid, and hiring Steve's lot to harm Richard. Steve chooses instead to target Richard's son, Marco, the one innocent character in the novel who adores Richard. Being a comedy, "[d]ecorum will be strictly observed" (*I* 262), we are assured, and Marco is saved from suffering for Richard's envy, leaving Richard with "the information, which is nothing, and comes at night" (*I* 374).

While not as extreme as Richard, Amis has never invested much literary capital in plot. Adam Mars-Jones summarized the plot of *The Information*: "things can't get any worse, and then they do" (Mars-Jones 1995: 19). Catherine Bernard identifies the effect Amis aims at: "His trademark style of using redundancy, of emphasis through incremental repetition, may be defined as maximalist" (Bernard 2006: 128). Part III illustrates this tendency by intensifying but not advancing the distinctions between Richard and Gwyn. Their horrific flight to Provincetown where they barely survive a hurricane only convinces Richard that "Death is good" (*I* 284). Various forms of death are everywhere in this novel. Its main concern is to offer a picture of the contemporary Western world, and all its characters are representatives of what living in it does to people. Steve is as much a part of this world as is Gwyn. Steve, the orphan boy turned criminal, is violence personified, "the first of many [. . .] waiting to happen" (*I* 77), "the hero of a novel from the future" (*I* 350). His literary origins (he also models himself on the Wild Boy of Aveyron, a feral boy who emerged from the woods in France in 1800) ironically conform exactly to the schema Richard had in mind for a book called "The History of Increasing Humiliation": "It would be a book accounting for the decline in the status and virtue of literary protagonists. First gods, then demigods, then kings [. . .] Then maniacs and murderers, tramps, mobs, rabble, flotsam, vermin" (*I* 92) (see Works and Criticism, **pp. 83–4, 111**). This deterioration in literary protagonists accompanies a deterioration in literary genre. *The Information* is a comedy, but, Amis insists, comedy "now has to do everything. It's as if all the genres have collapsed" (Fuller 1995). Like Steve's, Richard's life is not just a life devoted to literature. It is described as a literary construct. "His life, his whole life, was approaching its third-act climax [. . .] What genre did his life belong to? [. . .] In fact, it was comedy. Or anti-comedy, which is [. . .] a more modern kind of comedy" (*I* 131) (see Criticism, **p. 137**).

Given such a literary mouthpiece in Richard, it is not surprising that the first-person narrator disappears halfway through the novel. As the narrator says early on, "how can I ever play the omniscient, the all-knowing, when I don't know *anything*?" (*I* 43) (see Criticism, **p. 131**). Amis explains the disappearance of the narrator as paralleling the effects of Richard's midlife crisis: "as I absent myself in the novel, the information is telling me to stop saying 'hi' and to start saying 'bye'" (Wachtel 1996: 57). The narrator's last appearance in the book ends with this phrase (*I* 207). Before his exit, the narrator makes numerous references to the solar system in which the world features as "a dying star" (*I* 45). Even the sun is in decline, and the quasars are receding fast (*I* 148–9, 120). The novel's characters are placed within this vast context to emphasize the shrinking significance of human life: "The history of astronomy is the history of increasing humiliation. First the geocentric universe, then the heliocentric universe. Then the eccentric universe—the one we're living in" (*I* 93). The deteriorating literary world becomes a synecdoche for a dying universe. Writing is "like dying" (*I* 204). "In literature as in life everything would go on getting less and less innocent" (*I* 350). Literature starts with Homer and ends with Gwyn for whom the universe is homocentric and for whom "the stars were all about *me*" (*I* 329). As Richard's walk through the plane taking him to America humorously reveals, reading is on the way out (*I* 214–5). Human life too appears to be on the way out.

Amis's extensive use of intertexts in this novel adds metaphorical weight to the role literature plays in it. Joe Moran claims that the contrast between the two main characters and their outcomes constitutes an updating of *New Grub Street* (1891), George Gissing's celebrated novel about conflicting artistic and commercial pressures in the literary profession. Moran argues that Richard is modeled on Gissing's Edwin Reardon and Gwyn on Jasper Milvain who ends up marrying Reardon's wife (and her inheritance) after he dies (Moran 2000: 308–9). Both James Diedrick and John Nash have written respectively about the novel's references to two of Borges's self-reflective stories, "The Aleph" (about "a terrible poet, who wins a big prize [. . .] for his terrible poem" [*I* 165]) and "The Circular Ruins" (concerning the impossibility of original creation), the latter of which an author plagiarizes, giving Richard the idea of accusing Gwyn of doing likewise (Diedrick 2004: 150–1; Nash 1996: 220) (see Criticism, **p. 94**). One final example: Amis has said that he reread Milton's *Paradise Lost* before writing the last draft of *The Information*. One appearance of this intertext occurs when Richard compares the bums and drunks hanging out under the elevated underground railway to the convocation of rebel angels in Pandemonium. Once again, the intertext contributes to the novel's portrayal of the fallen modern world. If *Paradise Lost* is "the basic tragic story of our culture," *The Information* is its comic counterpart (Laurence and McGee 1995).

## *Night Train* (1997)

*Night Train* is Amis's first novel that is not in the comic mode. It is a spoof or parody of a detective novel. Amis researched not just numerous thrillers, especially those of James Ellroy, "the poet laureate of *noir*," but also nonfiction books on crime including David Simon's *Homicide*, the one work to tell him how cops "talk to each other and, by swift extension, how they talk to themselves" (Amis 1997: 18) (see Life and Contexts and Criticism, **pp. 26, 94**). The novel accordingly negotiates a path between the clichés of detective fiction (especially as dramatized on television) and the voice of a fictional policewoman detective who is made to confront a metaphysical angst that haunts her and others in a generic American city. Mike (she has many masculine characteristics) Hoolihan, the narrator/detective, is a deep-voiced, trunk-legged, large woman with a history of alcoholism, a damaged liver, and deeper feelings than any of Amis's past women characters (see Criticism, **p. 122**). Her police chief, Colonel Tom Rockwell, asks Mike to investigate the shooting death of his daughter, Jennifer.

He cannot believe that Jennifer committed suicide, as she had everything going for her: good looks, a loving boyfriend (Trader Faulkner), and a job as an astrophysicist at which she excelled. In keeping with the genre, Amis says that he employed "more structure" than was his usual practice (Weich 2003). But Mike's meticulous investigation into the possibility that Jennifer could have been murdered consists of a series of dead ends. It seems that Jennifer has anticipated Mike's lines of investigation and deliberately left a number of false trails: a quarrel with her boyfriend, a brief affair that goes nowhere, an uncharacteristic act of negligence or vandalism at her job, traces of lithium in her blood, and three bullets in her head. After Mike has pursued all these leads and found them to be so many red herrings, she comes to the conclusion that Jennifer committed suicide for no specific reason.

In *Experience*, Amis comments on the number of his friends who had taken their lives, including Lamorna Seale, the mother of his illegitimate daughter, Delilah (see Life and Contexts, pp. 27–8). There, he observes, "The murderer kills just one person. The suicide kills everybody [. . .] But no blame attaches. If what she was suffering had been endurable, then she would have endured" (*E* 281–2). The same turns out to be true of Jennifer. Life itself has become unendurable for her. As Mike says, "suicide is perhaps uniquely incoherent. And the act is without shape and without form" (*NT* 94). Jennifer's father, Colonel Tom, cannot face this fact, which is why he demands that Mike come up with a murderer. At the end, when she has closed her investigation and concluded that Jennifer acted out of no specific motive, Mike lies to Tom that "it all measures up" (*NT* 174) (see Criticism, p. 111). Being a policeman, Tom cannot deal with a conception of life that refuses to add up. Mike started out with the same mindset. But, as she gradually enters into Jennifer's consciousness, she begins to identify with and experience for herself Jennifer's existential despair. Jennifer is another of Amis's doubles, an idealized equivalent of the fallible Mike (see Criticism, p. 105). The two women are like honorary sisters in that, when Mike became critically ill from alcoholism, Jennifer's father took her into his home and Jennifer nursed her back to life. Mike betrays the way Jennifer comes to possess her when she sees her ghostly figure at the end of her bed and when Mike contemplates changing her name to "Jennifer Hoolihan" (*NT* 125). The final paragraph of the novel suggests that Mike may be about to follow Jennifer's example by heading off to the dives in the Battery where she can get drunk and "say goodbye" (*NT* 175). The ending leaves Mike's fate undecided, but the sound of the approaching night train of the title is indicative. Part II, titled "Felo de Se" (meaning intentional self-murder), opens: "Suicide is the night train, speeding your way to darkness [. . .] This train takes you into the night, and leaves you there" (*NT* 83). The narrative traces how Jennifer gets "inside" Mike "trying to reveal what [Mike doesn't] want to see" (*NT* 83).

In the course of her investigation, Mike is forced to abandon the conventional police distinction between murder and suicide: "with homicide, now, we don't care about motive [. . .] We don't care about the why" (*NT* 127). But "we all want a why for suicide"—not just the police. Yet, by this point in the book, Mike refuses to believe that "[a]nswers are coming together" (*NT* 128). She comes to understand that death, the unknowable, resists all linguistic attempts to infuse it with meaning, that self-inflicted death has no necessary why. Where does this demand for motive come from? From the world of television drama: "Motive might have been [. . .] in okay shape half a century ago. But now it's all in the fucking air. With the TV" (*NT* 127). Television's hammy treatment of death in which murders are neatly wrapped up within the hour has nothing to do with the unmotivated violence that Mike has witnessed as a detective (see Criticism, **p. 94**). Yet "TV has also fucked up us police" (*NT* 29). Even Mike early on still tends to envisage Jennifer's death in televisual terms as the blood splattering on the wall behind her head (*NT* 80)—or, rather, ketchup. In this novel, television shapes rather than reflects reality. Television is "the master criminal, beaming out gameplan to the somnambulists on the street. You're thinking: This is ketchup" (*NT* 164). Mike also resorts to television crime jargon when she interrogates Trader Faulkner and threatens to "grandjury" him. Instead of driving him to the conventional breakdown and confession, she ends up convinced that he is innocent (*NT* 70–1). Still, Mike persists with "the procedural ketchup of questions and numbers and expert testimony," not because she believes in it all any more, but so "we can do the *noir*," as Colonel Tom commanded her to (*NT* 164). *Night Train* not only refuses to make use of motive, one of the basic conventions of the genre, but in doing so it also exposes the artificiality of the genre it is parodying (see Criticism, **p. 137**).

As is the case with *London Fields* and *The Information*, this novel incorporates astrophysics as a trope for what is happening to its characters. Jennifer's job involves "asking if the universe is open or closed" (*NT* 108), whether it is expanding forever or not. As her boss explains, "it's *reality* we're investigating here" (*NT* 110). Staring at "revealed creation" (*NT* 112) means coming face to face with the sheer insignificance of "all this rat-race, turf-war, dog-eat-dog stuff we do all day" (*NT* 111). You need to be as tough as Newton or Hawking: "Hawking has been staring at death all his adult life" (*NT* 114). But Jennifer believes, "No man can stare at the sun or at death with a, with an unshielded eye" (*NT* 113). To see humans within the framework of the universe's "eighty-billion-year heartbeat," as Mike imagines Jennifer doing at the moment she took her life (*NT* 115), is to see them first being drawn further and further apart and then contracting to nothing: "From big bang to big crunch" (*NT* 108). Seeing human life in this larger perspective will take "a revolution of consciousness" (*NT* 111). While Trader, Jennifer's boyfriend, a philosopher of science, can "live with unanswered questions" (*NT* 117), are these two possibilities (infinite expansion or contraction), either of which spells death for humankind, too much for Jennifer? Do they make even her near-perfect-seeming life irrelevant? Redundant?

## Yellow Dog (2003)

*Yellow Dog* reverts to the comic or burlesque genre that characterizes Amis's trilogy of major novels: *Money*, *London Fields*, and *The Information*. After a false start in 1999, Amis began work on *Yellow Dog* in earnest the day after the terrorist attacks of September 11, 2001 (see Life and Contexts, **p. 37**). While not yet prepared to write directly about the attacks, he did incorporate in the book "the mental environment that seemed to come after September 11th" (Weich 2003) (see Criticism, **p. 138**). As he told *The Times,* "The emphasis in [the first] chapter was to do with male insecurity. It seems to me that the key to radical Islam is that it is quivering with male insecurity" (Malvern 2002: 3). The world of the novel is accordingly a "yellowworld of faith and fear, and paltry ingenuity" (*YD* 10). One of his working titles was "Men in Power" (Heawood 2002: 18). The principal character in the most prominent plot strand, Xan Meo, encounters men in power in the opening chapter when he is severely beaten over the head by two hired criminals (Mal from "State of England" being one) for (unintentionally) naming Joseph Andrews, a major London gangster, in his debut book of short stories, *Lucozade*. The blow sends Xan back to an atavistic state of mind in which his male fantasies and desires come to dictate his behavior. In fact, he becomes similar to Amis's conception of "Islamist" extremists, men who are obsessed with their powerlessness and humiliation and who dream of compensatory mastery over women. Xan sets out to counter violence with violence. The world of this novel is characterized by a proliferation of violence both physical and sexual, which connects its several plot lines.

This is much the most heavily plotted novel that Amis has written to date. Normally, the plots in his novels serve as token structures on which to construct the comic satire and linguistic effects with which he is most preoccupied. He is indebted to Dickens for this book's structure: "I knew I was going to be invoking a kind of Victorian tradition: you set three stories in motion—or three-and-a-half if you include the airplane—and the reader is going to think, *How are these going to be brought together?*" (Weich 2003) (see Criticism, **p. 93**). The opening paragraph invokes as its intertext the opening paragraph of Dickens's *A Tale of Two Cities* ("It was the best of times, it was the worst of times"). *Yellow Dog* is divided into three parts and eleven chapters. Part I, the longest with five chapters, is set largely in London, much of Part II in Los Angeles, and in the course of the short Part III many of the characters return to London. *Yellow Dog* introduces the reader to three major and one minor plot strands in the four sections of Chapter 1. Xan Meo is an actor and writer, married happily (at least until his beating) to Russia (many of the characters' names are bizarre) with two small daughters. His father was a thug, like Joseph Andrews, but Xan has risen above his violent upbringing to become more feminist than Russia (*YD* 209) until the blow to his head causes him to revert. The most disturbing effect is that he finds himself attracted to his own four-year-old daughter. The second plot strand introduces readers to King Henry IX, whose queen is comatose from a riding accident; his equerry, Brendan (nicknamed Bugger); his fifteen-year-old daughter and heir apparent, Victoria; and his Chinese mistress called He (pronounced "her" to further confuse matters). The King receives a photograph of his daughter nude in the bath with a threat to release it to the media. The third strand introduces Clint Smoker, who writes under the pseudonym of Yellow Dog and is the star reporter for the *Morning Lark*. This is a sexist tabloid newspaper that resembles the *Daily Sport* and is, according to Amis, "well below the *Sun* in its intentions and strategies" (Heawood 2002: 18). Amis's hilarious satire of the gutter press, from the slanders of which he had suffered over recent years, may have been responsible for some of the more vicious attacks on the novel, what Kate Muir called "this mugging of a professional writer by aimless gangs of critics" (Muir 2003: 9) (see Life and Contexts, **p. 32**). With the paper's all-male editorial staff, "it was universal practice, at the *Morning Lark*, to refer to readers as wankers" (*YD* 24).

The last minor strand introduces Flight CigAir 101 bound for Houston, Texas with a coffin carrying the corpse of Royce Trainer, whose wife is accompanying his body and waiting to rejoin the captain, her lover. This subplot is the only one connected purely thematically to the other three. As Xan reflects in the opening section, "all of us [are] just flying blind" (*YD* 10).

Once Amis has developed these plots to the point where the *Morning Lark* gets possession of the compromising photos of "the Goer Princess," as Clint calls her (*YD* 319), and Xan has recovered sufficiently to learn that his beating was ordered by Joseph Andrews, now a producer of pornographic films in Los Angeles, Amis sends Xan and Clint to the "San Sebastiano Valley" to act in or report on, respectively, the porn industry located in "Fucktown" (*YD* 250, 149). Much of the satire Amis directs at this $10-billion a-year industry derives from the essay he wrote on the Los Angeles porn business based in the San Fernando Valley titled "Sex in America" (see Life and Contexts and Criticism, **pp. 12, 32, 140**). In it, Amis reports on an industry that prefers anal to vaginal sex and sees as an advance its "evolution toward rougher stuff [. . .] A strong, male dominant thing, with women pushed to the limit"—similar to the Islamist fantasy of masculinity triumphant (Amis 2001b: 100; see *YD* 269). Against a backdrop peopled by porn stars with names like Dork Bogarde making movies with titles like *Fallstiff* and a series of *Princess Lolita* films featuring a look-alike of Princess Victoria (whose photos of her naked have gone public), Xan finally confronts Joseph Andrews who turns out to be his father, and Clint comes face to face with his "cyberpal," k8 (Kate) who turns out to be a "w" (double you) or hermaphrodite from whom he flees in fear for his residual masculinity (*YD* 327). The denouement consists of a violent confrontation between Clint and Joseph Andrews (who turns out to be the royal blackmailer having obtained the photographs from the King's mistress) in which the former murders the latter with a car tool but in the process loses both eyes which brings an end to the cycle of vengeance, the abdication of the King and Princess, a recovery by Xan (after almost having sex with his niece), and a scary landing on a freeway of the plane after it has been depressurized and its steering incapacitated by the breaking loose of the coffin (containing another vengeful man). The plane's narrow escape from disaster connects thematically to the escape of Xan and his family from further violence on them at the hands of Joseph Andrews.

The question remains how successfully Amis has combined these parallel strands. Is Alan Hollinghurst right when he claims that *Yellow Dog* "gives signs of quite bristling organization" (Hollinghurst 2003: 9)? Or is David Matthews closer to the truth when he writes of a "nagging feeling that there are four novellas here in search of a novel" (Matthews 2003: 27)? Misogyny, personified by Joseph Andrews and temporarily by Xan, not to mention by the porn industry and the gutter press, is laughed away in the finale. The plot strand concerning the King portrays an effete, older aristocratic society that has been replaced by the crudities of the *Lark* and the pervasive reign of porn which "is heading for the mainstream" (*YD* 237). The abdication of the King and Princess spell the end for the aristocracy. Those few critics to date who have given serious attention to the novel appear to agree that the ending suffers from an excess of commentary, what Xan calls "general thoughts" (*YD* 306). As Diedrick asks, does the novel really require Amis to spell out one of its major concerns: "men miss women being tractable, and women miss men being decisive" (*YD* 307; Diedrick 2004: 241)? Gavin Keulks calls this "heavy-handed moralizing," which it may be (Keulks 2003: 169). But does this sermonizing extend beyond Xan's letter to Russia, a mere two pages, and the somewhat sentimental treatment of Xan's altered relationship with his daughters in the final page and a half of the novel? Even those reviewers who considered the book's structure "overly complex and needlessly opaque" praised it for its "brilliant and often hilarious" prose (*Publishers Weekly* 2003: 55). The title itself turns out to refer to not just the yellow journalist, Clint, but an actual yellow bitch tied up in the backyard when Xan was a young boy that was "trying to free itself of this thing—the thing on its back"—a male dog taking advantage of the female's captive state (*YD* 337). Amis can give, as here, subtle narrative expression to the theme that he is also accused of belaboring (see Criticism, **p. 123**). The "moral grandstanding" he is charged with (Gessen 2003: 50) is confined to a few pages, while his comic portrayal of a Western civilization in a state of sexual and social confusion extends over the novel's 339 pages.

## House of Meetings (2006)

*House of Meetings* shows Amis revisiting the subject of the Russian gulags already described in his nonfictional work, *Koba the Dread* (2002) (see Works, **p. 75**). "After a couple of years," Amis has said, "all that reading and thinking goes down into the subconscious and something else emerges" (Goring 2006: 6). Since *Koba* had been published, Amis had read Anne Applebaum's *Gulag: A History* (2003), three pages of which describe the House of Meetings, the buildings where prisoners were allowed conjugal visits after Stalin's death in 1953. This was the starting point for the novel. His other intervening inspiration was Michael Specter's piece in the *New Yorker* (November 10, 2004) titled "Is Russia Dying?" in which he describes the demographic crisis threatening the nation's future (cf. *HM* 208–9). This is only Amis's second departure from the use of the comic genre (the first was in his spoof detective novel, *Night Train*) and his first use of tragedy, which felt like a new territory to him. The tragedy is not confined to the three protagonists. "The deeper grief," Amis has said, "is the loss of Russia's soul" (Goring 2006: 6). According to the narrator, "*Russia tried to kill herself in the 1930s*" (*HM* 237). The country is portrayed as a place in which everything "*is not what it seems; and all you know for sure is that it is worse than it looks*" (*HM* 206). The average age at which Russians die is so low that they have no time for a midlife crisis, which comes in the form of death (*HM* 72). To add to the novel's realist approach, Amis says that he used "a reliable narrator" which preempts his normal ironic play with narrator and reader (Battersby 2006: 10). The novel was perceived by most reviewers to be "a vast upswing in form" from *Yellow Dog* (Baker 2006: 51) (see Criticism, **p. 100**).

The novel is recounted by an unnamed narrator aged eighty-five who is revisiting Norlag, the Russian concentration camp in the Arctic Circle in which he was incarcerated as a political prisoner from 1948 to 1956. He was joined there by his half-brother Lev, a poet who rejects the use of violence, which the narrator uses as "currency, like tobacco, like bread" (*HM* 79). In fact, the narrator had served in the Russian Army and writes that "in the first three months of 1945, I raped my way across what would soon be East Germany" (HM 35). According to Amis, "he has some excuses. Like the Second World War." At the same time, Amis needs a monster for the narrator "to live on the page" (Grossman 2007: 1). The story concerns a love triangle between the two brothers and Zoya, the beautiful young Jewess they both fall in love with and who Lev marries the same day he is arrested and sent to Norlag. The central event of the book is the night of July 31, 1956 when Lev is allowed a conjugal visit with Zoya in the House of Meetings at the camp. After their release later in 1956, the narrator becomes rich while Lev becomes increasingly withdrawn until Zoya leaves him in 1962. Lev remarries, and his only son, a conscript in the army, gets killed in 1982 during the Russian occupation of Afghanistan. Later that year, the narrator looks up Zoya, now married to an aged playwright. When she collapses exhausted in his apartment, he reverts to his past self and rapes her. The narrator reaches the same conclusion that the reader of *Time's Arrow* is encouraged to do: "The conscience, I suspect, is a vital organ. And when it goes, you go" (HM 211). This lapse motivates the narrator to emigrate to the USA where he marries and acquires a stepdaughter, Venus, to whom he addresses the book and who writes the footnotes in it.

Amis has said that making her the recipient of the narrative made the book work, "because it lodges it in the present day" (Grossman 2007: 1). The four-part narrative is dated September 1–6, 2004, and makes frequent reference to another contemporary event—the Chechen rebels taking 1,200 children hostage in Beslan, Russia on 1 September, ending on 4 September with the death of 344 people, 186 of them children. Venus's wholly American experience makes it necessary for the narrator to explain to her (she is additionally meant to be black) the effect on both himself and Lev of the eight years they spent in Norlag. This effect becomes the main theme of the novel, which is only fully revealed at the end of the book when the narrator, near to death, opens the letter left for him by the long-dead Lev. Where most writers, such as Solzhenitsyn, wrote about their exceptional life force that helped them recover from their experience in the camps, Amis wanted to show the "more typical experience" epitomized by the narrator unable to "transcend this brutality" (Lehmann 2007). Lev recalls "the first law of camp life: to you, nothing—from you everything" (HM 223). A fellow prisoner has tattooed on his arm: "*You may live, but you won't love*" (HM 85). This is what the camp has done to both brothers: left them with a "weakened power to love" (HM 234). The narrator's capacity for sexual love had been fatally damaged in the army and extinguished when, by raping Zoya, he "*crossed from satyr to senex in the course of an afternoon. As early as the next day I couldn't even remember what it was I liked about women*" (HM 241). This novel is still concerned with what Amis has called the central subject of his fiction: masculinity (Dougary 2006). More than one reviewer commented on the fact that the narrator's principal affections are for his brother. In his closing letter to Venus, the narrator even writes enigmatically, "*I was queer for my brother*" (HM 240). Lev is the character with whom most readers sympathize, although the narrator is not an unrelieved monster as he makes his "reckoning with the dead"—both Lev and Zoya being dead by the time he writes his narrative (HM 144). He has genuine love for his stepdaughter, whom he tries to wean from her subscription to Western ideology, "*a mild ideology*" compared to the ferocious ideology of Soviet communism (*HM* 5). But, as Amis points out repeatedly when addressing the similarly ferocious ideology of Islamism, "Ideologies are powerful because they liberate you from reason" (Bilmes 2006: 39). Amis has subsequently explained, "You can't have ideology [even the mild ideology of the USA] without violence," because "ideology will necessarily contain an element of illusion" (Silverblatt 2007). Allow ideology to take control and everyone will suffer the effects that the characters in the novel experience—that "they've all been twisted into horrible shapes by the state" (Grossman 2007: 1) (see Criticism, p. 109). On the last page, Amis echoes Chaucer's words at the end of *Troilus and Criseyde*, "*Go, little book, go, little mine tragedy*" (*HM* 241). Chaucer's lines continue by hoping that before he dies he may "make [. . .] som comedye!" (Book V, lines 1786–8). As Amis was, by then, at work on his next autobiographical novel, *The Pregnant Widow*, does this promise a return to his favored comic genre?

## Collections of short stories

### Einstein's Monsters (1987)

*Einstein's Monsters* consists of an essay, "Thinkability," and five stories written between 1984 and 1987. Two ("Bujak and the Strong Force" and "Insight at Flame Lake") are set in a pre-nuclear realistic context, and three ("The Time Disease," "The Little Puppy that Could" and "The Immortals") in a post-nuclear context, employing the genre of science fiction which Amis had been reviewing anonymously from 1972 (see Life and Contexts and Criticism, **pp. 7, 134**). "Thinkability," which outlines Amis's outright opposition to the concept of nuclear deterrence, provides the theoretical stance underlying all the stories (see Life and Contexts, **pp. 18–19**). Two stories ("Bujak" and "The Little Puppy") end happily, while the remaining three are dystopian. Rachel Falconer sees their effect as cumulative: "The sequential disconnectedness between each story and the next allows us to reject each possible future as it unfolds, yet the cumulative effect is of a present that branches into numerous possible futures" (Falconer 1998: 709). What all the stories reveal is that for Amis the relatively new threat of nuclear annihilation has affected individual human relationships everywhere. Our hubris, he has said, is that "you think you can enslave this cosmic force. It's clear instantly that we have become enslaved by it." "I think nukes are responsible for a very great many modern defamations [. . .] Our ideas about what it is to be human are much changed by it already" (McGrath 1987: 194, 195). Asked whether his writing at this time was not pessimistic, he replied, "I don't think unadorned pessimism has any place in writing; it's always a complicated pessimism, or a qualified pessimism" (Ross 1987: 24–5).

"Bujak and the Strong Force" is a semi-allegorical story set in 1980 in which "Bujak, the strongman" possesses what the narrative refers to as "the strong force, the energy locked in matter" (*EM* 33, 42). He has worked in the circus, "bending bars, butting brick walls, tugging trucks with his teeth" (*EM* 34). The tendency of the story to creak under its part-allegorical weight is seen when

Bujak states his opposition to the very force he possesses and uses: "All peculiarly modern ills, all fresh distortions and distempers, Bujak attributed to one thing: Einsteinian knowledge, knowledge of the strong force"—nuclear energy (*EM* 46). This knowledge is why the "world looks worse every day," why it's "suicidal" (EM 47). Out of the blue, violence enters his life in the form of two Scottish louts ("Terrible mutations" [*EM* 58]) who, invited home by Bujak's daughter to have sex, have murdered his mother, wife, and daughter and then fallen into a drunken sleep where he discovered them. Instead of using his strong force on them, he turns them over to the police, at which his strong force deserts him. In effect, Bujak denounces the theory of deterrence. The story ends with an imaginary reversal of time in which his family is restored and they all travel back to the innocence of infancy—both theirs and the world's (see Works, p. 54).

"Insight at Flame Lake" concerns Dan, a schizophrenic boy who stays with his uncle, Ned, and Ned's wife and child, after his father, who worked in nuclear-weapons delivery systems, has committed suicide. The narration consists of alternating entries in Dan's and Ned's diaries. Its revelation of conflicting interpretations of events is reminiscent of *Success*. Amis has called Dan "a kind of nuked schizophrenic" (Profumo 1987: 41), a boy whose mind is so deformed by his proximity (through his father) to nuclear weapons that he sees Ned's innocent baby as the embodiment of Evil. Dan sees even the lake beside which he is staying as "an explosion;" the sun "is really going nuclear," and Dan dreams of "nuclear supercatastrophe" (*EM* 61, 71, 64). The story ends with Dan drowning himself and Ned finally having the insight that Dan suffered from the disease of living in the twentieth century when cereal boxes advertise "tips for avoiding cancer" and show "mugshots of smiling children, gone, missing" (*EM* 79).

"The Time Disease" is typical of Amis's penchant for reversing conventional conceptions. In this story, he imagines a world suffering the aftereffects of nuclear warfare. The principal effect is a reversal of how humans treat time. This reflects, Amis has said, the "damaged set of time we have [. . .] People behave as if there were no future" (Blades 1987: 3). The narrator is a television producer whose ex-wife goes down with time disease, which inverts the aging process and restores unwanted vitality, when all that humans desire is a lack of intense feeling in a world in which the sky reveals its "great chemical betrayals" (*EM* 87). Amis has said that the story enacted his "revenge on Los Angeles" with its "'live-for-ever culture." "I thought it would be funny if there was a disease around that encouraged you to live a very unhealthy life" (Profumo 1987: 41). So, the narrator's idea of health is illness and aging. His ex-wife dies from a return to youthfulness, while the narrator recovers from the time disease and returns to ill health.

"The Little Puppy that Could" parodies a children's story, "The Little Engine that Could," and appropriates the Greek myth of Andromeda (the name of the young female protagonist) who was saved by Perseus from being consumed by a sea monster. Set in a futuristic world in which humans were "traveling backward down their evolutionary flarepaths" (*EM* 109), the story portrays a matriarchal society preyed on by a monster, a mutated giant dog, that eats one human a week. Andromeda adopts a stray puppy who, when it comes to be her turn to be offered as sacrifice to the dog, lures the beast to its and the puppy's destruction in a flaming pit. But, at the end of the story, the puppy is reincarnated as a young man whose "arms were strong and warlike" who leads Andromeda to a hilltop from which they "gazed down at their new world" (*EM* 134). Is this happy ending meant to suggest the return of Adam and Eve, as Falconer (1998: 718) claims? Or does it represent a sexist fantasy, an imagined return to a patriarchal society where "a proper polarization of the sexes will make possible some sort of renewal," as Mars-Jones (1990: 11–17) suggests?

"The Immortals" confronts the dilemma involved in attempting to narrate the end of time. Such an endeavor is both impossible and pointless. Amis takes up the challenge by making his narrator "the Immortal" (a claim undercut by the title) who has come to New Zealand to die with the last humans on Earth who are suffering from radiation poisoning. Born simultaneously with the creation of the world, the narrator adopts a long historical perspective: "I sat through geology, waiting for biology" (*EM* 136). This evolutionary time scheme offers Amis the opportunity to wittily put humans in their place when seen from a macro perspective outside human history: "Jesus Christ, you were only here for about ten minutes. And look what you did" (*EM* 148). His account of life in the twentieth century is even more damning: "I swear, the entire planet seemed to be staging some kind of stupidity contest" (*EM* 143). He hints at the beginning of the story that the other remaining humans "all believe that they are …"—immortals, the context suggests. At the end, he is revealed as another delusional human, "just a second-rate New Zealand schoolmaster who [. . .] is now painfully and noisily dying of solar radiation along with everybody else" (*EM* 148).

## Heavy Water and Other Stories (1998)

*Heavy Water and Other Stories* was published the year after *Night Train* (1997). It included three early stories ("Denton's Death" [1976], "Heavy Water" [1978, rewritten 1997], and "Let Me Count the Times" [1980]) and six stories, all but one of which ("Career Move" [1992]) were written between 1995 and 1997 (see Life and Contexts, **p. 28**). All nine stories had been first published in magazines (four in the *New Yorker*). Although the stories do not have the thematic cohesion of those in *Einstein's Monsters* (which, however, critics attacked for their strong didactic content), they all show Amis's dystopian view of late-twentieth-century life and are stamped with his stylistic signature. Most reviewers detected a marked improvement in the later stories, in some of which they found a new compassion that they claimed first surfaced in *Night Train*. This is most in evidence in "What Happened to Me on My Holiday," a story based on his own son Louis's coming to terms with the death of his half brother, ending in a return from his stylized speech to adult normality. As Diedrick observes, the appearance of this "new emotional emphasis" coexists with "several outrageous comic fantasies" (Diedrick 2004: 178). Some of these comic stories depend on Amis's penchant for inversion, most obviously in "Career Move" and ""Straight Fiction." While some reviewers found *Heavy Water* mostly a "dismaying volume" (Mars-Jones 1998: 14), later critics have tended to side with the opinion of reviewers like Russell Celyn Jones who wrote in *The Times*, "*Heavy Water and Other Stories* is highly inventive, inimitably stylish and funny, exhibiting a wider voice range than anything he has done so far" (Jones 1998: 40).

Of the three early stories, "Denton's Death" describes a man waiting in his London apartment for the arrival of his murderers whose reasons for killing him remain undisclosed, "Let Me Count the Times" (originally written for *Penthouse*) focuses on a married man who, obsessed with the number of times he has sex with his wife (or himself), quantifies love, and "Heavy Water," a story he wrote for the left-wing *New Statesman* in 1978 and then rewrote in 1997. Diedrick has written at length on this story, comparing its two versions. He shows how it grew out of a two-week trip Amis made on a British cruise ship in the Mediterranean about which he wrote a travel article for the *Sunday Telegraph Magazine* in January 1979, where he observed, "The ship remains a capsule of England" (Diedrick 2004: 170). The story recounts the relationship between a mother and John, her forty-three-year-old mentally retarded son, on a similar cruise ship described as "a lurching chunk of England" (*HW* 130). The British working-class passengers are drunk by lunchtime, and Diedrick discerns a parallel between John's retardism and "a kind of moral idiocy [which] has followed upon the decline of British working class culture" (Diedrick 2004: 167). While some reviewers were moved by the love the mother shows for John, Dern sees her as "vampiric," "her thirst for John's vitality [. . .] evidenced by her bloodless lips" (Dern 2000: 117). John's attempt to kill himself in the finale is brought on by a momentary realization he has in the aquarium that he suffers like the turtle "with all its appendages retracted" beneath its protective shell (*HW* 139). So, does the heavy water of the title refer to John's tears (he constantly cries)? Or to the gin with which his mother laces his bottle? Or to the nuclear age they inhabit?

The two stories relying on inversion imagine, in the case of "Career Move," a world in which poets are treated by Hollywood as hot screenwriters subject to financially lucrative deals, while screenwriters belong to an impoverished underclass attending basement readings of their unpublished work. "Straight Fiction" conjures up a New York where gays are the majority and heterosexuals are a despised but rebellious minority. Amis has called "Career Move" "a revenge fantasy" and "affectionate satire" on Hollywood which commissioned him to write *Mars Attacks!* only to make no use of it (Bauer 1999). Anticipating a similar use of inversion for *The Information* (see Life and Contexts, p. 23), the story has some hilarious moments when studio executives are discussing the latest hit poem-turned-movie, "'Tis," and its prequel "'Twas" and sequel "'Twill" (*HW* 22, 31). Amis creates similar mayhem with his reversal of sexual orientation in "Straight Fiction," although this idea had already been used by Anthony Burgess in his 1962 novel, *The Wanting Seed*. Cleve, the gay protagonist of Amis's story, is gradually drawn to a despised "breeder," Cressida, who is pregnant. In an age when most babies are produced in test tubes, Cleve finds the paraphernalia surrounding her baby repugnant but, at the end, is irresistibly drawn to Cressida who "had undergone the internal struggle of biology" (*HW* 195).

"The Coincidence of the Arts" concerns a successful aristocratic British artist, Sir Rodney Peel, living in New York. He encounters Pharsin, an African American who asks him to read the manuscript of his long novel, *The Sound of the Words*. This is a task that Rodney is too lazy to perform. Meantime, he unknowingly meets and starts an affair with Pharsin's English cockney wife who refuses to speak during their times together. In the end, he discovers her identity when Pharsin forces his way into his apartment and insists on hearing Rodney's opinion of his novel. It turns out that he has been beating his wife in a rage at Rodney's refusal to give him that opinion. The entire story hinges on Rodney's ancestors having enslaved Pharsin's. When Pharsin's wife leaves Rodney, taking all his savings, she effects a partial compensation for Rodney's continuing exploitation of the African race. "The Janitor on Mars" is a science-fiction story reminiscent of some of those in *Einstein's Monsters*. It parallels the events at a pedophilic English orphanage with the appearance of the Janitor on Mars who invites representative humans to visit him and learn the fate of the Earth. In the Janitor's eyes, the Earth is a scientifically backward planet due shortly to become extinct from an increase in oxygen. Amis has explained the connection between the story's two strands: "The Janitor on Mars messed with human history, and that's what the pedophile does, too; he rewrites your history" (Brady 1999: H2).

Even reviewers who disliked the collection thought that "State of England" was "a triumph of compression and extravagance" (Mars-Jones 1998: 14) (see Life and Contexts, **p. 28**). The story, the title of which suggests its debt to the Victorian condition-of-England novel, is ostensibly about an uneducated London criminal Mal, who has left his wife Sheilagh for Linzi, an East Ender of Indian extraction. Mal is attending his son Jet's school sports day where he talks to Sheilagh (also present) on his cell phone. The school is expensive, and half of the dads putting in an appearance at sports day with their cell phones "weren't even English" but "spoke better English than Mal" (*HW* 43). Mal is another of Amis's comic antiheroes who "sensed he was a cliché—and sensed further that he'd even fucked *that* up" (*HW* 41). Mal appears to represent the newly empowered working class of post-Thatcher Britain: "So class and race and gender were supposedly gone (and other things were supposedly going, like age and beauty and education)" (*HW* 53). Yet, some workers, like Mal, "would never be admitted" due to their "deficiencies" (*HW* 54). According to A. O. Scott, "The state of England is that it's become a classless society obsessed with sports, children, cell phones and the profit motive" (Scott 1999: 5). However, the story is less clear-cut than this, as Amis's use of "supposedly" above indicates. In the conclusion, Mal attempts a reconciliation with Sheilagh that is destined to end up with him escaping once more to Linzi's "freeing his mind of all thoughts about the future" (HW 69). Mal reappears in *Yellow Dog* where he is more fully developed (see Works, **p. 62**).

# Autobiographical works

## Experience: A Memoir (2000)

At a time when critics were beginning to claim that Amis's writing powers were waning, the publication of *Experience* compelled most of them to acknowledge that his memoir showed a high degree of originality without sacrificing his linguistic wit and ingenuity. His stated motive for writing the memoir was "to set the record straight" (*E* 7). The way he does this is very different from the traditional autobiography. Amis has said that by avoiding a chronological approach he could "leave stuff out without saying why" (Richards 2000) (see Life and Contexts, pp. 28–9). In fact, he leaves out much of his private life, especially the circumstances surrounding his divorce from his first wife, Antonia Phillips, and marriage to his second, Isabel Fonseca, although he does address some passages of the book directly to Isabel in the second person. His nonlinear organization of material, which gives him a degree of novelistic freedom, allows him, as he says, "to follow themes rather than merely the calendar" (Reynolds and Noakes 2003: 22). He knew that he "would have to write it with the same kind of priorities with which you write fiction" (Weich 2003). In fact, its form derives from "the novelist's addiction to seeing parallels and making connections" (E 7). His use of both chronological and structural discontinuities aims at presenting "a clear view of the geography of a writer's mind" (E 7). What he means by "mind" includes, even gives precedence to, the unconscious: "The big jobs are done by the unconscious. The unconscious does it all" (E 80). He offers an instance of its working in the memoir when he recalls how shocked he was to recognize the truth of Maureen Freely's observation in the Observer that his fiction was haunted by "a stream of wandering daughters and putative or fugitive fathers," something equally true of this book (E 280).

While far from stream of consciousness, the book's method of progression employs association (of ideas, individuals, events, images) as a key organizational principle. For instance, Chapter 4 ("Learning About Time") opens with a recollection of a 1968 holiday in Spain he took with Rob when he ended up broke and hungry for the only time in his life. He next remembers his family's poverty when he was a baby; his father's need to ask Philip Larkin for a loan takes him to Rob asking him for a loan and takes him forward to the time when Rob landed up in jail. Reverting to the topic of going abroad, he compares his time in Spain staying with his mother, living in Ronda after he won the Somerset Maugham Award, with his father's reluctant stay in Portugal after he had won the same prize that required its recipient to spend time out of Britain. Remembering that Kingsley took his family of five to Portugal leads Amis to compare Kingsley to his generation, which married and had children much later (the entire chapter is partly a meditation on time). This leads him to dwell on some of the affairs he had before marrying, including the one with Lamorna Seale, who had given him a photograph of her daughter. He shows this photo to his mother on his trip to Spain where she is then living, upon which she confirms that the daughter is likely fathered by Amis. The arrival of his aunt in Spain takes him back to the time her daughter, Lucy Partington, disappeared for good. That loss reminds him of a later occasion in Spain when his son went momentarily missing. The chapter ends with him listening to his aunt confessing, "not a minute passed without her thinking of Lucy." His inability to comprehend what she was feeling leads him to end reflecting on "youth, that time of constant imposture" (E 54).

This apparent use of random association is far from random. Amis might claim that in this book he wants "to speak, for once, without artifice" (E 7), but the fact that he uses fictional methods of organization inevitably brings into play his novelist's penchant for parallels and contrasts, that is, for artifice. Not only is this representative chapter connected by its reflections on the nature and influence of time, but it constructs polarities: his privileged life contrasted to Rob's "genius for adversity" (E 44); his embrace of the prize money to spend time abroad with his father's foot-dragging visit to Portugal; his gift of a new daughter balanced by his aunt's loss of a daughter. James Wood first suggested that Amis is indebted to Nabokov's autobiography, *Speak, Memory* (1967) for burying "his patterns deep in the aesthetic textures of his book" (Wood 2000: 8). In a review he wrote the same year he published *Experience*, Amis wrote that *Speak, Memory* is "the least revealing, because the most artistic" (*WAC* 257). All autobiographies have to strike a compromise between the poles of factual truth and artistic form. Amis clearly privileges the latter as instanced in Nabokov's "deliberately oblique and stylized autobiography" (*WAC* 247). Diedrick adds that Amis also praised Gore Vidal's autobiography, *Palimpsest* (1995), for what Amis called "its elaborate double-time scheme, its cunning rearrangement and realignments of the past" that equally characterize *Experience* (*WAC* 282). Amis has said that the numerous footnotes were intended to act as a relief from the emotional intensity of the main text, a way of "[l]etting the temperature drop for an instant" (Richards 2000). In the book, he writes that he used the footnotes "to preserve the collateral thought" (*E* 7). In effect, they provide the more cerebral reflections of the conscious self on the less conscious, emotional narrative of the book.

To what kind of experience does the title refer? Experience, he writes, "so unanswerably authentic," is what he as a novelist is "trained to use"; yet, it "is the only thing we share equally" (*E* 6). He has explained that "innocence is a *tabula rasa* on which is piled, stacked, over the years, experience, in the Blakeian sense of being more and more aware of your fallen state" (Reynolds and Noakes 2003: 25). Joan Acocella surmises that the title "is probably taken from a remark that Amis tells us his father, Kingsley, made upon the bust-up of his second marriage: 'Well, it's all experience, though it's a pity there had to be so much of it.'" (Acocella 2000: 182). For Amis, experience came in concentrated form at the height of his midlife crisis in 1994–5. Wood calls these years "the pregnable pivot, the wound to which the text recurs again and again" (Wood 2000: 8). Amis experienced an exceptionally intense midlife crisis in his mid-forties which he summarizes at one point in the book: "'Breakup, separation from children, health-crisis.' Lucy Partington, Bruno Fonseca, Saul Bellow in the ICU" (*E* 269). Elsewhere in the book he also mentions the break with his agent Pat Kavanagh and her husband and his close friend, Julian Barnes, and the horrific dental work he had done (see Life and Contexts, p. 24). The paragraph ends, "All I need now is the death of a parent" (*E* 269). It was his father's death in 1995, which affected him deeply, that determined him to write the memoir. This was the finale to "all the discontinuities and disappearances of 1994" (*E* 199). In particular, the disappearance of his father brought about the experience that "[d]eath is nearer, reminding you that there is much to be done" (*E* 345). Yet, as Christopher Hitchens observes, *Experience* "makes the stale phrase 'midlife crisis' redundant for all time, if only by showing that crisis is a condition of all stages of life" (Hitchens 2000: 10). Like Amis's symbolic use of his dental work (loss and restoration), his treatment of his midlife crisis becomes a means for discussing the larger crisis that we all undergo when brought face to face with our threatened disappearance.

Amis has explained that *Experience* was "also a cognitive stretch of grieving for the father" (Richards 2000). "I have packed a lot of mourning into it [. . .]

and also reread him from start to finish and communed with him" (Gerard 2001). In *Experience*, Amis illustrates the extent to which his father's writings influenced him and his writing. He recalls reading Kingsley's *The Anti-Death League* at the age of sixteen and being mesmerized by the two questions put by the heroine: "Is it now? Is it you?"—questions he kept asking himself as he grew older (*E* 33). He draws comparisons between his father's *Ending Up* and his *Dead Babies*: "Both Amis novels were black comedies set in country houses. In his book they all died. In my book they all died except one" (*E* 349).

Considering how unsympathetically his father spoke of his novels in public, Amis's portrait of him is a marvel of compassion and love, "one of the most remarkable father–son accounts we have; as good as Gosse, but without the rancour," according to one reviewer (Lanchester 2000: 5). Tempted once only to make a clean break with his father, he rejected the idea because they "would soon be needing each other in complicated ways" (*E* 25). Both writers, they had both gone through painful divorces. It seems natural that Amis should confess only to his father how terrible he felt about his: "Only to him could I talk about what I was doing to my children" (*E* 99). The difference between the two is that Amis is honest about his own complicity in the catastrophe. He might have done it for love, he writes, but "you are also the enemy of love and—for your children—its despoiler" (*E* 256).

His close competitive relationship with his father also surfaces in his allusions to *Hamlet*. Once he is fatherless, he identifies with the fatherless Hamlet surrounded by death and faced with the imminence of his own death. He alludes to *Hamlet* when giving Rob the news that his father had died: "The King is dead" (*E* 358). He also identifies with Hamlet's failure to quickly come to terms with his father's death when he adapts Claudius's remonstrance to Hamlet: "The father is dying, as did his (and as did his)" (*E* 345; see *Hamlet* 1.2.89–90) (see Life and Contexts, **pp. 3, 26**). Amis's use of this intertext goes further, because he calls his youthful self "Osric," the ridiculously mannered and pretentious courtier whom Hamlet made look foolish, and he quotes "Osric's" letters to his father and stepmother from his crammer and Oxford. A conscious stylist who believes that style is a signifier of a writer's ethics, he writes that he punctuated the memoir with "Osric's" early letters to "allow the reader [. . .] to enjoy a few moments of vacuity," that is, to compare his early, irresponsible use of language to his mature style (*E* 151). In the manner of Osric, the young Amis made a practice of "mincing up and down the King's Road in skintight velves and grimy silk scarves" (*E* 13). Compare this updated "water-fly" (*E* 15) with the mature modern-day Hamlet visited near the end of the memoir by his father's ghost who gives his son to understand that Martin "had all his trust—in the prosecution of his wishes, and in everything else" (*E* 363).

Amis practices what he preaches about the morality of style. For instance, he allows the reader to observe him as he corrects the way he expresses himself. Reflecting on his inability to absorb the significance of cousin Lucy's disappearance at the time, he asks, "Can you think about something you can't assimilate? I don't think you can. Or I don't think you do" (*E* 52). That correction involves a judgment on himself. Writing plays a vital protective role for this writer. At the age of twenty-four he was "pretending to know everything, while knowing nothing [. . .] But there was another world, one I felt I could control and order—

which was fiction" (*E* 36). In addition, the fact that his father was a writer meant that "his [Kingsley's] shadow served as a kind of protection" (*E* 35). Once he has lost his own father he seeks a father substitute in another writer, Saul Bellow (see Life and Contexts, **pp. 26–7**). The writing of others also provides Amis with one of the means by which he makes sense of his accumulating experience. As he himself has said of the memoir, "You're trying to make sense of it [an event in your life] after the event, and you reach for similar analogous experiences, or representations of those experiences in literature" (Reynolds and Noakes 2003: 24). He writes of how, although he sees Bellow perhaps twice a year, "that accounts for only a fraction of the time I spend in his company," as in reading his work he communes with him constantly: "And here are the other writers who swirl around you, like friends, patient, intimate, sleeplessly accessible, over centuries" (*E* 268). *Experience*, Amis told one interviewer, is "a meditation, an essay on the literary life as I have led it" (Orr 2000: 7).

Most reviewers and critics expressed admiration for this unusual, finely crafted yet honest autobiography. In particular, not just the forgiveness of, but the love Amis shows for his cantankerous father won widespread praise (see Life and Contexts, **p. 29**). Karl Miller is typical: *Experience* "might seem a miracle of forebearance, but what comes across is more in the nature of a candid and finely qualified generosity of heart" (Miller 2000: 14). One or two reviewers did find fault with Amis's inclusion of his postscript (on Auschwitz), appendix (on his father's biographer, Eric Jacobs), and addendum (his letter to his aunt). In such passages, John Lanchester, for instance, found the writing to go "flat and strained," an "aesthetic mistake" (Lanchester 2000: 5–6). Joan Acocella, who praised the main text for making its points "by accumulation, as in a Symbolist poem," also felt that the three appendices "should have been deleted" (Acocella 2000: 182). Keulks is more representative when he praises the book's connection between theme and method: "love triumphs over isolation, and form emerges strengthened from shapelessness" (Keulks 2003: 223).

## Koba the Dread: Laughter and the Twenty Million (2002)

Amis has said that his memoir *Experience*, "created an appetite for the form," which made him go on to write what he thought would be a pamphlet but turned into *Koba the Dread*. He called it both "a political memoir" and "a site memoir" (Richards 2000). It is a hybrid form, combining the personal and the historical, what Keulks describes as "equal parts autobiography, biography, political science, and historical fiction" (Keulks 2003: 243). The idea for the book first germinated at a political meeting Amis attended in 1999 at which his friend Christopher Hitchens joked about spending time at the London venue of the meeting "with many 'an old comrade.' [. . .] the audience responded with affectionate laughter" (*KD* 256). Why is it, Amis wonders, that a reference to the horrors of Stalin's USSR can elicit laughter, where a similar joke about Nazis would alienate the same audience? Amis personalizes this question by addressing it to Hitchens, a Trotskyist, and his dead father, who had been a member of the Communist Party between 1941 and 1956 before veering to the far right (see Life and Contexts, **p. 30**). Both must have been aware at the time of Stalin's purges and pogroms. The second moment of the book's germination came after Amis attended the anticlimactic millennium celebrations in the Millennium Dome: "that night did seem to mark the end of the twentieth century; and the twentieth century is unanimously considered to be our worst century yet" (*KD* 5). A day or two later, he began work on this book, which aims to address what he considers to be the chief lacuna in the popular memory of the twentieth century. That lacuna was the murder of at least 20 million citizens of the USSR during Stalin's reign from 1924 to 1953. Amis comments, "they deserved more reverence than they got" (Richards 2000).

That accounts for the reference to "The Twenty Million" in the title. He explains his ironic use of Koba for Stalin in the title, as Koba was the childhood nickname Stalin borrowed from a Russian novel in which the Robin Hood hero had that name (*KD* 98). Amis draws on his earlier fictional yobs, such as John Self or Keith Talent, for his portrait of Stalin, the difference being he has absolute power. "The Dread" derives from Ivan the Terrible also known as Ivan the Dread, a "hands-on torturer" and "paranoid psychotic" after whom Stalin modeled himself (*KD* 168). The word in the subtitle that caused the most confusion and criticism was "Laughter." Amis refers to the laughter with which the audience (and he) greeted Hitchens' use of "comrade" as "the laughter of universal fondness for that old, old idea about the perfect society. It is also the laughter of forgetting" (*KD* 256). But even Diedrick appears to confuse this with Amis's use of laughter in the book for satiric purposes: "'Laughter' identifies the literary paradigm that organizes—and strains the reader's patience with—Amis's analysis of Stalin's evil" (Diedrick 2004: 189–90). Amis directs his satire in the book at the ideas of a Communist society: "what is all this about the earthly paradise, which [. . .] is a horrible notion? An inhuman, alien notion" (Richards 2000). As in his subsequent *The House of Meetings*, he is showing his opposition to all forms of ideology: "ideology brings about a disastrous fusion: that of violence and righteousness" (*KD* 86).

The book is divided into three parts. Parts I and III mix historical and political material with personal memoir. In both these parts Amis evokes, in particular, his father, Hitchens, and his sister Sally, who died while he was at work on the book (*KD* 5). Part III opens with "Letter to a Friend" (Hitchens) and closes with "Letter to My Father's Ghost." Part II, which occupies half the book, consists of his recapitulation of the horrors of Stalin's reign in the Soviet Union. Amis acknowledges his indebtedness to historians, such as his father's friend Robert Conquest, and to Russian novelists who had experienced the deprivations of the gulags, such as Solzhenitsyn. Michiko Kakutani finds that "[w]here Mr. Amis is at his best is in using his arsenal of literary skills to create a compelling narrative, summarizing vast amounts of information and presenting them in lucid, accessible form" (Kakutani 2002: 9). He recounts the toll of the civil war, the 1922 famine, the effects of collectivization, Stalin's purge of the peasantry ending with the Terror Famine of 1933, the deadly purges of 1937–8, the show trials, the gulags, the losses sustained during World War II, and the period between 1945 and 1953 when "Stalinism entered its rancid, crapulent phase" (*KD* 215), ending with Stalin's death just as he was about to launch a massive pogrom against the Jews. *Koba the Dread* continues Amis's extended meditation on death begun in *Experience*. He quotes Stalin as once saying, "while every death is a tragedy, the death of a million is a mere statistic" (*KD* 276–7). Amis attempts to deny this chilling aphorism by drawing parallels in this book between the Twenty Million and his own dead—his father and Sally. Confessing to the devastation he was still experiencing at the absence of Sally and of his two sons from his first marriage, he writes, "I thought I was sick, I thought I was *dying* (maybe that is what bereavement actually asks of you)" (*KD* 247). However awkward the appearance of his personal recollections may be in this book, they are intended to bring the writer into some form of parallel empathy with those like Solzhenitsyn who had experienced Stalin's reign of terror firsthand, to imbue "a mere statistic" with a sense of personal tragedy.

The book garnered mixed to negative reviews (see Life and Contexts, **p. 30**). Criticisms targeted his "narcissistic self-positioning" (Cowley 2002), and charged that his "arguments are hackneyed, his emotions narcissistic" (Service 2002: 33), that the book "leaves you with a sense of too much artifice, of ideas in love with themselves" (Thubron 2002: 11), that he got some of his facts wrong such as mistaking Ivan III for Ivan IV, and—the most frequent complaint—that he had the bad taste to compare his daughter's tears to the screams emanating from the gulags (cf. *KD* 260). In a number of public responses, Hitchens, while unable to rebut the charge that he turned a blind eye on the horrors of Communist rule in the Soviet Union, asked, "What did you imagine would happen if you elected to write on such a Himalayan topic, and then pygmified it by addressing so much of it to me?" (Hitchens 2002: 6). Some reviewers defended Amis's combination of a personal and historical memoir, one claiming that these mixed elements "do end up establishing a rhythm [. . .] It is the rhythm of grief as experienced by a man who would rather experience anything else." The same reviewer offered a balanced evaluation of it as "one of the oddest books about Stalin ever written, indignant, angry, personal and strangely touching" (Berman 2002: 7).

## Essay collections

### The Moronic Inferno and Other Visits to America (1986)

Amis's first collection of nonfiction took the form of twenty-seven articles, profiles, and reviews on American subjects first published between 1977 and 1985. Two-thirds of the items in *The Moronic Inferno* were initially written for the *Observer* (see Life and Contexts, **pp. 6–7**), and all but one (on Brian de Palma) were commissioned by English papers or magazines. Sixteen of the pieces are about American writers and their work. The remainder cover topics from "The Killings in Atlanta," "Palm Beach," and "Elvis Presley" to "Here's Ronnie: On the Road with Reagan," "In Hefnerland," and "Double Jeopardy: Making Sense of AIDS." They vary in tone from respectful (Bellow, Heller, Updike) to sarcastic and satirical (Capote, Presley, Mailer, Hefner), with many showing Amis balancing the admirable against the derisory. Most items are reprinted as they originally appeared, although occasionally Amis has felt compelled to add postscripts updating already-dated material. The title, Amis writes in the Introduction, derives from Wyndham Lewis's description of interwar society via

Saul Bellow's *Humbolt's Gift* (see Life and Contexts, **p. 18**). Although Amis explains that the phrase "is not a peculiarly American condition" (*MI* x), at least one American reviewer questioned his right to call America a moronic inferno (Bawer 1987: 22).

Reviewers each side of the Atlantic tended to adopt different positions in their responses. Americans claimed that in this collection Amis "seems not so much to be observing America as to be observing himself in America" (Bawer 1987: 25) or talked of his "very stereotyped assessment of the purported 'reality' of America's 'dreamlife'" (Baker 2005: 551). English reviewers generally praised the book: "He is never a more British writer than when he is writing satirically about America" (Brown 1994: 98). Insisting on his American connections, Amis is equally acerbic when surveying similar aspects of the British scene. His judgments on literature are usually fresh and rely on his acute awareness of a writer's use of English. The collection opens and closes with essays on his literary hero Saul Bellow, who, he argues, unlike most impoverished modern writers, writes "in a style fit for heroes: the High Style," which "attempts to speak for the whole of mankind" (*MI* 5) (see Works and Criticism, **pp. 83, 97–2**). When he wants to put down a writer, such as Norman Mailer, he uses style as his measure: "The prose gurgles with clichés, tautologies and uneasy mandarinisms" (*MI* 60). His judgments combine frankness with fairness. Writing of John Updike's *Rabbit Is Rich*, Amis observes, "At its best the narrative is a rollicking comedy of omission, as author and reader collude in their enjoyment of Rabbit's pitiable constriction." In the following paragraph he complains, "Updike repeatedly lapses into winsome editorials, as if to fill the spiritual gaps" (*MI* 156).

Inevitably, Amis's critical assessments of other writers' work reveal his own literary preoccupations. In his piece on Philip Roth he discerns three kinds of women in Roth's work: "the Girl Who Will Do Anything," "the Ball-Breaker," and the "Big Woman," the tender, self-abnegating woman who is scared by the Roth man (*MI* 43). These types of female characters are curiously similar to the women found in Amis's fiction. For instance, in *London Fields*, the Girl Who Will Do Anything characterizes Nicola, the Ball Breaker Hope, and the Big Woman Kath. Similarly, he quotes Bellow as saying, "Death is the dark backing a mirror needs if we are to see anything" (*MI* 202). Amis wrote that piece between writing *Other People* and *Money*, both books in which death provides just such a backing to the lives of their comically rendered characters. In the same way, Amis's profiles in this book show a similar approach to his subjects as does his fiction. He actually compares the profile to the short story: "You hire out your senses to take a reading of this person or event and so that is rather like fiction" (Bigsby 1992: 174). He has also said of the subjects of his profiles that he would "rather watch them being interviewed than interview them. It's postmodern now [. . .] You write about their PR act, because that's as close as you're going to get" (Cash 1992: 5). This resembles ways in which characters such as Gwyn Barry in *The Information* and Luke in "Career Move" are constructed through their mediated image (see Criticisms, **pp. 114–15**).

Amis shows the same acute ability to analyze his subject in his cultural and political essays. Following Reagan campaigning to become California's governor, Amis observes how the crowds "Love this actor. And I don't mean 'ex-actor.' I mean *actor*." Watching him talk, Amis writes, is "like coming out of *Kramer versus Kramer*, denouncing the film with tears drying on your cheeks" (*MI* 92). Amis can see that Reagan appeals to something deep in the people, which will give him the governorship, as it did. He is equally astute in his article about the Evangelical Right with its belief that evolution is "a vicious lie" (*MI* 110). Amis rightly predicts in 1980 that this movement could determine the outcome of the presidential election of 1984, although he underestimates their power when opining that he does not "think the Evangelicals will be soon running the country" (*MI* 118). Despite his admitted British liberal scorn of the Evangelicals' vulgarity and the use of the "holy sting" by their tele-evangelists (*MI* 114), he discerns that the "movement constitutes a genuine revolution from below," that "will have to be heeded" (*MI* 118). But Amis's most admired article in the book is his piece on AIDS, which one English reviewer called "the most levelheaded and, up to 1985 at least, the most accurate account by a non-specialist to be found anywhere" (Moore 1986: 14). In it, he targets the public fear that produces myopia in government and in the heterosexual population both in London and New York. He sees the same "resistance to corporeal truth" in the offices of the *Observer*, which printed while slightly bowdlerizing his article, as he does in the streets of both cities (*MI* 197). What distinguishes this piece is Amis's instinctive identification with the feelings of the AIDS sufferer, which helps to increase his awareness of his own heterosexual prejudices. Diedrick calls this essay "an example of sustained imaginative sympathy" (2004: 201).

## Visiting Mrs. Nabokov and Other Excursions (1993)

Amis's second collection of journalistic writing consists of an Introduction and thirty-three prose pieces. Of these, eleven are literary profiles, eight are on popular culture, five on sports, four are celebrity profiles, two are reviews, two political, and two autobiographical. The earliest of these articles is "The Rolling Stones at Earls Court" published in the *New Statesman* on May 28, 1976, and the latest is "Madonna" published in the *Observer* on October 11, 1992. Most date from the mid-1980s to the early 1990s. The majority were written for British publications, especially for the *Observer*, which employed him as a special writer in the 1980s. Amis had been writing journalism since 1971 and claims that in this book "much has been left out" (*VMN* ix). Because his articles are commissioned, he says that writing them "never feels like writing in the proper sense" (*VMN* ix). Yet, reviewers considered that the best of them show journalism of a high order, distinguished by Amis's special brand of verbal wit and humor. As Geoff Dyer wrote, they have an "undisputed claim [. . .] to a stylistic terrain so pervasive that you're in danger of encroaching on it before you've even set foot in it" (Dyer 1993: 28). Amis's reliance on verbal wit and satire makes most of the pieces at once readable and somewhat emotionally removed. But his account of his "Emergency Landing" while flying to Malaga and his compassionate obituary of the unlovable Philip Larkin show that his feelings are held in check just below the surface. This may be why he strikes Hermione Lee as "the man of feelings with a cold eye" (Lee 1993: 40).

Almost half the book consists of literary and celebrity interviews, a genre which, according to Francine Prose, demands "wit at the expense of depth, more

facility than profundity" (Prose 1994: 17). Amis has his own reservations about
the literary interview, calling it a convention that "is dying, or growing old"
(*VMN* viii) and, quoting Updike approvingly, "It rots a writer's brain, it
cretinizes you," because you "say the same thing again and again" (*VMN* 50).
Amis concludes, "The literary interview won't tell you what a writer is *like*. Far
more compellingly, to some, it will tell you what a writer is *like to interview*"
(*VMN* 54). Unsurprisingly, many of Amis's judgments rely on an analysis of his
subject's use of language. "The response to language," he observes, "is, as
always, an ingredient of something larger" (*VMN* 198). He admires Anthony
Burgess for being "practically omnilingual" (*VMN* 241) and picks out for special
praise the fact that V. S. Pritchett "loves to impact language, and run the
cadences up the wrong way" (*VMN* 270). He uses his considerable satirical
powers to consign Isaac Asimov and John Braine to the status of Grub Street
hacks. After trying to read Asimov's two-volume autobiography, he asks, "How
could anyone *dare* to record a life with such fidelity to the trivial?" and he
reports caustically that Braine "saw the film version of *Room at the Top* [his
bestselling novel] several nights running, and wept every time" (*VMN* 219, 233).
His profile of Larkin combines honesty with genuine admiration for his poetry:
"Everything about Larkin rests on irony, that English speciality and vice," he
declares and concludes that "[t]he clinching paradox may be, however, that
Larkin will survive as a romantic poet, an exponent of the ironic romance of
exclusion, or inversion" (*VMN* 201, 204).

Amis's celebrity interviews contribute to his other readings of popular culture
in this book. He opens with the assumption that the star interview is dead
(*VMN* viii). Madonna even refused to see him on the grounds that he was too
famous (*VMN* 255). Amis was untroubled: "The great postmodern celebrities
are a part of their publicity machines, and that is all you are ever going to get to
write about: their publicity machines" (*VMN* viii). Characteristically, Amis turns
instead to examine Madonna's photobook, *Sex*. "From the start," he writes,
"Madonna has included pornography in her unique array of cultural
weaponry—because she understands its modern industrial nature" (*VMN* 263).
As Diedrick has pointed out, Amis's distrust of the impersonal forces of modern
technology surfaces not just here, but in "Nuclear City" and "*RoboCop II*"
(Diedrick 2004: 208). As Amis writes about the original movie, "Technology is
god in *RoboCop*, but it is also the villain, with its triumphant humourlessness, its
puerile ingenuity, its dumb glamour"—a typical Amis triplet of oxymorons
(*VMN* 164) (see Works and Criticism, **pp. 83, 152**). In his over-lengthy article,
"Nuclear City," written at the same time as *Einstein's Monsters* (1987), he mocks
Washington's nuclear experts for their euphemistic use of such terms as "surgi-
cal" (strike) and (nuclear) "umbrella": "How can anyone get hurt by an
umbrella?" he ironically asks (*VMN* 15). For Amis, these experts' linguistic
naivety reveals a more significant naivety: their failure to imagine the planetary
catastrophe that any large-scale use of nuclear weapons would unleash.

Language is the great giveaway for Amis. Reporting on the Republican
Convention of 1988, he ridicules the vice-presidential candidate, Dan Quayle,
for being "quite at sea in the English language, utterly confounded by the
simplest declarative sentence," and quotes a sentence of Quayle's that even
manages to use a cliché incorrectly: "The question today is whether we are going

forward, or past to the back" (*VMN* 108). Amis is as aware of his own use of language as he is critical of others'. He writes paradoxically of "the hospitable void of the New World" (*VMN* 114). He uses topical food spreads to describe how Florida turns tennis spectators "into various shades of peanut butter and hotdog mustard" (*VMN* 61). In "Nuclear City" he notes ironically that the Committee for National Security is "situated, appropriately enough, above a pizza parlour called Vesuvio's" (*VMN* 19). He uncovers the "venue-fixing, spy-planting, rule-bending" ways of modern World Chess Championships, which have turned this intellectual pursuit into "the game of the *spite check* and the *shame mate*" (*VMN* 86–7). How much he manages to impart in those two paired phrases. His observations on sports matches, like those on cultural events, penetrate to their human essence. Darts, he explains, is a game that "is all about *scoring*." But, again, he is alert to multiple signification. Scoring means not simply numerical totals but "piss-taking one-upmanship" that is equally integral to the sport (*VMN* 225).

The most serious criticism directed at this book came from Hermione Lee. Commenting on Amis's explanation in the Introduction that journalism is the only part of his writing that gets him out of the house, she remarks, "Where they got him out to is a world that is 99 per cent male." She goes on to allege that Mrs. Nabokov is the only woman he talks to, "but the real object of desire and veneration [. . .] is, of course, Nabokov himself." (see Criticism, **pp.** 140–1). Yet, she grants that as a journalistic writer, "he is serious, fastidious, and moral" (Lee 1993: 40). Even if his canvas is limited here largely to his own gender, he still has a remarkable ability to penetrate beneath the surface of his subjects, to see behind Reagan's surgically altered face ("now the picture window to the soul" [*VMN* 104]), to interpret Madonna as "a masterpiece of controlled illusion" (*VMN* 264), while at the same time he "makes writing seem fun, serious fun" (Dyer 1993: 28).

## The War Against Cliché: Essays and Reviews, 1971–2000 (2001)

In the Introduction to *The Moronic Inferno*, Amis indicates that as early as 1993 he was planning a volume devoted to "the lowest and noblest literary form: the book review" (*MI* ix). Amis began life as a book reviewer and editor of others' reviews, and he has always felt "a sense of duty about it." He considers the book review the most difficult thing he does. "You don't have the freedom of fiction [. . .] It's a totally enclosed world, like chess or math" (Curiel 2001: 2). Amis acknowledges James Diedrick's help in compiling the pieces in *The War Against Cliché* (*WAC* ix). In an email dated April 11, 2007 James Diedrick wrote to me explaining his contribution: "I presented Amis/Wylie with a proposed organization for the volume, which Amis took and modified." Diedrick has observed that Amis omits from this collection all twenty-six of the science-fiction reviews he wrote for the *Observer* between 1972 and 1974 (Diedrick 2006: 181). In fact, Amis's selectivity is extensive: "two additional volumes would be required to contain the more than fifty essays, more than sixty book reviews, and more than forty film and television review columns from this period that remain uncollected" (Diedrick 2004: 220). The 500-page volume covering almost thirty years of Amis's reviews is divided topically rather than chronologically. Most of the pieces deal with novelists, although what is often considered the most impressive is about a poet, Philip Larkin, and two sections focus on masculinity (from Robert Bly to nuclear weapons) and popular culture (from football to world records). Amis includes all the essays he wrote for the *Atlantic Monthly* between 1986 and 1995 in which he was allowed more length than was allotted to the traditional review. Only three women writers are considered: Jane Austen, Iris Murdoch, and Fay Weldon. This prize-winning collection was greeted with widespread acclaim.

The title of the volume is the same as that he has given his essay on Joyce's *Ulysses* (which originally was published in the *Atlantic Monthly* as "Teacher's Pet"). In that essay, he writes, "*Ulysses* is *about* cliché. It is about inherited, ready-made formulations, fossilized metaphors—most notably those of Irish Catholicism and anti-Semitism. After all," he adds, "prejudices are clichés: they are secondhand hatreds" (*WAC* 444). For Amis, clichéd language has always entailed what he calls "clichés of the mind and clichés of the heart" (*WAC* xv) (see Life and Contexts and Criticism, pp. 29, 148). Early in life, Amis learned to spot the use of cliché. When he was working for the *Times Literary Supplement*, he recalls, "we made collective war on certain clichés. Nothing could ever 'throw light' on anything. Nothing could ever be 'oddly reminiscent' of anything" (Amis 1992a: 18). His reviews from almost three decades show him consistently using language as a litmus test for evaluating a book. As he notes in the Introduction to this volume, "When I dispraise, I am usually quoting clichés. When I praise, I am usually quoting the opposed qualities of freshness, energy, and reverberation of voice" (*WAC* xv). Almost invariably, a criticism by Amis of an author's use of cliché leads to a criticism of the work as a whole. So, he writes of one of Fay Weldon's novels, "Cliché spreads inwards from the language of the book to its heart. It always does" (*WAC* 137). Similarly, after listing the succession of clichés to be found in D. M. Thomas's *The White Hotel*, he draws the conclusion: "the sentences conjure nothing but an exhausted imagination" (*WAC* 145). Conversely, he praises Nabokov's insistence that style "is the only thing that matters in books," which makes him view cliché as "the key to bad art" (*WAC* 251, 245).

Amis calls literature "a pattern of words" and insists that "an author's more general procedures will always be reflected in its verbal surface" (*WAC* 87). For Amis, style is not something added to "content"; "it is intrinsic to perception." A tired imagination will produce tired use of language. But, style for Amis means more: "style is morality. Style judges" (*WAC* 467) (see Critcism, pp. 147–8). Accordingly, in Bellow's *The Adventures of Augie March*, "Things are not merely described but registered, measured and assessed for the weight with which they bear on your soul" (*WAC* 467). Amis's close attention to the way writers use language results in some acute critical insights. For instance, he singles out Elmore Leonard's use of the present participle to create what he calls "a marijuana tense." Sentences using this tense "seem to open up a lag in time, through which Mr Leonard easily slides, gaining entry to his players' hidden minds" (*WAC* 226). He gets constant pleasure from Bellow's prose style "because of its manifest immunity to false consciousness" (*WAC* 326) (see Criticism, p. 92). Equally, he faults Andrew Harvey for referring to "mangy, flearidden dogs," on the grounds that

Harvey's use of such clichéd adjectives reveal the fact that he had never truly looked at these dogs. Amis makes sure he practices what he advocates. He wittily puts down Hillary Clinton's committee-written "300-page press release," *It Takes A Village*. After quoting some of its banal observations, he observes, "we are out there on the cutting edge of the uncontroversial" (*WAC* 30, 31). Condemning Angus Wilson's *As If by Magic* for its "repetitions, unintentional rhymes, jangles, even solecisms," he punningly refers to an incident in the novel "at some smarmy, Swami gathering" (*WAC* 75). Whenever he can, he uses verbal wit to denounce narrative failings. So, he will comment on Truman Capote's depiction of the Very Rich: "Interestingly, they are not interesting; incredibly, they are not even *credible*" (*WAC* 311). He cites what he ambivalently calls Ballard's "creative narcissism" to condemn his indifference to his reader (*WAC* 101). He employs one of his characteristic triple descriptives to gently satirize George Steiner's erudition, calling him "the panoptic, polymathic, polysyllabic Doctor" (*WAC* 342) (see Works and Criticism, **pp. 80, 152**).

This creative use of language to comment on the language (and substance) of fellow writers offers Amis the confidence to make highly perceptive and authoritative judgments about their work. He disregards the accepted opinion about the greatest classics. "While clearly an impregnable masterpiece, *Don Quixote* suffers from one serious flaw—that of outright unreadability" (*WAC* 427). Similarly, he pronounces *Ulysses* "not reader-friendly," and calls Joyce's prose "this incredible instrument, half wand, half weapon" (*WAC* 441, 443). Amis often employs the evenhanded assessment constructed from opposing qualities as a device to offer a complex response to the work of his competitors. Most of his reviews of Updike's writing show a deep ambivalence. Updike is "above all an *embarrassing* writer: it is his recurrent weakness, and his unifying strength. He is always successfully taking you to where you don't quite care to follow" (*WAC* 378). Even when he comes to write about *Lolita*, one of his favorite works, he describes it as "both irresistible and unforgivable" (*WAC* 471). However, when he turns to his most loved novel, Bellow's *The Adventures of Augie March*, he assumes the authoritative tones of F. R. Leavis in pronouncing it the Great American Novel (*WAC* 447, 469) (see Criticism, **p. 91**). Yet, how different is such a verdict from the practice of Leavis who "sought to reduce literature to a moral audit," to whittle it "into a hard core of mature and wholesome texts" (*WAC* 77)? At the same time, unlike Leavis, Amis can combine schoolmasterly reproof with humor. He will accuse Ballard of a "morbid fear of the common pronoun" (*WAC* 108), Cyril Connolly of the frequent use of the "factotum adjective" (*WAC* 133), and, in more general terms, dismiss Thomas Harris's *Hannibal* with his verdict that "Harris has become a serial murderer of English sentences, and *Hannibal* is a necropolis of prose" (*WAC* 240).

Inevitably, Amis reveals his views on a wide range of larger literary and cultural concerns in the course of reviewing individual books. Amis finds Anthony Burgess's distinction between A and B novels a useful analytic tool. Burgess believes that the A novelist "is interested in character, motive and moral argument, and how these reveal themselves through action," while the B novelist is interested in "the autonomous play of wit, ideas and language" (*WAC* 113). It is evident that Amis considers the B novel the preferred type and elsewhere refers disparagingly to the A novel as merely "illustrative" (*WAC* 300). He sees plot as of central importance only in genre fiction, because "mainstream fiction, famously, has only about a dozen plots to recombinate" (*WAC* 225). He also dismisses Updike's insistence that a novel should imitate reality. Amis comments, "Life goes on regardless, and reality won't mind if a novel spurns it" (*WAC* 372). Amis's views on the degenerative history of the second half of the twentieth century inevitably color his definitions of the modern novel. During the last half century, he observes in a review of Don DeLillo's *Underworld*, an "ambient mortal fear constrained us. Love, even parental love, got harder to do" (*WAC* 319). In modern fiction in the West, realism is now modified by irony (*WAC* 428). Because the future nowadays seems bleak, "no one creates utopias any more." "Pretty well inevitably, the speculative novelist becomes a satirist" (*WAC* 117). So, Joyce wills into existence "the frame of epic: degraded epic, modern epic" (*WAC* 442) (see Works and Criticism, **pp. 59, 111**). Even *The Adventures of Augie March* is an "epic about the so-called ordinary" (*WAC* 448). And, when Amis comes to discuss his favored literary mode, comedy, he demonstrates what a capacious genre it has become in modern times: "Human beings laugh, if you notice, to express relief, exasperation, stoicism, hysteria, embarrassment, disgust and cruelty" (*WAC* 488).

Amis's attitude to postmodernism is ambivalent (see Criticism, **pp, 116–23**). The contemporary writer, he suggests, should draw on "the [realist] strengths of the Victorian novel together with the alienations of post-modernism" (*WAC* 79). The postmodern world itself gets a poor press from Amis. For instance, it has turned otherworldly chess into a "spectator sport" involving "genuinely bitter conflict" (*WAC* 339). It is a "world of wised-up rabble and zero authenticity" (*WAC* 226). In an egalitarian age when "*everyone* has become a literary critic," this world has naturally left its mark on his fellow reviewers whom he calls "book-chat mediocrities" whose crucial defect is "dullness" (*WAC* xiii, 241, 369). He expresses his amazement at the adulation with which UK reviewers greeted Thomas Harris's vulgar novel, *Hannibal*: "Is this the next thing? Philistine hip? The New Inanity?" He is especially enraged by critics (such as the *Guardian*'s Mark Lawson, whom Amis quotes without naming) who enlisted *Hannibal* as literature (*WAC* 234). Yet, as a reviewer, Amis gets more tolerant, more evenhanded as he matures (see Life and Contexts, p. 7). He prefers the artist-critic, because he expects "artists to stand as critics not just of their particular milieu but of their society, and of their age" (*WAC* 439). Because "finding a voice" is "what all novelists have to do," novelist-critics will search the text for the voice of an author, whereas the critical theorist [. . .] fails to find literature very interesting, all by itself" (*WAC* 133, 77). Like Nabokov, Amis distrusts the academic critic because of the "professorial impulse to pontificate and generalize" (*WAC* 250) (see Criticism, **pp. 110–11**). Amis's attention to style and language ensures that he rarely does either.

Nowhere is Amis's skill as a critic more in evidence than in his *New Yorker* essay on Philip Larkin, which Frank Kermode called "the most permanently valuable part of the book" (Kermode 2001: 28). In it, Amis examines the character assassination that followed the 1992 publication of Larkin's *Selected Letters* and Andrew Motion's 1993 biography of him, *Philip Larkin: A Writer's Life*. Amis skillfully rebuts Motion's criticisms of Larkin for being misogynistic and sexist by describing in detail the drabness of Larkin's life, his shyness, his miserliness, and his fear of failure, while ridiculing Motion's anachronistic charges that Larkin was sexist at a time when "'sexism' had no currency" (*WAC* 162). How, he asks, can Motion accuse Larkin of misogyny when Larkin "devote[d] his inner life to women" (*WAC* 163)? Employing his own form of verbal wit, Amis shows Motion sharing the faults he discerns in Larkin: "Motion is extremely irritated by Larkin's extreme irritability; he is always complaining that Larkin is always complaining" (*WAC* 166). He concludes by showing how Larkin criticizes himself in his poems far more effectively than does Motion in his life of him, because "the internal story, the true story, is in the *Collected Poems*" (*WAC* 169). Amis demonstrates his fair-mindedness as a reviewer (seen throughout the book) by balancing his dissection of Motion's politically correct distortions with praise for Larkin's honesty as a poet.

## Further reading

The best introduction to Martin Amis's work is the second edition of James Diedrick's *Understanding Martin Amis* (2004). A selection of reviews and critical essays related to each of Amis's major books up to *Heavy Water* is available in *The Fiction of Martin Amis: A Reader's Guide to Essential Criticism*, edited by Nicholas Tredell (2000).

# 3

# Criticism

## Intertextuality

### Kingsley Amis

The concept of intertextuality has largely displaced that of literary influence in critical discourse. What is the difference between them? Put over simply, influence operates in one temporal direction while intertextuality operates equally between both texts and not just temporally. When did the term "intertextuality" enter the vocabulary of literary criticism? Julia Kristeva coined it from her reading of Mikhail Bakhtin in the later 1960s (being most fully articulated in *Revolution in Poetic Language*) to refer to the way "any text is the absorption and transformation of another" (Kristeva 1986: 37). This means that literary language "is at least double," the transposition of one or more sign systems into another (Kristeva 1986: 37). Kristeva points to the way that the status of any word or signifier is defined both horizontally by its dialogic connection between writer and addressee and by its vertical relationship to the entire corpus of literary work. She claims that all texts are composites of other signifying systems, not the end product of a number of discernible sources. In referring a reader to another text, the text in question generates polysemy (multiple meanings) that amounts to more than the semiotic content of either text on its own. Seen in this light, no text is wholly intelligible unless seen in relation to other texts with which it is inscribed. In particular, the differential relations between one text and others are productive of multiple meanings. In Part 2, for instance, it was suggested how the name of the narrator of Amis's *Other People*, John Prince, suggests both Prince Charming and the Prince of Darkness (see Life and Contexts and Criticism, **pp. 45, 126**). The ambivalent status resulting from these mutually conflicting intertextual associations in turn draws attention to the ambivalent control of the narrative exercised by this ghostly narrator who also enters the narrative as a character beyond the narrator's determination. So, John Prince accrues more meanings than the combination of the meanings attached individually to Prince Charming, the Prince of Darkness, and John Prince.

It would be surprising if Martin Amis had not used his writer-father's novels and essays as intertexts in his own writings. As he points out, "we're the only father-and-son team who both have a substantial body of work" (Bellante and

Bellante 1992: 4), although in *Experience* he does mention Frances and Anthony Trollope and Dumas *père et fils* (*E* 23). The nature of the relationship between Martin's and Kingsley's work is necessarily complex, involving admiration and rejection by the son in almost equal measure. Martin simultaneously considered his father "the leading comic novelist of his generation" (*E* 344) and rejected everything that his father's generation stood for both socially and esthetically (see Life and Contexts, p. 1). His father was just as opposed to Martin's politics and esthetic practices, and, unlike Martin, he said so in public. Amis tries to suggest in *Koba the Dread* that the difference between father and son was more generational than attitudinal, writing in his "Afterword: Letter to My Father's Ghost": "If our birthdates had been transposed, then I might have written your novels and you might have written mine" (*KD* 272). But, this tribute to his father forms part of his mourning for his recent death. Martin was more balanced in an early interview he gave in 1985 when he said that, compared to his father, he took "greater liberties with reality" and that his work showed "more of a frisson about the awareness that what I'm offering is a fiction," which his father thinks is "all balls" (Smith 1985: 78). Martin's desire to differentiate his work from that of his father works against his genuine respect for it. In the case of his first novel, he even admits to "quite a lot of imitation" of Kingsley (Cash 1992: 4) and to revising it after his father had told him that a good writer avoided such doggerel as the repeated use of suffixes. But he is quick to add, "It was the only piece of literary counsel he ever gave me" (*E* 23) (see Life and Contexts, p. 8).

Intertextuality concerns itself with the interaction between texts rather than writers. It simultaneously involves the new text's rereading of, and displacement of, the intertext, thereby producing both a new understanding of the intertext and a contextualizing of the new text. In *Understanding Martin Amis*, James Diedrick appropriates Harold Bloom's Freudian concept of writers' "anxiety of influence" to describe the relationship between the work of Kingsley and Martin Amis. In his book, *The Anxiety of Influence* (1973), Bloom argues that poets (writers) suffer from a sense of belatedness, because they fear that their literary predecessors have preempted their freedom of expression. Just as the boy child, according to Freud, fears castration by the father, so the new strong writer experiences the Oedipal fear that his work will be overshadowed by that of his literary forefathers (Bloom is as unconsciously androcentric as Freud). His response is to create an imaginative space for himself, which involves misreading the earlier work. Bloom lists a variety of ways in which such "poetic misprision" (misreading) works. But the most important aspect of his theory for our purposes is that all literary works come into being in the course of conducting a psychic struggle with antecedent texts. Bloom insists, "there are *no* texts, but only relationships *between* texts" (Bloom 1975: 3). Intertextuality is literally an integral part of the creative process. Part 2 points out that both Kingsley's and Martin's first novels employ the *Bildungsroman* which both treat in comic mode (see Works, p. 36). But, at the same time, Martin employs a different, darker form of comedy while denying that it is significantly different, which can be interpreted as an instance of his misreading his father's early work in the act of creating his own.

In *Father and Son*, Gavin Keulks argues that Bloom's theoretical framework cannot explain the complex ways in which the two Amises' works relate to one another. Martin's works "must be read as more than successful instances of efficient misreading," in part because both writers' work overlapped and caused each to compete with the other (Keulks 2003: 23). In Keulks' view, the Amises' literary rivalry "was neither hidden nor an example of surreptitious misprision" (2003: 29). It has to be seen as a more overt and conscious competitiveness conducted by both writers. Accordingly, Keulks persuasively argues that *The Rachel Papers* "consciously undermines the aesthetic [. . .] foundations of Kingsley's *Lucky Jim*," initiating "a literary battle over genre and mode that inspired, not silenced, production" (Keulks 2003: 119) (see Works, **p. 36**). As *Lucky Jim* had never gone out of print up to the time Martin published his first novel, he could not ignore it. His own first novel had to distinguish itself from his father's if he was to be seen as a novelist in his own right. Far from misreading his father's novel, Martin challenges its literary affiliations, especially its use of the comic mode. Whereas Kingsley's Jim Dixon acts as his creator's satiric mouthpiece and "labors to deflate pomposity, pretension, and egotism," Martin's Charles Highway "nurtures every possible pretension," and is the principal target of the narrative's satire (Keulks 2003: 125). Jim is portrayed as a cultivator of instinctual responses and twice declares his belief that "nice things are nicer than nasty ones" (Amis, K. 1976: 140, 243). Charles stands for all those controlling characteristics that Jim dislikes. In an act of conscious literary revision, Charles reverses Jim's dictum when he proclaims, "Surely, nice things are dull, and nasty things are funny. The nastier a thing is, the funnier it gets" (*RP* 87). In his review of Martin's novel, Blake Morrison emphasizes the radical nature of the son's separation from his father's form of comedy when he declares that *The Rachel Papers* shows clearly that "'nastiness,' the comedy of the grotesque," is to be Martin's specialty (Morrison 1973: 1389) (see Life and Contexts and Criticism, **pp. 9, 132–3**). These complementary quotations from the two novels illustrate how intertextuality generates more meaning than either produces independently.

To show the way in which the father's and son's literary rivalry became contemporaneous, Keulks focuses on the manner in which Martin's *Dead Babies* responds to and inverts Kingsley's *Ending Up*, which was published in 1974, a year before *Dead Babies* appeared in print, and thereby contests his father's current achievements. Keulks contends that "the two novels should be considered as companion texts, contrapuntal variations of a distinctive genre, the country house novel" (2003: 133). He cites Martin's observation in a joint interview with his father to the effect that both novels were about people living in a house getting on each other's nerves and ending up killing each other (Byrne 1974: 219). He also refers to *Experience* in which Martin talks about the time he spent at his father's house in Hadley Common when each of them was writing their novel in rooms one above the other: "Both Amis novels were black comedies set in country houses" (*E* 349). Keulks sets out to show how the two novelists' "satirical divergences illuminate the antithetical nature of their worldviews" (2003: 134). Where the characters in Kingsley's novel are all old, those in Martin's book are all young. "Saturated by self-indulgence, egotism, and excess, *Dead Babies* vividly depicts the emotional by-products of a doomed hedonistic generation" (2003: 137). Keulks discerns an underlying humanism permeating Kingsley's sympathetic portrayal of his elderly characters, as opposed to Martin's total withdrawal of sympathy for his vicious and unlikable young characters. In treating its characters so savagely, *The Rachel Papers*, according to Keulks, "directly engages Kingsley's conceptions of pathos, human nature, and satire" (2003: 140). Keulks concludes that "Martin's satirical technique [. . .] departs from his father's brand of comic realism [derived from Horace and Fielding] and adopts instead a more playful, amoral, and ludic form, energized primarily by words, not ideas" (2003: 149). Following Diedrick, Keulks discerns the use of Menippean satire in *Dead Babies* (its epigraph is from Menippus). Menippean satire posits "a carnivalesque, amoral realm in which bacchanalian chaos displaces accepted reality" (Keulks 2003: 151). The endings of each novel confirm this difference between the two writers. Death is an accident treated with humanist pathos in *Ending Up*, whereas death represents utter destruction, "a Mansonesque bloodbath without logic or reason," in the case of *Dead Babies* (Keulks 2003: 158–9). No wonder that Kingsley could not finish his son's second novel, seeing that it implicitly indicts *Ending Up* for literary falsification (see Life and Contexts, p. **12**).

Keulks goes on to consider two more "companion texts," Kingsley's *Stanley and the Women* and Martin's *Money*, both published in 1984, which show the two novelists' differences in their attitudes to "postmodernism and their controversial portraits of women" (Keulks 2003: 162). He argues that the postmodern esthetic distance that Martin establishes from his sexist male protagonist and narrator demonstrates the advantages of his choice of narrative mode (see Criticism, p. **128**). Kingsley's realist treatment left him open to charges of male prejudice that even Martin made later in *Experience*, where he called *Stanley and the Women* "a mean little novel" in which Kingsley "didn't kill the world. He just killed half of it" (*E* 310). Keulks maintains that where in *Stanley and the Women*, "Kingsley created a realistic text that rejects and ridicules the exertions of fabulation and metafiction," Martin responded with "a metafictional text that scrutinizes realistic conventions," effectually dismissing his father's "literary regression" (2003: 198). David Galef and Merritt Moseley have written articles about the lives and work of the two Amises in which each argues that the intertextual relationship between their two oeuvres shows more similarities than conscious conflicts. Galef believes that both "Amises' hallmark" is "social satire" and speculates, "Perhaps both authors desire to turn the clock back" (Galef 2002: 560, 562). Moseley argues, "Martin Amis was more like Kingsley than Kingsley ever suspected or admitted," and goes on to explain, "Each has been a primarily comic novelist with deep and powerful moral interests" (Moseley 2005: 305, 312). In a review essay of Keulks's book, Robert Baker also appears to suggest that Keulks may be overemphasizing the conflict between Martin and Kingsley when he claims that "Martin's aesthetic is inherently sympathetic to Kingsley's, despite the public disagreements" (Baker 2005: 549). Because Martin is simultaneously protective of and deeply attached to his father while equally deeply needing to separate himself as a writer from his father's form of fiction, it is easy to find evidence for either stance. However, Keulks offers a book-length analysis of his interpretation that is the more convincing.

## Vladimir Nabokov

In *Experience*, Amis asserts that Vladimir Nabokov and Saul Bellow are his "twin peaks," his two novelists of the twentieth century (*E* 119n). He has written seven essays on Nabokov and six on Bellow. Nabokov was his first literary love, and he first reviewed one of Nabokov's books, *Transparent Things*, in 1973. He makes intertextual reference to Nabokov and his work in many of his books. He named his third novel, *Success* (1978), after the title used by Nabokov for a novel written by a fictitious author featured in his *The Real Life of Sebastian Knight* (1941). *Other People*, his fourth novel, has its female protagonist read this novel of Nabokov's and refer to *Lolita* (1955), as well as adapting a sentence from Nabokov's *Pnin* (1957) to describe Trev's tongue uselessly flapping around inside his mouth (*OP* 63). In *Einstein's Monsters*, Amis acknowledges that his story "The Little Puppy that Could" owed something to Nabokov. In *London Fields*, the narrator discusses Nabokov's insomnia and quotes a line from Nabokov's *Transparent Things* (1972): "Night is always a giant but this one was especially terrible" (*LF* 303). Amis has coupled *Time's Arrow* with Nabokov's *Pale Fire* (1962) on the grounds that both are conscious "literary tours de force" (Bellante and Bellante 1992: 16). The theme of literary competition and jealousy that informs *Pale Fire* reappears in Amis's *The Information*. Part 2 mentioned James Wood's suggestion that in his memoir, *Experience*, Amis is indebted to Nabokov's autobiography, *Speak, Memory* (1967) (see Works, **p. 73**). Keulks discerns in *Experience* the presence of the same intertext, *Speak, Memory*, which "furnished Martin with a model for interrogating time" (2003: 205). And, in a review of Nabokov's *Selected Letters*, Amis praised *Speak, Memory* for exhibiting the same reticence he would observe in *Experience*: "it traces the formation of the talent, not the personality" (*WAC* 257). In *Koba the Dread*, he also cites the political pulse present in some of Nabokov's work that offered him a precedent for writing this, his most political book (*KD* 37).

Amis has said that Nabokov has been an inspiration to him, not an influence, "because you simply can't do that stuff as well as he did" (Bellante and Bellante 1992: 16). What he means by inspiration is that when he gets to a difficult paragraph he will think, how would Nabokov do it? (Curiel 2001: 2). *Lolita*, in particular, provided Amis with almost unlimited inspiration. His father had attacked it in a review he wrote in 1959 which Amis called "willfully philistine" in *Experience* (*E* 121n; Amis, K. 1970). In 1992, Martin wrote an extended essay for the *Atlantic Monthly* titled "Lolita Reconsidered" in which he rebutted his father's two main accusations in his review: that Nabokov failed to establish any esthetic distance between himself and his protagonist, Humbert, and that consequently the novel failed both stylistically and morally. Martin opened his counterattack by provocatively stating that *Lolita* is "a cruel book about cruelty" (*WAC* 473). He admits that Humbert is cruel to Lolita in using her "for the play of his wit and the play of his prose." But, he continues, "However cruel Humbert is to Lolita, Nabokov is crueler to Humbert" (*WAC* 474). Amis repeatedly recalls Nabokov's dictum that readers need to identify with the writer, not the characters. As Nabokov wrote in *Lectures on Literature*, they should share with the author the pleasures and problems of creation. "In art," Amis wrote, echoing Nabokov, "nothing really matters; no one gets hurt; it is only a game. But an artistic reckoning must be completed" (*WAC* 487).

Amis's brilliant handling of language in all his work has been inspired by Nabokov's similarly dazzling style. In his earliest essay on Nabokov, "The Sublime and the Ridiculous: Nabokov's Black Farces," written in 1980, Amis argues that, because *Lolita* eschews any kind of moral didacticism, it belongs to the literary mode of the sublime. "Sublimity," Amis writes, "replaces the ideas of motivation and plot with those of obsession and destiny. It suspends moral judgement in favour of remorselessness, a helter-skelter intensity" (Amis 1980a: 76). All that matters for Nabokov, Amis argues, is that the writer remains true to his fictive world by preserving "an absolute trust in style," and he cites Nabokov's creed: "For me 'style' is matter" (WAC 260) (see Criticism, **p. 120**). Both Nabokov and Amis believe that their society is in a state of decay. Their narrator-protagonists are made to reveal this through their language, style, and vocabulary. As Dern points out, the opening paragraph of *Lolita* contains "a line that easily might have been by Samson Young [in *London Fields*]: 'You can always count on a murderer for a fancy prose style'" (Dern 2000: 165). Humbert's verbal affectation and insane self-assurance resembles that of Prince in *Other People* who, like Humbert, manipulates a hapless female protagonist for his own sadistic narrative purposes. Amis discerns in *Lolita* a sublime "method of moral focus" which allows Nabokov to invoke ethics through style, "letting style prompt our choice" (Amis 1980a: 82). Like Humbert, Gregory in *Success* shows a haughty narcissism through his manner of speech: "I used to love the man I would become" (*S* 180). Style judges. Style is morality. Style is a war against clichés of the mind and of the heart. Those deeply held convictions of Amis originated in Nabokov's esthetic position. Amis's use of and defense of Nabokov's identification of style with narrative matter may well have provided him with "a means to upend and supplant Kingsley's literary authority," as Keulks suggests (2003: 46). Ultimately, it became the centerpiece of Amis's stance as a writer (see Criticism, **pp. 147–8**).

## Saul Bellow

Amis came later to the work of Saul Bellow than to that of Nabokov. Christopher Hitchens introduced him to Bellow's work in 1977 (see Life and Contexts, **p. 91**). He starts mentioning admiringly Bellow's fiction in reviews of others' work that he wrote in 1980. In 1982, he wrote his first review of a Bellow novel (*The Dean's December*). In 1983, he paid his first visit to Bellow in Chicago (see *E* 175–6, 179–80) (see Life and Contexts, **p. 16**). From then on, Bellow played as important a role as Nabokov in Amis's literary life. After his father died, he found in Bellow a substitute literary father figure with whom he communed constantly through reading his work (*E* 268) (see Life and Contexts, **p. 27**). The same year (1995), he pronounced Bellow's *The Adventures of Augie March* (1953) the Great American Novel (WAC 447) (see Works, **p. 83**). The conjunction of Bellow and Nabokov in Amis's pantheon of inspirational writers may appear, at first, paradoxical. Where Nabokov typifies postmodernists' emphasis on art as play, Bellow was never a postmodernist. As Amis writes in *Experience*, Bellow's "only *ism* was realism." But, he adds, "Meditative Realism, or Inner Realism, perhaps" (*E* 176). Amis called this inward movement by the writer the "higher autobiography," a fictional form of self-inspection the best practitioner of which was Bellow. Drawing on his "private being," Bellow, Amis wrote in 1993, "has made his own experience resonate more memorably than any living writer" (*MI* 200). By becoming an Everyman, Bellow makes his personal experience that of everyone. Quoting this passage in *Experience*, Amis goes on to suggest that his use of a first-person female narrator in *Night Train* and his personal preoccupation with bachelorhood and childlessness in *Money* were indebted to Bellow's use of the higher autobiography (*E* 177).

In *Experience*, Amis records the fact that Bellow had as many reservations about Nabokov's work as Nabokov had about Bellow's (*E* 119–20n). It is hard to think that two such antithetical writers had equal appeal for Amis. David Hawkes, however, suggests how both novelists offered Amis features in common: "Like Nabokov, Bellow invents narrators who constantly undermine their own credibility." Bellow, he goes on, "also shares Nabokov's interest in literary rivalry and his habit of constructing his plots around the conflict between a pair of contradictory yet complementary characters." Hawkes parallels Humbolt and Citrine in Bellow's *Humbolt's Gift* (1975) with Shade and Kinbote in Nabokov's *Pale Fire* (1962) and Amis's pairs of characters in *Success, London Fields* and *The Information*. All such characters, Hawkes claims, "are not credible or consistent 'characters' in the realist tradition" (1997: 27). Amis admires Bellow's characters because they combine realist representation with an aura of universality, which is what he means by the "higher autobiography." One could argue that Amis combines Nabokov's linguistic playfulness with Bellow's preoccupation with concerns of the soul. And yet, in his *Atlantic Monthly* essay on Bellow's *The Adventures of Augie March*, Amis insists that Bellow's style is also extraordinary, because it "loves and embraces awkwardness, spurning elegance as a false lead" (*WAC* 466). He cites Bellow's use of compounds such as "lair-hidden," and "pimple-insolence," and his verb-couplings such as "cars 'snoring and trembling' or 'fluddering and shimmering'" (*WAC* 466). If one turns to Amis's own writing, one can find not just the elegance of Nabokov's puns and apothegms but also Bellow's awkward conjunctions of words such as those used for John Self's arrival in New York in the first paragraph of *Money*: "still drunk and crazed and ghosted from the plane" (*M* 7). Amis's use of "ghosted" is as inventive and awkward as is Bellow's neologism, "fluddering." Bellow's use of the High Style "attempts to speak for the whole of mankind [. . .] to remind us of what we once knew and have since forgotten" (*MI* 5) (see Works, **p. 78**).

Another assumption shared by Bellow and Amis is that they inhabit a degenerated world. In his review of Bellow's *Him with His Foot in His Mouth*, Amis quotes a Canadian landlady in the novel who tells the narrator, "The wrought work is brightly divine but Divinity is not now active within it. The world's grandeur is fading." Amis comments that "the myth of decline [. . .] has never looked less like a myth and more like reality" (*MI* 10). What he admires about Bellow is that he still believes in a divinity in humans, a soul which Amis cannot subscribe to as literally as Bellow but which stands for a belief in human decency that Amis still holds. As Keulks puts it, Amis learns from Bellow's quest for a "secular night of the soul" that "even the gutter can accommodate transcendence" (2003: 49, 50). At the same time, Bellow, like Amis, concentrates principally on constructing flawed characters. Amis explains that "in literature, goodness has always been bad news," because happiness, as Henri de Montherlant said, "writes white" (*WAC* 457). Dern sees a similarity between Bellow's Joseph in *Dangling*

*Man* (1944) and Amis's John Self and Richard Tull in that they all "struggle to retain a semblance of [humanity] in a world that fights them at every turn" (Dern 2000: 168). What is significant about both of Amis's protagonists is that they survive everything the deteriorating world throws at them. In Self's case, he even escapes the fictional world of the novel itself in the italicized final section of *Money* (see Criticism, pp. 113, 128). Like Bellow's protagonists, they emerge to testify to their realization that "being human [. . .] is not a given but a gift, a talent, an accomplishment, an objective" (*MI* 208).

## Other instances

Amis is an author who is widely read and consistently draws on his reading when constructing his own fictions. Apart from Nabokov and Bellow, he frequently mentions his debt to Charles Dickens. Charles, the protagonist of *The Rachel Papers*, is described as, like his author, exploring the literary grotesque, particularly Dickens (*RP* 62). Dickens, Amis has said, "likes to write about the whole of society. He likes to see what links Lady Dedlock and Joe the Sweep, and that's very much what I am interested in, too" (Bigsby 1992: 183). Amis repeatedly connects working-class and upper-class characters, such as Terry (a double of Oliver Twist, according to Diedrick [2004: 48]) and Greg in *Success*, and Keith and Guy in *London Fields*. When he was writing the latter book, he has said that the writer he thought most of was Dickens (Bigsby 1992: 183). One thinks of Keith treating *Edwin Drood: The Musical* as on the same plane of reality as the riots in Kazakhstan (*LF* 55). In a 1973 review of a study of Dickens by John Carey, Amis refers admiringly to Northrop Frye's essay on Dickens in which he argued that Dickens's novels are structured by "a conflict between two social groups, the family-oriented 'congenial' society [. . .] and the institutionalized 'obstructing' society." "The congenial society," he continues, "is mostly featureless and uniform; the obstructing society is far more exuberantly imagined, peopled not so much by caricatures as by humours—of hypocrisy, parasitism, pedantry" (*WAC* 194). Amis is similarly attracted to a fictional world peopled by humorous characters, especially those exuberantly imagined as belonging to the obstructing society, such as John Self, Keith Talent, and Clint Smoker. In addition, several reviewers and critics have seen the multiply plotted *Yellow Dog* as an evocation of Dickens's repeated use of several plot strands that lent themselves to the serialization of his novels, but this is used more parodically by Amis (see Works, p. 63). Intertextuality depends for its full effect on a well-read reader. In *The Information*, Richard's first visit to America is seen by those who have read Dickens's *Martin Chuzzlewit* to parallel its protagonist's visit to America to seek his fortune only to be cheated and disappointed. Richard Menke sees the American section of Amis's novel as paralleling Dickens's American interlude, both offering "an intensification of themes established during the English action" (2006: 147). When Richard first arrives in his New York hotel, the effect of the shaving mirror, which enlarges his face, gives rise to the sentence: "This was the best mirror, and it was the worst mirror" (*I* 217). This is an intertextual adaptation of the opening sentence of Dickens's *A Tale of Two Cities* which begins, "It was the best of times, it was the worst of times." But, whereas Dickens is invoking the hopes and horrors of the French Revolution, a momentous turning point in Western history, Amis is mocking Richard's impoverished confrontation with his own personal hopes and horrors. The effect of the intertext here is to comically place Richard in a vastly inferior world to the one Dickens evokes.

Luc Verrier devotes part of his essay on *The Information* to its sophisticated use of intertextual references. It is hardly surprising that a novel about two writers should be sprinkled with allusions to other writers and canonical works. But, in this novel, as Verrier suggests, "intertextuality dramatises the apparently impossible originality of the contemporary writer, [. . .] especially since *The Information* gives pride of place to plagiarism" (Verrier 2005: 280). When Richard goes to work for the Tantalus Press, he receives some poems from Keith Horridge for publication by the press. One of them, titled "Ever," turns out to have been plagiarized from a famous story by Jorge Luis Borges (*I* 319) (see Works, p. 60). When Richard spots this, he is inspired to attempt a form of reverse plagiarism by writing a supposedly earlier novel, bearing a close resemblance to Gwyn's best-selling *Amelior*, the title of which is a quote from Andrew Marvell's "The Garden": *Stumbling on Melons*. He invents the author's name by making an anagram of Marvell's title –"Thad Green" (*I* 327). But "MA," the narrator, stages his own plotted denouement in which Richard's plot comes to nothing. So, Amis has used intertextuality to offer three tiers of intertextual usage: the straight plagiarism of Horridge, the reverse plagiarism of Richard, and the skillful deployment of intertexts both real (Borges and Marvell) and fictional ("Ever," and *Stumbling on Melons*) achieved by the narrator. Through this elaborate literary game, Amis, Verrier claims, has restored originality to his heavily intertextual novel (2005: 282).

Intertextuality can involve texts other than works from the literary canon. Beata Piatek maintains that reviewers of *Night Train* failed to understand that Amis was primarily using intertextual allusions to television crime drama, not to the likes of Raymond Chandler (see Works, pp. 60, 62). Specifically, Piatek claims that "Amis is involved in an intertextual game with the American television cop show: *Miami Vice*, *Kojak*, *Starsky and Hutch*," although the latter two, dating from the 1970s, seem unlikely (Piatek 2004: 163). But she is more credible when pointing to the way that Mike Hoolihan's methodical survey of the murder room ending with her looking at the body parallels the way a camera, especially a television camera, would handle the shot. Compared to film, television employs a stripped-down image that Amis uses parodically in *Night Train*, "a novel so bereft of detail that it immediately attracts the reader's attention." All its stylistic traits "from the way the [. . .] narrator introduces herself, [. . .] down to the weird syntax in the unrealistic dialogues, point to trashy cop shows on television" (Piatek 2004: 170). Hoolihan frequently complains about the effects of television: "TV has ruined American juries for ever. And American lawyers. But TV has also fucked up us police" (*NT* 29). According to Piatek, the effect that these repeated intertextual references to television cop shows have is to show the way "TV appears increasingly in the role of a medium shaping reality rather than reflecting it" (Piatek 2004: 168). In the case of this novel, Amis's intertexts operate parodically. But they still perform the same function of proliferating meaning through the oscillation of text and intertext.

# Contemporary reception of Amis's work

## The Rachel Papers

Any attempt to offer a critical analysis of a living writer's work is compelled to take into account the variety of responses to that work found in the reviews accompanying its initial publication. Often reviews constitute the only (pseudo-) critical reactions available to date. Besides, reviews offer a glimpse of the literary climate in which the writer is living and to which he is responding in his work. Amis has been blessed with a number of intelligent, articulate, and discerning reviewers (such as Blake Morrison, Karl Miller, Adam Mars-Jones, Frank Kermode, and Michiko Kakutani) and plagued with some exceptionally vicious attacks (even by fellow novelists such as James Buchan and Tibor Fischer) that almost invariably confuse his fiction with his life. Considering the degree of vitriol that has been directed at him by the press, Amis has generally refrained from becoming embroiled in, or being demoralized by, the harsh treatment he has received in print. He attributes his detachment to being raised as the son of a famous novelist, which helped him realize that journalistic misrepresentation and antagonism were simply an unpleasant and unavoidable appendage to the business of making a living as a writer: "He [Kingsley] taught me to have a thick skin and I'm glad I have it as much as I do" (Davis 2003: 27D). Besides, he has been a lifelong reviewer himself, and, although he has never indulged in personal abuse in that role, he admits that "[e]njoying being insulting is a youthful corruption of power" that he sometimes exercised in his early days (*WAC* xiv). In *The War Against Cliché* he even draws the reader's attention to a review he wrote back in 1972 of William Empson's edition of Coleridge's works in which he unjustifiably criticized Empson's omission of the prose gloss which he had actually included (*WAC* 178–81) (see Life and Contexts, p.8). Occasionally, the bias of the press response to Amis has seeped into the more serious academic appraisal of his work, but he has been fortunate to have as his principal critics James Diedrick, Nicholas Tredell, and Gavin Keulks, all of whom maintain a distance between their assessments of his work and those of the reviewers and gossipmongers.

The earliest responses of reviewers to Amis's first novel, *The Rachel Papers*, focus on some of the features that reviewers will continue to consider core ingredients of Amis's writing (see Works, p. 37). As mentioned in Part 1, inevitably the father and son's first novels were compared and the son was perceived to be challenging his father's preeminent position as the leading comic novelist of his day (see Life and Contexts, p. 9). Many of these early reviewers drew attention to Amis's unusual facility with language. Writing for *Encounter*, Clive Jordan anticipates a later trend among reviewers by praising Amis's language at the expense of his creation of character: "What holds the attention are not these limited characters, but the author's verbally inventive scrutiny of them" (Jordan 1974: 64). Another less defensible response is to identify the narrator/protagonist with the author. Seeing that Charles is the object of Amis's continuous satire, it seems perverse to charge Amis, as Peter Prince did in the *New Statesman*, with failing to distance himself at all from his narrator. In *Experience*, Amis writes that Prince "saw no irony, no stylization—no difference at all between me and my narrator, with his 'cheesy little *bons mots*' and 'dingy little *apercus*.'" Amis writes that he only intermittently disagrees with that distant judgment (*E* 34), and Diedrick also sees the distance Amis creates from Charles as ambiguous (2004: 38) (see Life and Contexts, **p. 35**). But appearing in the weekly paper of which he was Deputy Literary Editor, the review must have made Amis determined to avoid a similar charge in his future work. The other major criticism, which recurs in the reviews of *The Rachel Papers* and which will dog reviews of his future work, is the accusation that it is "casually crude, scatological and obscene" (Sissman 1974: 102), together with the more serious charge that it is "unabashedly sexist" (Fremont-Smith 1974: 76), a charge that had been repeatedly leveled at Kingsley. Much later, Amis admitted that there is some misogyny in his first novel, which was written for a predominantly male readership, but that this ceases to manifest itself in his subsequent fiction (Weich 2003).

## From *Other People* to *Time's Arrow*

By the time his fourth novel was published, the reviewers' responses to his work had become enough of a phenomenon for Claude Rawson to devote an essay in the *London Review of Books* to their treatment of *Other People*. Rawson notes that within three weeks the novel had received twenty-one reviews (or interviews about it) and four broadcasts. Thirteen of the reviews were solo treatments, which is an indication of how important Amis was perceived to be by 1981. Rawson attributes this partly to Amis's acquisition of a public personality, being much photographed for this occasion. Rawson claims to discern in Amis "a remarkable management of the reputation game" (1981: 21). His public persona, whether consciously cultivated or not, was destined to blow up in his face in 1994–5. What made Amis so attractive to the press was the controversy that swirled about him and his work since the publication of his first novel. Paul Ableman, in his piece on *Other People* for the *Spectator*, wrote that "Reviewing Martin Amis is like trying to hear a bird sing in the midst of an artillery duel. 'Most powerful, wonderful, titanic English novelist alive' boom the guns on one side. 'Talentless, jumped-up, nepotistic little nobody' comes the answering fire" (Ableman 1981: 22). As was the case with *The Rachel Papers*, Rawson cites at least one reviewer, Richard Rayner of *Time Out*, who was unready "to accept any simple distinction between author and characters," especially when it comes to the same old charge of misogyny (Rawson 1981: 20). In an interview in the same issue of *Time Out*, Amis strongly defended himself, insisting, "my fiction isn't anti-women, it's anti-people. Everyone has a bad time in it" (Rawson 1981: 20). One of his woman interviewers, Helen Chislett, concluded, "Talking to him, the woman-hating image does seem nothing more than a good publicity stunt," popular in a militant feminist climate (Rawson 1981: 20). Finally, Rawson considers the spurious charge of a form of plagiarism in the *Times Literary Supplement* by Blake Morrison, who alleges that Amis is a "self-confessed raider of others' texts" and lifted the Martian technique used in the novel from Craig Raine (Rawson 1981: 21). Rawson dismisses this accusation on the grounds that this literary tradition antedates Raine by centuries. Morrison appears to be confusing plagiarism with not just established literary conventions but also intertextuality (see Works, **pp. 43–4**).

Amis's fiction from *Money* to *Time's Arrow* drew a range of similar responses with more favorable than unfavorable ones. Amis noticed an increasing divergence between the British and American reactions to his work, starting with *Money*. Whereas American reviewers appreciated the irony with which he treated John Self, "one or two reviewers in London, even intelligent reviewers, said that it was really depressing," missing the irony completely (McGrath 1987: 191). The furor over the failure of the selection committee to include Amis's *London Fields* in the shortlist for the Booker Prize (see Life and Contexts and Criticism, **pp. 22, 143**), because of its alleged sexism, "got him more column inches than most of those on it" (Bragg 1989b: 1). The public controversy helped make the novel a bestseller and turned Amis into "the rock star of English literature" (Thomson 1998: 14). *Time's Arrow* was shortlisted for the Booker Prize but failed to win it. This might have been partly due to his ironic treatment of a sensitive subject—the Holocaust (see Works, **p. 54**). While most reviewers felt that *Time's Arrow* had, as the *TLS* reviewer wrote, "the hallmark of something earned, struggled for, originated" (Harrison 1991: 13), James Buchan was the most egregious of the few reviewers who unjustifiably accused Amis of anti-Semitism (see Life and Contexts, **p. 22**). While some English reviewers used the slur of anti-Semitism, no such imputation came from reviewers in America or Israel.

## The later period

Amis's *annus horribilis* (terrible year) was 1995. His separation from his first wife and choice of another American heiress for his second wife, his sacking of his British agent (the wife of his friend, Julian Barnes) in favor of a supposedly cutthroat American agent and ensuing huge advance on his next work (*The Information* and one subsequent book), and his expensive dental reconstruction by a New York specialist brought out the latent jingoism in the yellow press in Britain and typecast him there as a disloyal turncoat and money grabber who deprived his fellow writers in Britain of their share of the publishers' pool for authors' advances (see Life and Contexts, **pp. 24–5**). Disgusted by the spurious furor, Rushdie wrote: "This was an attempt to murder a writer" (Wilson 1995: 102). All this xenophobic hysteria in the British tabloids had an immediate impact on the reception of *The Information*, which came out that year. Hardly a single reviewer avoided mentioning the brouhaha in reacting to the book. As Tredell points out, the fact that "the novel itself takes literary success and failure as a key theme" further encouraged reviewers to fuse Amis's life with his fiction (Tredell 2000: 154) (see Life and Contexts and Works, **pp. 25, 57**). The novel was widely treated as a *roman à clef* in which Richard and Gwyn were mistakenly supposed to be modeled on Amis and Julian Barnes. The new publisher of the novel rushed the release of the novel two months ahead of schedule to cash in on the controversy surrounding Amis's huge advance. This only fueled a widespread assault on Amis's eighth novel by the British press. It was dismissed as "the overpriced sale of second-hand shoddy" (Kaveney 1995: 24), a work of "unpalatable arrogance" (Curtis 1995: 8), "self-laceratingly autobiographical" (Ratcliffe 1995: 17), and so on. Reviewing for the *Guardian*, David Sexton epitomizes the confusion of the hype surrounding the author with the novel that he wrote: "*The Information* is not about a mid-life crisis—it is a mid-life crisis" (Sexton 1995: 6).

Joe Moran has written an interesting and thoughtful essay about the relationship between the British press response to *The Information* and the change in book marketing and ownership during and after the Thatcher decade. He argues that in the novel Amis is not just targeting the rise of international publishing conglomerates and their use of the British book market as an extra source of revenue. He is also incorporating in it "a scathing view of the coziness and corruption of the old literary establishment and its forms of quality control and peer review" (Moran 2000: 310). Since many of the reviewers were still part of that peer review, it partly explains why they defended themselves by going on the attack when the novel appeared. In *The Information*, Amis is reflecting contemporary conflicts between the serious writer (represented by Richard) and the multinational publishers' promotion of the writer as a media personality (represented by Gwyn). But Moran charges that Amis, by dividing writers into these two antithetical types, cannot explore ways in which these two types can no longer be kept apart in a competitive publishing marketplace. "It is interesting to note," he writes, "that Amis complained about the unwelcome attention given to events surrounding the publication of *The Information* in the interviews arranged as publicity for the novel" (Moran 2000: 315). Reasoned criticism of this kind is worlds apart from the hysterical bombast with which British reviewers greeted a novel that is now considered (with *Money* and *London Fields*) part of Amis's "mighty triptych" of novels about modern urban life (Mars-Jones 1995: 19) (see Life and Contexts, **p. 25**). Part 1 cited several American reviews of *The Information*, many of which, free of a poisoned press campaign targeting Amis in person, were favorable (see Life and Contexts, **p. 26**).

Shortly after the publication of Amis's next short novel, *Night Train*, James Diedrick produced a survey of its early reception in Britain. He located five negative reviews, two mixed ones and six positive ones (see Life and Contexts, **p. 28**). The review that most approximated to the personal attacks that greeted *The Information* and reached an all-time low came from David Sexton in the *London Evening Standard*: "*Night Train* is an all-American novel, fit company for Amis's American agent, intimates and ivories" (Diedrick 1997). Most of the reviews this time avoided ad hominem attacks. But John Updike appeared to be settling scores over a mixed review Amis had given his *Rabbit* trilogy (cf. *MI* 155–9) (see Works, **p. 78**) when he criticized *Night Train* in the *Sunday Times* for "a number of American locutions new to this native speaker," and complained about "the unmentionable way the plot proceeds" (Porlock 1997: 8.2). Diedrick calls this latter criticism disingenuous, "since he must know that Amis is parodying, not parroting the hard-boiled American detective novel whose rhythms he has adopted" (1997). Many of the British reviewers complained about Amis's use of American jargon, although most still repeated the jaded opinion that, as Philip Hensher wrote, "The pleasure [. . .] is not in its metaphysical dilemmas but in the polish of the delivery" (Porlock 1997: 8.2). Natasha Walter voiced a feeling expressed by several others that, with its female narrator, *Night Train* "asks you not to keep your distance, but to come close and suffer with the narrator" (Walter 1997: 29). Both Diedrick and Tredell single out

Adam Phillips' review for the *London Review of Books* as the most "insightful review that grasps something of the complexity and power of the novel" (Tredell 2000: 178). Unlike Updike, Phillips appreciates that the book is simultaneously "a spoof of a detective novel" and "a metaphysical thriller" which "makes a mockery [. . .] of the expected satisfactions of narrative," especially that of closure when the matter under investigation is suicide (Phillips 1997: 6).

Apart from the publication of *Heavy Water and Other Stories* in 1998, there is a six-year gap before Amis returns to fiction. In that time, he published his memoir *Experience* and his collection of reviews and essays, *The War Against Cliché*, both of which won prizes, as well as *Koba the Dread*. While the former two nonfiction works attracted wide respect (see Life and Contexts and Works, pp. 29, 75), the latter was given a more hostile reception by reviewers (see Life and Contexts and Works, pp. 30, 77). This laid the ground for British reviewers' astonishing mass savaging of *Yellow Dog* when it appeared in 2003. Part 1 cited two sentences from Amis's fellow novelist, Tibor Fischer's premature review in the *Telegraph* (see Life and Contexts, p. 32). He also wrote that being seen reading this novel on the Underground felt "like your favourite uncle being caught in a school playground masturbating" (Fischer 2003: 18). This set the tone for most of the British reviewers. George Walden, while commenting that "it is a sign of the galloping contamination of tabloid ethics that Amis's book should have been widely and lovingly trashed before it appeared," went on to trash it as a rehash of Amis riffs (Walden 2003: 49). Suzi Feay, the literary editor of the *Independent* on Sunday, observed, "what's going on now—it's like watching someone clubbing a seal" (Walsh 2003: 2).

Jean-Michel Ganteau sums up the response:

> All quality dailies published quasi-unanimously negative reviews in which Amis's novel (or rather, in most cases, Amis himself) was disqualified on account of its (his) fascination with hateful violence, twenty-first century horror, the world of pornography, various forms of the contemporary emetic, and a taste for hackneyed, contrived jokes.
>
> (Ganteau 2006: 132)

Although most British reviews were negative, Sarah Lyall pointed out that there was little middle ground: *Yellow Dog* "is either an embarrassment or a masterpiece, depending on which critics you listen to" (Lyall 2003: 1). Despite the first review to appear in the *Sunday Times*, quoting the dismissive opinions of several anonymous Booker Prize judges, forecasting that the novel would not be nominated, it was chosen for the twenty-three-long book list (see Life and Contexts, pp. 32–3). One of that year's judges, John Carey, called the novel "a great comic extravagance," adding that Amis, "in addition to being 'very brilliant,' was also extremely resilient" (Lyall 2003: 1). Offering an overview in the *Independent* of the British press reaction, John Walsh suggested that it might have to do with the way in which Amis had dominated the British book world for almost three decades. Younger novelists, worried about his pervasive influence and fearful that their work would continue to be put in the shade by his, thought that with *Koba the Dread* "he'd been buried [. . .]" but he's back, and the anxiety of influence can be felt all over town" (Walsh 2003: 3). Walsh cites Suzi Feay again, who remarks that the "new generation are more proper novelists than Amis, in terms of plot and character, [. . .] but then, so what if he's an improper novelist? He's still full of crazy energy. I'd much rather read him falling over the place than read someone more correct and cautious" (Walsh 2003: 3).

Three years later, and Amis's *House of Meetings* was widely greeted on both sides of the Atlantic as what the *Economist* called "The Comeback Novel." Calling it "terrific," a "slight novel in size only," the *Telegraph's* reviewer concluded: "Painful, trenchant, and elegantly written, *House of Meetings* is every bit as affecting and rich with emotional content as *Yellow Dog* was inconsequential and empty" (Shriver 2006: 26). John Banville went so far as to call *House of Meetings* "his best book yet" (Banville 2006: 1), and in the *New York Times* Michiko Kakutani also thought that, after "his embarrassing 2003 novel, *Yellow Dog*," Amis had "produced what is arguably his most powerful book yet" (Kakutani 2007: 1) (see Life and Contexts, **p. 34**). It is rare to meet so much unanimity of opinion among reviewers in Britain and America. Naturally, there were a few exceptions, including Tibor Fischer's snide description of the book as reheated leftovers from *Koba the Dread* (Fischer 2006: 55). This time, no one else quoted Fischer. Instead, the book was praised for having "the density and texture of a far more hefty work" (Kennedy 2006: 5), "a version of the great Russian novel done in miniature" (Banville 2007: 15). As with *Night Train*, *House of Meetings* was praised for its emotional conviction, and Amis was commended for his "sheer courage as a writer" in tackling a subject just as fraught with difficulties as was *Time's Arrow* (Acocella 2007: 85). The most commonly voiced question was why he chose to imagine himself into a situation that had already been written about so vividly by Russian writers who had experienced the gulags at firsthand. Yet, James Marcus echoed several reviewers when he wrote in the *Los Angeles Times* that, instead of employing "foolish ventriloquism," "Amis really does carve out his own little piece of the northern Eurasian plain" (Marcus 2007: 3). Finally, nearly all the reviewers felt that Amis had left behind his stylistic excesses and produced "a disciplined narrative in which every word is weighted with deliberation" (Battersby 2006: 10). While the adverse reaction to *Yellow Dog* seems, in hindsight, excessive, the near adulation of *House of Meetings* appears to be partly the product of reviewers' perceived need to atone for their previous overreactions. Reviews share the partiality of their papers competing to outsell one another and rarely anticipate the more considered judgments of posterity.

## Major thematic concerns

### Doubling

Reviewers began to discern Amis's penchant for creating doubles in his fiction with the publication of *Success* in 1978. Tom Paulin, for instance, noted at the time that its "two central characters, Terry and Gregory, duplicate Quentin and Little Keith in *Dead Babies*" (1978: 74). Later, Diedrick assumed that it was Andy, not Keith, and Quentin who form doubles of one another (2004: 48). But it was Karl Miller, in his innovative book, *Doubles: Studies in Literary History* (1985), who first drew considered attention to Amis's repeated use of doubles in *Success*, *Other People*, and *Money*. He points out that *Success* is "the first of three fictions [. . .] in which orphan and double meet" (Miller 1985: 409). Not only is Terry "Siamesed to a dandy foster-brother," but also both "dote on, and unite to destroy, Gregory's sister" (Miller 1985: 409). While *Success* duplicates two forms of insanity (inherited and societal), *Other People* suggests that "every girl was really two girls" (*OP* 80): Mary and Amy; in this case, what Miller calls "psychic duplication" is produced by the device of Mary's amnesia (1985: 410). Miller classifies *Money* as "an obscene orphan delirium [. . .] The movie [Self and Fielding] are making is a family romance in which Self's own orphan-oedipal predicament is mirrored" (1985: 411). Not only is Self "a narcissist who is never done playing with himself," but the narrator and "Martin Amis" constitute two Selves (Miller 1985: 411–12). Miller concludes that an identifiable subgenre exists in literature "in which the individual who feels himself invaded, from without or from within, is perceived as an invader," and cites as another example Nabokov's *Despair* (1966) which Amis much admires (Miller 1985: 414–15).

In a 1996 interview, Amis claimed that his by-then widely noted penchant for creating doubles in his work must have originated in his sibling rivalry with his older brother, Philip. But he goes on to give a more theoretical explanation that, as a writer of comedy, his use of characters as doubles offered him a useful comic device. Where most other writers choose to combine antinomies within the same character, he says that he prefers to "write of huge disparities and vicious invidiousnesses" (see Life and Contexts, p. 50). "Comedy comes into the gap that you create between people when you force them apart, when you make the division extreme." As a comic writer, he says that he is always in search of "the comedy of the disparity" (Wachtel 1996: 56). Again and again, Amis deliberately magnifies and distorts the differences between two characters even as he is establishing similarities between them beneath the surface. The first instance of this occurs in *Dead Babies* where Quentin, the only seemingly sympathetic character, turns out to be the malignant Johnny who has been playing sadistic practical jokes on other characters throughout the novel. This is one of several occasions, as Richard Todd notes, when "Amis appears to make use of Robert Louis Stevenson's *The Strange Case of Dr. Jekyll and Mr. Hyde* (1886), which has become a *topos* for the gothic use of the double" (2006: 23). In this particular instance, Amis's use of the comedy of disparity is so dark that comedy seems a misnomer. But the society of youthful deviants in this novel, which dismisses all humanist sentiments as "dead babies," ensures that any well-intending Quentin will turn out to be a Johnny. The reader is Johnny's final victim by believing that Quentin could possibly be himself rather than his true double (see Life and Contexts, p. 39).

*Success*, with its alternating chapters told from respectively Terry's and Greg's point of view, is Amis's first novel in which doubling acts overtly as the primary motif and narrative mode. The diametrical pattern in which the two foster brothers follow the arms of an X in their ascending and descending paths draws attention to both their opposite and similar natures. At the crossing point of the X stands Ursula whose incestuous sexual relationship with Greg is exchanged for an equally destructive sexual liaison with Terry (see Life and Contexts, p. 40).

Just as Ursula dies as a result of her treatment by both stepbrothers, so Terry's sister had died at the age of seven at her father's hands. The novel opens with Greg, aristocratic and privileged, meeting success in the work, social, and sexual spheres, and with Terry, working-class, an adopted orphan, his diametric opposite, a failure in the same spheres. Yet, early in the novel, Terry undercuts this seeming disparity by informing us that "Mr Riding and my father were the same age, and Greg's and my birthdays were only twenty-four hours apart; Ursula, Greg's sister, and mine were both seven at the time, and were alike the survivors of abbreviated twins—and so on" (S 27). The fact that he sees these similarities as "some Fieldingesque parentage mystery" that "would one day resolve our destinies" (S 27) reveals the extent to which Amis in this book is using the burlesque form of comedy that Fielding employed in *Tom Jones* to exaggerate the differences between so-called hero and villain for comic purposes. The brothers cannot even agree on who won in their accounts of a game of cards (cf. S 109, 113).

Both Terry and Greg speak dismissively of Greg's father's insistence on "certain imagined affinities" between the two families (S 50). Yet, their affinities become all too apparent to the reader. In the first half of the book, Greg compares his "love of fabrication" to Terry who "could never lie" (S 97). Yet, in the later part of the book, Terry lies about his refusal to come to Ursula's support (S 207), while Greg resolves "to try to tell the truth from now on" (S 184). Not only does Greg seduce Ursula as a girl, and Terry seduce her when she is a woman, but the language each uses to describe their seduction is improbably identical (cf. S 186–7, 196) (see Life and Contexts, p. 42). Or maybe not that improbable, as Miller reports of descriptions in the *Sunday Times* of twins reared apart who called their children by the same names (1985: 402). Both brothers are followed by unfriendly eyes (S 32, 214). Greg uses similar language in describing Terry as a child on the lawn at Rivers Hall and himself in the same spot at the end (S 95, 224). Has Greg reverted to childhood while Terry has reached maturity? Does that suggest that Terry himself is destined to revert to childhood now that he occupies the unenviable position Greg occupied at the beginning? The parallels, which become more insistent as the narrative progresses, affect not only our understanding of the two characters but also seep into the style each uses and even the way each addresses the reader as the sole confidant of their apparently conflicting but slowly conjoining narratives. Diedrick goes one step further by suggesting that the novel also contains some significant intertextual doublings, and cites Terry who "implicitly doubles himself with Oliver Twist," only ultimately to come "to resemble the Artful Dodger more than Oliver" (2004: 48).

Richard Todd claims that "many, possibly all, of these double relationships in Amis's fiction are metafictional in nature [. . .] one or more characters attempts explicitly to control the fate of other characters, or allow themselves to be so controlled" (Todd 2006: 23). Obvious examples include Prince's narrative, as well as his narrated manipulation of Mary/Amy in *Other People*, "Martin Amis's" similarly sadistic treatment of John Self in *Money*, and Nicola Six's psychosexual manipulation of all three male characters in *London Fields*, where she is both the controller and controlled. However, *Time's Arrow* offers an even more interesting variation on the theme of doubling, as the narrator in this case is the unconscious victim of the protagonist, Unverdorben, being his soul. In the novel's afterword, Amis expresses his debt to his friend Robert Jay Lifton's *The Nazi Doctors* (1986) (see Life and Contexts, p. 22). In particular, Lifton explained in his book that "the key to understanding how Nazi doctors came to do the work of Auschwitz is the psychological principle I call 'doubling': the division of the self into two functioning wholes, so that the part-self acts as an entire self" (2000: 418) (see Works p. 54). Unverdorben's soul shares with the Nazi doctors of history what Lifton calls "the repudiation by the original self of anything done by the Auschwitz self" (2000: 422) (see Criticism, p. 130). As Greg Harris writes, "Amis presents a narrator who functions as a split-self that disavows Tod [Unverdorben] as his opposing 'Auschwitz self'" (Harris 1999: 494). Doubling, combined with narrative inversion, creates a startlingly ironic effect. Richard Menke astutely remarks, "With its implicit, structural antithesis (*unverdorben* means 'not *verdorben*,' 'not polluted or corrupt'), the name encapsulates the dual structure of the narrative, which opposes the life history of Odilo (hideous and banal, lived forward) in the narrative of his *doppelganger* (striking and scrupulous, lived backward)" (1998: 965). The ultimate irony of this doubling of Unverdorben and his alienated soul, Menke observes, is that "the technique of the narrative forces readers into many of the same misperceptions the narrator makes" (1998: 968).

When *The Information* was published in 1995, discerning reviewers like Adam Mars-Jones were quick to point out how the "trope of rancorous twins creates a polarized world based on the exaggerated differences between two essentially similar characters" (1995: 19). Compared to its use in *Money* and *London Fields*, the doubling in this third novel of his loose trilogy, Joe Moran observes, "seems particularly marked and permeates all aspects of the narrative" (Moran 2000: 307). As with Terry and Greg in *Success*, so Richard Tull and Gwyn Barry, the rival novelists and protagonists of *The Information*, are more alike than either would care to admit. Born a day apart, fellow students at Oxford, both writers are married and turning forty as the novel opens. But where Gwyn is what Virginia Woolf called disparagingly a middlebrow who is showered with success for his mediocre literary effusions, Richard, so highbrow that readers of his books get ill trying to read them, is a failure driven to prostitute himself to a modern-day Grub Street (see Works, p. 58). In a 2005 essay, Luc Verrier suggests that Amis employs doubling for both comic and darker purposes. Focusing on the occasion when Demi's father, on being introduced to Richard, mistakes him for Gwyn (*I* 204), Verrier calls Gwyn Richard's twin brother, citing the play on the homophony between Gwyn and twin.

> Richard is thus denied any individual notion of self, which is also the case for Gwyn since Richard recognizes their mutual lack of ontological completion ('Whatever happens we balance each other out . . . You're part of me and I'm part of you' [*I* 358]) [. . .] Paradoxically [. . .] their lack of individuality derives from their duplicated personality, an annihilation of their respective identity best encapsulated by the oxymoronic phrase 'Same difference' that crops up again and again in the novel.

> (Verrier 2005: 276)

Verrier cites Richard's hilarious mistaking of Darko for Ranko (Ranko explains: "He's Croat. I'm Serb" [*I* 128]) as further evidence of how Amis exploits the staging of multiple twins in the novel to extract maximum comic effect from this lack of individuality (Verrier 2005: 275).

Yet, the same use of doubling can have a less comic, decidedly sobering effect. Amis engineers "the total destruction of identity via the recurrence of onomastic doubles, as when Richard, in the post office, meets 'a queue of Hildas and Gildas, of Nobbies and Noddies' [*I* 32]" (Verrier 2005: 276). Verrier offers other examples of interchangeable twins, "mere 'nobodies' endowed with a mock identity" whom Richard encounters, clones from the London underworld, such as Del and Pel (*I* 175) who spend their days with Ben and Den (*I* 346). This threat of the annihilation of all sense of identity spills over from Richard not just to such anonymous thugs but also to his own twin sons, especially Marco, who occupies the same threatened position as does Richard, compared to Marius and Gwyn. "Thus impersonality is staged via overkill, which paves the way for the somber abjection of Marco [. . .] who wants to erase his identity by being renamed 'Nothing' [*I* 304]" (Verrier 2005: 276). Verrier goes on to argue that such "ontological collapse" is also achieved by the way in which characters are reduced to media images and the way in which both the urban setting and the universe are portrayed as impersonal forces that reduce to nothing the significance of individual identity (2005: 276–8). What Verrier does not do is to connect this universal loss of identity through doubling with the information that we are all due to die. Anstice, Richard's secretary and one-time lover, dies. Marco almost dies at Steve Cousins' hands, and Richard undergoes a book-length death-in-life after waking up to the fact of his mortality (see Works, p. 57). Doubling, by depriving either member of a separate identity, leaves both with the prospect of their own demise. But Amis still handles this somber theme comically.

Amis has continued to employ doubles for comic effect in some of the stories collected in *Heavy Water* (Alistair and Luke in "Career Move"; Big Mal and Fat Lol in "State of England"; Rock and Rod in "The Coincidence of the Arts"), and in minor elements of *Yellow Dog*. Considering that he defended his use of doubles as essentially a comic narrative device, it is fascinating to note that he has made doubling a major feature of the two serious novels he has written: *Night Train* and *House of Meetings*. The pairing and one-upmanship of the two brothers who both love the same woman in *House of Meetings* is as overt in its use of doubles as is *The Information*. *Night Train* offers a subtler instance of Amis's use of doubling for noncomic purposes. Patrick McGrath was the first to draw attention to the similarities between Mike Hoolihan, the female detective and narrator of *Night Train*, and Jennifer Rockwell, the daughter of the police chief whose suicide Mike is appointed to investigate. McGrath claims that in all previous instances of competing doubles, the more brutish characters win out and comments, "This recurrent triumph of the primitive and mediocre over the civilized serves to point up the idea that qualities like integrity, breeding, decency, sophistication and confidence are redundant in the face of emergent social barbarism" (McGrath 1998: 6).

However, he continues, Amis's use of the double in *Night Train* is deployed "in an almost Platonic manner." By this, he means that doubling makes us see "the brainy, lovely and seemingly untroubled Jennifer Rockwell as an ideal form of the tough and battered Mike Hoolihan." Made siblings by Colonel Rockwell's virtual adoption of Mike during her recovery from alcoholism, the "two women, stark opposites in everything from their wardrobes to their lovers to their jobs [. . .] are now drawn into a haunted intimacy as Mike penetrates the fabric of the dead woman's existence" (McGrath 1998: 6). The slow realization of how similar they really are simultaneously removes Mike from the comedy of disparities and draws her to the same fate as Jennifer when faced with a meaningless universe (see Works, p. 61). Gavin Keulks, mounting a different argument, adds an interesting observation. Mike "seeks a mimetic, rationalist universe containing answers, logic, and order, yet in the end, she symbolically—and ironically—inherits Jennifer's contingency and indeterminacy" (Keulks 2006: 164). It is fascinating to note that in *House of Meetings* Amis uses a similar strategy—having the narrator in the course of the novel draw closer to, and eventually identify with the narrator's double, whose defeat has been brought on by the realization that life is like that experienced in the Soviet camp in which the two brothers spent eight years: "the first law of camp life: to you, nothing—from you, everything" (*HM* 223). Both Mike and the narrator of *House of Meetings* make their "reckoning with the dead," and in doing so become virtually indistinguishable from their double (*HM* 144) (see Works, p. 66).

## Late modernity

Early in life, Amis developed a strong conviction that he had entered a world that had taken a decisive and irreversible turn for the worse. Born, as he reiterated, four days before the Russians successfully tested their first atom bomb, he grew up, he recollects, at a time when "my form-master regularly told me to get down on the floor and hope that my desk would protect me from the end of the world" (*E* 59) (see Life and Contexts, p. 1). The absurdity of this response to the threat of global catastrophe seeped into, indeed determined the tone and mode of his fiction from the beginning. The use of grotesque comedy for his first novel, the savage satire of the futureless younger generation of the 1970s in his second novel, and the dehumanizing effects of the British class system in his third novel offer evidence of a writer convinced that he is living in an age of depleted values and hope. Early on, he attributed the deteriorated state of the later twentieth century to three events: Stalinism, the Holocaust, and the invention of nuclear weapons. Their narratives, he writes, "are full of terrible news about what it is to be human" (*KD* 92). He has made each of these mid-century events the subject of one or more books. *Koba the Dread* and *House of Meetings* center on Stalinism; *Time's Arrow* represents a longing to undo the Holocaust; and *Einstein's Monsters* confronts directly, just as *London Fields* treats indirectly, the threat of nuclear devastation. Convinced that "history is reaching a climax of some kind" (Ross 1987: 25), Amis became and remains convinced that "[n]ovelists have a duty, not every time, but they should be thinking about the near future" (Bilmes 2006: 39). Amis's written responses to the disastrous age in which he finds himself have varied from the farcical to the savagely satirical to the near tragic. But he has never thrown in the towel in his fight against a trend he deplores but does not see as totally irreversible.

As a British writer, he has always had strong views about the changes that have occurred in British culture and society during his lifetime. While declaring, "I've always been a little bit left of centre myself, not far, and can't imagine ever changing" (Doshi 2002), Amis has never taken as prominent a left-wing stand as his friends Christopher Hitchens and James Fenton. But he has always had strong views on wider matters affecting British society. He opposed Margaret Thatcher's administration because of the effect it was having on social values. He criticized her monetary policy, what he called her formula that money equals democracy, as "facile." "The money age we're living through now," he said in 1990, " is [. . .] a 'live now, pay later' thing [. . .] you can feel the whole of society deteriorating around you because of that" (Stout 1990: 36) (see Life and Contexts, **pp. 13–14, 20**). (He is equally critical of George W. Bush's administration, floating in a "sea of illegitimacy" [Muir 2003: 9]). Amis embodies this view of the new Britain in *Money*. In it, England is seen to be "scalded by tumult and mutiny, by social crack-up in the torched slums," caused by the massive unemployment that Thatcher's policies produced during the 1980s (*M* 67). Amis's opposition to the inequalities of the British class system surfaced most overtly in *Success* (1978) where an outdated aristocracy is replaced by the new rule of the yobs (see Life and Contexts and Works, **pp. 13, 42**). Amis further used the contrast between the privileged upper-class Guy and the working-class Keith in *London Fields* to comically satirize the disparities in Thatcher's Britain (see Works, **p. 52**). In an interview the year the novel was published, he asked, "why should the Honorable Guy Clinch have all the money? Why? Who says? It's not a political feeling. It's a social unease [. . .] savage contrasts between what some people have and what they don't excites me as a writer" (Bragg 1989a). More recently, he has been a vocal critic of what he sees as Britain's inclination to appease the Muslim population in its midst even as that sector of the population produces terrorists aiming to destroy the society to which they belong. "In England," he said in 2003, "you have individualism running up against egalitarianism, totally contradictory ideas. And it's in that mess that the future of England lies" (Birnbaum 2003).

Amis has said that he first became aware of the threat of nuclear annihilation in 1984 (see Life and Contexts, **p. 18**). This awakened interest found its most insistent outlet in "Thinkability," his introductory essay to *Einstein's Monsters* (1987). There he portrays the nuclear age as a second fall for humankind but one that promised an immediate Day of Judgment: "Our time is different. All times are different, but our time is *different*. A new fall, an infinite fall, underlies the usual—indeed traditional—presentiments of decline" (*EM* 21). He saw the nuclear age as "a new moral universe. We can unmake the world. Extinction is a possibility" (Basel 1989: 22). Motivated by the birth of his first son in 1984, Amis became obsessed for the next few years by the threat of a nuclear holocaust, offering scathing summaries of what Mutual Assured Destruction amounted to: "The only thing that could precipitate general nuclear attack would be the fear of general nuclear attack" (*WAC* 45). His father excoriated his public pronouncements on the subject, accusing his son of taking democracy and freedom lightly (*EM* 14) (see Life and Contexts, **p. 19**). Several reviewers questioned some of his assertions, such as the claim that the nuclear stockpile is spreading cancers among the surrounding population, a claim that John Carey dismissed as scaremongering (1987). But, apart from his astute dissection of the perverted language employed by military-industrial writers (*EM* 5–6), Amis's main contribution to the nuclear debate is to offer a psychological reading of the effect that the prospect of imminent dissolution has had on Western consciousness. As he writes in "Thinkability," "the hyperinflation of death [. . .] has cheapened all life" (*EM* 8). This is because, as Jonathan Schell argued in *The Fate of the Earth* (1982), the anticipation of nuclear war is all we are going to experience. "As yet undetonated, the world's arsenals are already waging psychological warfare [. . .] it is already happening inside our heads" (*EM* 22).

Amis, then, insists that the possibility of a nuclear apocalypse "has inserted something in us morally [. . .] It gives a bit more power to the elbow of the man who is smashing in the head of a ninety-year-old woman" (Hoare 1991: 132). Ours is what Guy in *London Fields* calls "an age of mediated atrocity" (*LF* 214). Peter Stokes offers an interesting argument, which connects Amis's interest in the discourse of nuclear annihilation with his postmodern use of literary discourse. Because Amis's novels suggest a close proximity between literary and social discourse, they "exploit the self-reflective character of literature as a means of revising and redirecting nuclear apocalyptic discourse" (Stokes 1997: 300). Focusing on the way Amis in his fiction deprives the author of full authority, he associates the fragmented character of the author in *London Fields* (Samson Young/Mark Asprey/M.A.) with "the precarious character of literature at the close of the twentieth century—a literature made precarious, in large part, by the tonnage of nuclear weapons pointed toward the sky" (Stokes 1997: 302). He recalls that Amis told one interviewer, Szamuely, that the germinating idea for *London Fields* was the notion that a murder requires not just a murderer, but a "murderee": "Given the environmental and nuclear catastrophes threatening the world at the close of the 1980s, Amis began to wonder, 'Is the planet the murderee?'" (Szamuely 1990: 47). "*London Fields,* then," Stokes argues, "is a meditation on the possibility that the world—in an anthropomorphized sense—*wants* to die, with Nicola representing a kind of suicidal earth-figure, but a suicide in need of assistance" (1997: 307). Reading the rest of the novel in the same allegorical manner, Stokes points out that the way the novel in its finale avoids the global disasters threatened by the nuclear superpowers leaves Sam, as pseudo-author, free to appropriate the discourse of nuclear apocalypse into his own literary narrative by entering it as murderer. Stokes concludes, "Rather than a global apocalypse, then, *London Fields* delivers a simulated apocalypse in microcosm—represented in the deaths of Nicola, the author, and his book" (1997: 308).

As early as 1987, Amis linked the effects that the nuclear threat was having on human thought and behavior with the way we were destroying the environment. According to him, "we're hurtling towards an entropy watershed when all the fossil-fuels and the oil run out, and no-one's thinking about change." The cause of our ostrich-like response is the existence of nuclear weapons, which, "by possibly embodying an end to the human story, seem to have fucked up everyone's idea of where the future is supposed to be" (Profumo 1987: 42). As he wrote in a 1990 review of a book titled *The End of Nature*, "The frontier we face is no longer spatial. It is temporal" (*WAC* 33). Once the Berlin Wall had fallen in 1989 and Russia had opted out of the nuclear-arms race, Amis turned his attention to the equally serious ecological disaster facing civilization. *London Fields* (1989) incorporates in its mildly futuristic scenario both a nuclear and environmental mishap. By the following year, he is saying, "Now that nuclear weapons are beginning to look like a huge distraction, the real nightmare is the wasting disease of the earth" (MacSweeney 1990: 222). On the one hand, he claims, we altered the entire chemical balance of the Earth so drastically that "[i]t's as if the planet aged four billion years in the last two centuries" (Stout 1990: 48). On the other hand, astronomical discoveries have extended our knowledge of the immensity of the universe to such an extent that we humans cannot help feeling vastly diminished: "The history of astronomy is the history of increasing humiliation. We have gone from amply filling the universe to a remote outpost on an average galaxy." Amis thinks that "it's an intriguing possibility that, as we get smaller in the universe [. . .] our opinion of ourselves goes down" (Wachtel 1996: 50) (see Criticism, **p. 111**).

This gradual removal of humans from centrality in the universe has been reflected in the changing modes of depicting them in literature, according to Amis. In classical times, there were epics; since Copernicus and Galileo there was social realism; and "in the twentieth century you get the age of irony, low life" (Wachtel 1996: 50). In *The Information*, Richard reiterates this "history of increasing humiliation" (*I* 93) (see Works, **p. 59**). For Amis, an age in which low life is triumphant naturally encourages the novelist to portray characters who are representative of this widespread turpitude. A dying universe breeds humans (or at least characters) who show their connection to it by staging their own figurative or physical deaths: the entire cast of *Dead Babies*, Ursula Riding, Mary Lamb, John Self, Sam Young, Nicola Six, Odilo Unverdorben, Richard Tull, Mike Hoolihan, Joseph Andrews, Clint Smoker, and the two brothers in *House of Meetings* are among the more obvious instances in his novels. Amis only came to the realization that this was what he had been unconsciously doing in his fiction after he identified his anxieties about the threat of nuclear devastation and global disaster. Not until the mid-1980s did he realize that the world situation expressed itself in "the hysteria and wantonness of my characters. It's as if they're heading towards an ending too" (Bragg 1989a). His jaundiced vision of a planet turned into a toilet by its callous inhabitants equally spills over into the cityscapes through which his characters move. In *Money*, the London sky "is no more than the sum of the dirt that lives in our human eyes" (*M* 72). *London Fields* paints a doomsday city where "life has been revised downwards" (*LF* 282), London's fog has become "scalding heatmist," and the sun looks "like a nuclear detonation" (*LF* 103, 365) (see Works, **p. 52**). In *The Information*, Richard takes his children for walks in the local Dogshit Park where the London air, "equipped with new chemical elements" (*I* 43), is indistinguishable from the smoke produced by Richard's chain-smoking (*I* 49). The London of *Yellow Dog* is closer to contemporary reality, littered with hills of black garbage sacks and ten-mile traffic jams (*YD* 327) but still peopled by characters governed by the planet's death wish.

*Yellow Dog* was written after the terrorist attacks on September 11, 2001 had injected a devastating new dose of reality into everyone's perception of what it was like to live in this late modern age. Amis's immediate reaction to the attacks on September 11 was to declare, "The verities that you depended on a few weeks ago are gone—and gone, I think, for our lifetimes" (Curiel 2001: 2). That date immediately became a historical turning point for him, far more so than the start of the new millennium. It was "another great injection of arbitrariness and randomness and madness and annihilation," which "politicized, or re-politicized" him (Birnbaum 2003; Grossman 2007: 1) (see Life and Contexts, p. 31). Gradually, Amis developed his own interpretation of what Islamism (Islamic militancy) represented. He claimed that it arose from Islam's subordination to the West since the thirteenth century, which led to radicals' unrepressed rage (Getlin 2007: 16). It represented an extreme ideology, and Amis is opposed to all ideologies, even the mild ideology of America, as the narrator tells his stepdaughter in *House of Meetings* (*HM* 5), because they involve "the rejection of reason" (Bilmes 2006: 39). He sees Islamism as a recrudescence of the irrationality of Stalin and Hitler, both of whom "hated reason because it set limits." Because ideology appeals to mass emotions, impatience with it "is inescapable for a rationalist in the West" (Bilmes 2006: 39) (see Works, p. 67). Along with irrationality, Amis thinks, Islamism involves "hatred of women, religiosity [. . .] fanaticism [and] humorlessness." "Humour," he explains, "is the obverse of common sense" (Doshi 2002). Amis became so enraged at Britain's attempts to placate its Muslim population in the wake of 9/11 that in 2006 he delivered a diatribe to Ginny Dougary, published in *The Times*, in which he admitted to fantasies of banning Muslims from travel, deportation "further down the road," strip-searching Asian-looking people—"Discriminatory stuff, until it hurts the whole community and they start getting tough with their children" (Dougary 2006). Amis had just returned to Britain and had not lived through the aftermath of the London bombings of July 7, 2005. He denied being an Islamophobe, telling one correspondent, "the harassment and worse of Muslim women in the street—disgusts me. It is mortifying to be part of a society in which any minority feels under threat." On the other hand, he still declared himself "an anti-Islamist because [. . .] there is nothing irrational about fearing someone who professedly wants to kill you" (Amis 2007) (see Life and Contexts, p. 33).

In 2006, Amis jettisoned one novella, "The Unknown Known," in which Muslim terrorists unleash a horde of rapists on "Greeley," Colorado, and published another story concerned with Islamism, "The Last Days of Muhammad Atta," in the *New Yorker* (see Life and Contexts, p. 33). This story portrays Atta as an apostate who is a fundamentalist "[i]f you took away all the rubbish about faith" (Amis 2006c: 154). While he shares his fellow terrorists' hostility towards women, music, and laughter, he has nothing but contempt for their belief in a heaven where six dozen virgins will reward those dying in a jihad: "How could he believe in such an implausibly, and dauntingly, priapic paradise?" (Amis 2006c: 155). A hater of life, his core motivation is "all the killing [. . .] the war, the wars, the war cycles that would flow from this day" (Amis 2006c: 163). Amis, in effect, demonizes Atta and turns him into the mindless ideologue that he had previously argued characterized the typical Islamist. The story was most extensively reviewed by Daniel Soar, who accuses Amis of making Atta "not a person but a narrative black hole" (Soar 2007: 16). Soar is equally dismissive of Amis's longest and most considered essay on terrorism, "The Age of Horrorism," published in the *Observer* later the same year. In fact, it is a closely argued analysis of how Islamism arose with the disillusionment of Sayyid Qutb, an Egyptian who immigrated to the USA in 1949. While in jail after returning to Egypt, he wrote *Milestones*, which, Amis writes, "became the *Mein Kampf* of Islamism" (Amis 2006a: 6). It was Qutb who linked Islamism to a hatred of Western women's overt sexual allure. He was bin Laden's favorite philosopher. Amis is also critical of what he terms "Westernism" which has cultivated moral equivocation, producing episodes like that of the American use of torture in Abu Ghraib prison, which he sees as "the equivalent of a lost battle" in the fight for the moral high ground (Amis 2006a: 7). Amis's response to this new era has been to adopt a supra-nationalist and supra-religious position: "Rather than thinking about your nation or your continent you should be thinking in terms of species. Species consciousness is sort of the next goal where we don't have these conflicts and territorial disagreements and we see the planet as one" (Doshi 2002). It is hardly surprising that his next novel, *The Pregnant Widow*, has an Islamic theme (Grossman 2007: 1).

## Subjectivity and Amis's characters

The notion of the subject has become commonplace ever since the assumption that identity is a product of choice and individual agency was questioned by structuralists and post-structuralists. Where modernist writers cultivated the notion of a unique autonomous self, the post-World War II aesthetic denied its very existence. Louis Althusser is representative in asserting that "the individual *is interpellated* [hailed] *as a (free) subject in order that he shall* [. . .] *(freely) accept his subjection*" (1971: 182). While most post-structuralists argued that the subject is entirely or largely a construct (whether of language [Derrida], of the imaginary and symbolic orders [Lacan], of discursive power [Foucault], or of ideology [Althusser]), more recent theorists have attempted to strike some balance between a totally subjected subject and one with a degree of agency. Building on Freud's premise that subjects are split between a conscious and unconscious self, most post-structuralists have also maintained that the self, far from being unified, is split, or fragmented, or multiple, and that the earlier idea that we possessed a single identity was simply the effect produced by our performing the role of such a unified personality. Judith Butler, a post-structuralist feminist, typically asserts that "Identifications are multiple and contestatory" (1993: 99). Yet, she also believes that "being" may still be located in areas of the subject left untouched by the sum of interpellations that we embody (Butler 1997: 131). Obviously, these radically altered notions of the nature of subjectivity reflect the altered nature of life in the second half of the twentieth century, in which the encroachments on individual autonomy have become far more severe and evident with the globalization of production, media, and communications: All contribute to a sense that the power of the individual to choose his or her destiny has been hugely diminished (if not, as some maintain, taken away entirely).

Writers of Amis's generation grew up in this post-structuralist climate and naturally absorbed many of its assumptions. While Amis was still at university, he observed how "literary criticism began to be systematized" as he encountered the theories of the New Critics and Northrop Frye (*WAC* 79). His reaction to their successors was ambivalent, and he later called the critical theorist "half high priest, half cultural janitor," someone who "fails to find literature very interesting all by itself," feeling that it "needs some gustier infusion" of theory (*WAC* 77). Yet, he still manages to absorb and make use of some of these theorists' ideas about language and narrative. From the start, he is adamantly opposed to the idea that fiction should attempt to be mimetic or realist. "The reason why you can't put real people into novels [. . .] is because they don't fit," he declared (Haffenden 1985: 17). Real people, he explained, "don't have enough definition. They don't fit in fiction. They're the wrong shape" (Smith 1985: 79). This conviction, in turn, led to his unusual stance on the use of motivation for fictional characters.

> A. C. Bradley and that whole school of humanistic criticism tell us that people behave for reasons, whereas—if you read *The Sun* every day, and keep your wits about you on the street—you see that motivation has actually been exaggerated in, and by, the novel [. . .] Yes, motivation has become depleted, a shagged-out force in modern life.
>
> (Haffenden 1985: 5)

Amis not only explains this viewpoint to interviewers, he also has characters in his novels express it. In *Money*, "Martin Amis" uses virtually the same words to tell Self, who is demanding to know why Fielding chose to fool him, that "motivation is pretty well shagged out by now" (*M* 331) (see Works, **pp. 48–9**). In *Night Train*, Mike informs the reader that motive may have been a meaningful concept half a century ago but "now it's all up in the fucking air. With the TV" (*NT* 127) (see Works, **p. 67**). Modern murder needs no reason, being so often random and arbitrary. Only old television police series still make motive central, because they reflect an earlier era. So, the absence of motivation derives from Amis's conviction that "it isn't a set purpose to make this life look frightful. It is, to the writer, self-evidently frightful" (Haffenden 1985: 7). In a planet heading for an end to human life, his characters are doing the same. Lack of motivation is the outcome of a civilization bent on self-destruction.

Accordingly, Amis invents characters who serve as representations of contemporary subjectivity and yet who are, as he says, "constructs," being the product of his penchant for exaggerating and impersonating the two halves of the split personality. "So, there's something artificial about the kind of dance they do on each other" (Bragg 1989a). Amis's reiterated theory about the gradual degeneration of protagonists from the role of epic hero to present-day nonentities has already been described (see Works, **pp. 59, 83–4**), as has his association of this with humans' growing insignificance in a universe the estimated extent of which we keep increasing: "[T. S.] Eliot knew that the sun was not the center of the universe; that it was not at the center of the galaxy; and that the galaxy was not at the center of the universe" (*I* 329) (see Criticism, **p. 108**). This diminution in the significance of human life is given fictional expression by his use of "antiheroes, non-heroes, sub-heroes." This is because "even realism, rock-bottom realism, is felt to be a bit grand for the twentieth century" which has been termed "an ironic age" (*MI* 5) (see Works, p. 37). Caught between a debased contemporary world in which everything is "getting less and less innocent" (*I* 350) and their author's insistence on treating them as nonrealist verbal constructs, Amis's characters assume a distinctive set of characteristics that have been much commented on. As David Hawkes remarks, "The disturbing thing about Amis' characters is that they are extremely lifelike without being fully human" (Hawkes 1997: 27). Is that because they are meant to represent Amis's feeling that all of us in the modern era are getting less human, less in control of our own destinies? Or is he revealing a post-structuralist conviction that subjectivity is ultimately a construct of the wider forces of the will to power and ideology? As Keulks notes, Amis's characters "seem trapped in repetitive or fixed time. They are unable to effect meaningful change, and they often discover that identity and reality are illusory constructs, manipulated by authorial guile" (Keulks 2003: 233). A natural consequence of this approach to fictional characterization is that Amis, as Mars-Jones wrote when reviewing *The Information*, "doesn't develop his characters so much as wear them out" (Tredell 2000: 155).

Amis's conception of subjectivity informs all his characters and can be as easily discerned in his first novel's protagonist, Charles Highway, as in such later instances as Clint Smoker and Joseph Andrews in *Yellow Dog*. Neil Brooks views Charles as a typical verbal construct whose obsessive journalistic writing reveals "an identity that threatens to be subsumed by textuality" (Brooks 2006: 14). Charles, he believes, can "be seen as a quintessential representation of the postmodern subject whose perceptions are so mediated that, despite his seemingly likeable nature, he is not only unstable but also frighteningly dangerous, both textually and ideologically" (Brooks 2006: 9). Here, Brooks implicitly recognizes the way Charles is simultaneously a post-structuralist verbal construct and a postmodern representative of a civilization in crisis. Because Charles sees himself as the originator of signification, he is misled by his compulsive egotism. His "inflated notion of his self-importance [. . .] is logical because he perceives his solipsistic way of *writing* the world to be a superior form of understanding—far surpassing mere lived experience" (Brooks 2006: 10). A construct of Amis's writing, he turns everyone else in his fictional world into constructs of his writing. His "very embrace of intellectualism and egotism leads Charles to create elaborate fictions to control his sphere of existence and reduce people to mere papers, as the novel's title suggests" (Brooks 2006: 11). Amis appears to mock his own desire to give fictional form to a world he finds increasingly formless by satirizing Charles's parallel use of nonfiction writing. "Charles may be even more pathetic *because of* his delusion that he controls the external forces that restrict him" (Brooks 2006: 11). Charles attempts to acquire agency in his life by "making his papers the mark of his identity" (Brooks 2006: 10). Yet, as Brooks observes, he ends up as much of a victim of cultural productions as does John Self, but in Charles's case, the cultural productions are of his own arrogant making (see Works, p. 37).

Carlos Silva-Campañón argues that Self is equally a construct (see Works, p. 49), and his constant journeying between London and New York is a metaphor of "both his displaced self and his attempt to escape such displacement" (2004: 90). Self is "a shapeless, half-constructed, hybrid identity"; "his perception is limited," so that "he is absent or unable to access what surrounds him" (Silva-Campañón 2004: 91). His shuttling between London and New York represents an unconscious desire to escape from his inner contradictions (his loveless childhood), from external conditions restricting his freedom which he attempts to use money to evade, and from "the murderous nature of the narrative act itself" (Silva-Campañón 2004: 91–2). Moving between the two cities and their inhabitants, Self is shown to be "an essentially split consciousness. He is trapped between what he is and what he thinks he is or wants to be, this continual displacement being an irony on the impossibility of escaping from himself" (Silva-Campañón 2004: 92). Silva-Campañón draws on Jean Baudrillard and Jacques Lacan to argue that Self fails to distinguish between what Baudrillard calls "the narcissistic dream of the subject's projection into his ideal ego [. . .] the one in the mirror" (Lacan's mirror phase) and the real (Silva-Campañón 2004: 93). Self projects his imaginary self onto the cityscapes of London and New York, distorting them to suit the needs of his ego. This makes it impossible for him "to have an intuition of the mechanisms at work in the construction of the subject's identity [. . .] and so, the possibility of having access to the real structures of his self are barred to him from the start" (Silva-Campañón 2004: 93). In his 2006 essay, Richard Todd argues similarly that what he calls "mirror narcissism" and "reflectiveness" "have been a constant, brooding presence in Amis's work from the beginning, culminating in *Money*" (2006: 23).

A number of critics have argued that Amis's characters appear to write (or miswrite) themselves and their fellow characters into existence. Peter Stokes points to the fact that Self, at the beginning of *Money*, announces, "Recently my life has taken on form" (*M* 9). A postmodern "character in search of form," his escape at the end of the novel leaves him formless. "And so," Stokes concludes, "Self is left to rewrite his own future" (1997: 304) (see Criticism, **pp. 93, 128**). Similarly, Frederick Holmes argues that all of the characters in *London Fields* "are 'authors' of one sort or another who are vying with each other to shape events into the form of a story that will count as authoritative" (Holmes 1996: 53) (see Works, **p. 53**). Holmes cites Roland Barthes's contention that the writer's "only power is to mix writings" to argue that none of the characters in Amis's novel "is the real originator of the plots [they write], which issue from the intertextual web formed by the various codes operative in the culture at large" (1996: 53). In this way, Holmes illustrates the way Amis's fictional characters can be simultaneously purely verbal constructs and yet determined by the material conditions of late-twentieth-century Western society which are themselves reflected in the symbolic order of language. His characters are both unreal and yet representations of the real. Holmes shows the metafictional effect of making each character in *London Fields* assume the role of author:

> Although its narrator [Sam] disavows the power of invention and claims a factual status for the events which he says he records directly from life or copies from Nicola's diaries ([*LF*] 42), his many confidences about the process of writing the book only have the effect ultimately of highlighting its fabricated nature. So does the fact that all of the other major characters, as authors of one sort or another, focus our attention on the medium, on the process of writing.

> (Holmes 1996: 54–5)

The page in *London Fields* he alludes to contains Samson's observation: "All three characters have given me something they've written. Keith's brochure, Nicola's diaries, Guy's fiction" (*LF* 42). Holmes sees this "foregrounding of artifice" as an "intention to reflect [. . .] the culturally constructed nature of [. . .] psychological and social reality" (1996: 55).

Susan Brook reaches a similar conclusion about the way in which Amis's characters combine the artificiality of being textual constructs with behavior patterns evoking the reality of contemporary life. Focusing on Nicola in *London Fields*, she contends that she "is both author and text." On the one hand, she "is a radically deconstructive figure who embodies the slippery nature of textuality, breaking down oppositions between form and content, the mediated and the real, the natural and the unnatural, language and the body" (Brook 2006: 87–8). As author figure, she "embodies the disturbing, destabilizing effects of writing [. . .] She is linguistic style, with its slippery, parodic qualities, as well as plot, with its structure: she therefore breaks down the distinction between form and content" (Brook 2006: 91). In deconstructing the difference between the fictional (i.e., form) and the real (i.e., content) Nicola produces the hyperreal (that which makes no distinction between the real and the imaginary). On the other hand, she stands for a reality—for the death of love in the late twentieth century and for the love of death that produces. Brook writes, "although Nicola is a representation of representations [. . .] she is also the real as death. She embodies the destructive forces of natural phenomena" as "her crisis is mapped onto a global ecological crisis" (2006: 91–2). In other words, Nicola combines textual indeterminacy with determinate links to the real world beyond the text. She "is clearly a fiction but also bears witness to the reality of cultural traumas, including atomic destruction" (Brook 2006: 92). Because "she is an author as well as a text," "she realizes the way in which fictional forms mediate the world, rather than mistaking the representation for reality itself," as both Guy and Keith do (Brook 2006: 93). This is what gives Amis's characters their distinctive quality, one hard to define. They simultaneously undermine their status within the real and yet acknowledge the difference between the real and the hyperreal.

Like Silva-Campañón, Nicole LaRose uses the relationship established between characters and cityscape to identify how Amis constructs characters. Focusing on *The Information*, she notes how, in it, "the London space remains specific and knowable, whereas the characters wander aimlessly" (LaRose 2005: 173). What disorientates the characters is the false information given to them by the media, which LaRose compares to the false information or gossip about Amis given to the reading public by the press. She makes a direct connection between the media and the subjectivity it interpellates: "mass media has corrupted epistemological identity and blocked spatial comprehension. The digitalized information that pervades the mass media makes commodities out of individuality; with individuality digitalized all referents fail," and characters misread the world they inhabit (LaRose 2005: 160) (see Works, p. 78). Starting with minor characters, LaRose describes Darko and Belladonna as "two youthful, cartoonish characters, [who] epitomize the anti-intellectual audience targeted by sensational media" (2005: 163). Darko, who comes from the place he still calls Yugoslavia (*I* 126), is, LaRose argues dubiously, incapable of understanding that the difference between Serbs and Croats is religious, not ethnic. As for Belladonna, her "obsession with TV is so extreme that she confuses it with reality" (LaRose 2005: 164). Thinking Gwyn is in love with her because of the way he looks at her when appearing on television, she gives him oral sex during which, Gwyn tells Richard, she repeatedly took out his penis, "[h]olding it there, like a mike" (*I* 358). LaRose comments, "Gwyn is the celebrity medium that would allow Belladonna to transcend reality for the television reality she prefers" (2005: 164). She sees Steve, or Scozzy, as likewise the product of television's pervasive addiction to violence. When the narrator asks whether Steve is not Mars but Mercury, the messenger of the gods, LaRose argues that Amis is deliberately depriving Steve of agency, of representing him instead as "a manipulated medium that brings the violence of the urban environment to those outside" (2005: 166).

Turning to the major characters, LaRose claims that Oxford-educated Gwyn and Richard ought to be able to read aright the misinformation put out by the media. Instead, Gwyn writes *Amelior*, a novel about a utopia which, "much like TV, is an unrealistic substitution for the realities of life" (LaRose 2005: 166–7). *Amelior* "resonates with Thatcher's agenda for Britain" (LaRose 2005: 170). Due to its success, Gwyn becomes "famous for something other than writing: Gwyn becomes famous for publicity" (LaRose 2005: 167). In effect, he is constructed as a subject by the media, which is itself part of the Thatcherite hegemony. Thus, Gwyn "fails to become anything but the stereotype he lives" (LaRose 2005: 172). Richard may seem to represent the intellectual opposed to the "trex" (that is, poor substitute for the real thing) that *Amelior* represents. LaRose, however, argues that both writers cultivate writing as self-worship. Gwyn does this by obsessing over drafts of his authorized biography, while "Richard's writing becomes self-worship through its alienating difficulty" (2005: 167). Richard victimizes himself by envying Gwyn. His "discomfort with fame permits the mass media mentality to influence him immensely," causing him to become "as obsessed with celebrity as Belladonna and as internally violent as Scozzy" (LaRose 2005: 167). Determined to "fuck Gwyn up" (*I* 25), he proceeds to misread the information out there in his world, for instance hatching an unrealistic plot to seduce Demi (he is impotent) which ends with her giving him a black eye. LaRose suggests that even the televisual method of cutting that Amis uses in this novel serves to draw attention to the media-constructed nature of his characters: "The already fragmentary narrative excessively emphasizes the fragments, cutting from character to character as in a movie or TV broadcast constructed of sound bytes" (LaRose 2005: 173). Like Frederick Holmes and Susan Brook, LaRose sees Amis's characters as constructs who act as representations of contemporary social life, a key feature of which is its manipulation of individuals through the media.

Catherine Bernard cites Theodor Adorno and Max Horkheimer's view that the triumph of the culture industry "ultimately spells 'the abolition of the individual'" to argue more extremely, "*The Information* mourns the liquidation of identity" (Bernard 2006: 118–19). She cites an early passage from the novel where Richard reflects that "those gathered in the room were not quite authentic selves—that they had gone away and then come back not quite right, half remade or reborn [. . .] Not quite themselves. Himself very much included" (*I* 18). Like LaRose, Bernard sees the self in *The Information* as "endlessly processed by CCTV systems, video cameras, a whole array of lenses that frame the characters, ascribe them a place, subject them to control that, for all its digitalization, is all too real" (2006: 119). She cites the way in which Steve's face appears to Richard "smeared into squares" (*I* 116), and his apartment protected by a series of CCTV systems, just as Gwyn's house is guarded by cameras and filled with electronic communication devices. "Ever more transient, insubstantial, and alienated, identity is caught in a whirlwind of information" (Bernard 2006: 119).

Richard Menke elaborates on *The Information*'s figurative use of digitalized images to describe characters. He quotes the first description of Steve: "in certain lights his features seemed to consist of shifting planes and lenses, like a suspect's face 'pixelalated' for the TV screen: smeared, and done in squares, blurred, and done in boxes" (*I* 14). Menke comments, "A physical description of a character cites a technique from another medium, a moving image systematically reprocessed to give it lower definition, to decrease its informational content" (2006: 140). Amis is simultaneously describing his character and placing him as a part of a digitalized culture that degrades its mediated representations: "by invoking a modern medium, the passage at once concedes and transcends the character's lack of delineation, deliberate stylization, and origin in mass cultural stereotype" (Menke 2006: 140). Menke concludes that character in *The Information* is a product of the play of pattern and randomness that Katherine Hayles saw as one hallmark of information culture and points to the passage in the novel that reassures the reader that Steve is "not a type. Not an original, maybe; but not a type" (Menke 2006: 141). Menke appears to be saying what many of the other critics cited are suggesting, that Amis sees his characters as caught between the opposing forces of media and textual construction of subjectivity on the one hand and, on the other hand, the postmodern world, which is itself identified with the representations of the media, the Internet, and electronic forms of mass communication. They constitute mediated mediations of the material world.

## Amis and postmodernism

James Diedrick, John Dern, and Gavin Keulks all place much of Amis's fiction within the context of postmodern fiction. Diedrick offers a comprehensive definition of what he understands by the term. He traces it back to Theodor Adorno and Max Horkheimer's *Dialectic of Enlightenment* (1947), in which they argue that reason, which had been celebrated since the Enlightenment as a force for liberation from superstition, had proved itself to be enslaving. Jean-François Lyotard subsequently developed this argument in *The Postmodern Condition* (1984). He pointed to the Holocaust as an outcome of the cult of reason and advocated the abandonment of the grand narratives of the Enlightenment in favor of postmodern micro-narratives, each of which constructs its own rules as it invents itself. Diedrick further connects aesthetic to political postmodernity, instancing such historical factors as the arrival of the nuclear age, the West's shift from production to information-processing, and the hegemonic presence of electronic media. This more periodized conception of postmodernism is most closely associated with Fredric Jameson, an American Marxist critic, who argued in *Postmodernism, or, The Cultural Logic of Late Capitalism* (1991) that postmodernism arose during the third phase of capitalism—multinational capitalism—which became the principal world economic mode in the late 1950s. He characterizes postmodernism negatively as the cultural dominant determined by this capitalist base, charging that the modern world has become commoditized, depthless, lacking in emotion, ahistorical, and addicted to a world of images that lack originals. To these features, Dern adds postmodern literature's "combination of forms and its challenge to those forms" (2000: 2), and Keulks, among other aspects, emphasizes "self-reflexivity and authorial involution" (2003: 27)—involution involving the incorporation of the author within the text, depriving him of originary authority. A problem that persists through all the discussions of postmodernism is that the term is used, often indiscriminately, to refer to the postmodern world of the past half-century and to the artistic/literary techniques used to represent that world.

Amis has always maintained an ambiguous relation to postmodernism that he has found both an attractive artistic response to the contemporary world "with tremendous predictive power," and, ultimately, "something of a dead end" (Reynolds and Noakes 2003: 17) (see Works, p. 84). His most considered assessment of it came in a 1991 review of the American postmodern novelist, Don DeLillo's *Mao II*:

> Post-modernism in fiction was never a school or a movement [. . .] It was, instead, evolutionary: something that a lot of writers everywhere began finding themselves doing at roughly the same time. Even its exponents could see, in post-modernism, the potential for huge boredom. Why all the tricksiness and self-reflection? Why did writers stop telling stories and start going on about *how* they were telling them? Well, nowadays the world looks pretty post-modern [. . .] Post-modernism may not have led anywhere much; but it was no false trail.

> (*WAC* 313)

Amis adopted this ambivalent response to postmodernist literature from the mid-1980s on, telling Haffenden, "Yes, I have enough of the postmodernist in me—although I hope I'm on the humorous wing of postmodernism—to want to remind the reader that it is no use getting het-up about a character, since the character is only there to serve this fiction" (Haffenden 1985: 19). This explains, he has said, his relegation of plot in his novels to "something that will let comic invention flow" (Bigsby 1992: 179–80). In a review he wrote the same year he published *Money*, a novel widely hailed as postmodern, he advocated a midpoint between realism and postmodernism: "The contemporary writer [. . .] must combine [. . .] the strengths of the Victorian novel together with the alienations of post-modernism" (*WAC* 79). Robert Baker claims that Amis's "singular voice [. . .] masks an underlying conservatism that holds at political arm's length the more radical and more deeply thought through innovations of American postmodernist literature" (Baker 2005: 553). Yet, many of the characteristics associated with more extreme forms of postmodern fiction appealed to Amis as appropriate narrative ways of embodying the soullessness and absurdities of the postmodern Western world.

David Hawkes assumes that Amis first makes use of postmodern techniques in his second novel, *Dead Babies* (1975), his first novel in which plot is sacrificed to other concerns: "Whereas *The Rachel Papers* is generally realistic in mode, *Dead Babies* presents a world peopled by excessive, exaggerated parodies of human beings." He justifies this on the grounds that this novel prefigures "the demise of the soul [that] will figure alongside the death of love [. . .] as the characteristic developments of the postmodern era" (Hawkes 1997: 30). These are precisely the themes that also inform *The Rachel Papers*, although Diedrick claims that Charles is too close to his author for this novel to qualify as high postmodern art (2004: 38). Keulks thinks that Amis's form of comedy in *The Rachel Papers* is "a revisionist model more conducive to postmodern instability" (2003: 128). Keulks discerns a different form of postmodernism in *Dead Babies* and largely agrees with Hawkes when he asserts that its characters "reflect Martin's deterministic views of the amorality and disconnection of postmodern life" (2003: 141). Diedrick has argued that Amis was profoundly influenced by J. G. Ballard, especially his novel *Crash*, the 1974 French edition of which offered its author's interpretation of the postmodern condition: "Over our lives preside the twin leitmotifs of the 20th century: sex and paranoia [. . .] The century's most terrifying casualty [is] the death of affect" (quoted in Diedrick 2006: 188). Ballard is here referring to what Jameson called "the waning of affect," by which he means the contemporary decline in the ability to feel deeply leading to the depthlessness of postmodern art. The only novel of Amis that Ballard reviewed was *Other People*, which Ballard called a "metaphysical thriller" that "hurls another spadeful of earth onto the over-ripe coffin of the bourgeois novel" (can a coffin ripen?) (Diedrick 2006: 193). *Other People* is the first of Amis's novels that Diedrick specifically identifies as postmodern, commenting that because of her amnesia, "Mary [. . .] is a radical embodiment of the 'death of affect' Ballard associated with the postmodern condition" (2006: 192).

Almost every critic reaches for his or her postmodern lexicon when it comes to discussing *Money*. Diedrick sees Self's "temporal confusion, psychic fragmentation, and anxiety" as "common symptoms—of the postmodern condition" (2004: 78). Dern focuses on the way in which *Money*, like postmodernist literature in general, "freely uses aspects of other literary styles," just as Self has a plurality of voices that render him Self-less (2000: 90) (see Criticism, **p. 127–8**). Self is not just a director of television commercials, he is also a product of them who is unable to distinguish image from original. As such, he inhabits the postmodern age, which Amis defines as "an age of mass suggestibility, in which image and reality strangely interact" (*WAC* 16). Keulks, however, writes of Amis's use in *Money* of "a playful postmodern form, a hybrid of realism and fabulation" (2003: 189). He argues that Amis "blends elements from autobiography, realism and fabulation to produce an amorphous, hybrid amalgamation that cannot be easily classified" (2003: 191). The way Amis combines these seemingly contradictory modes, he continues, is by reworking realistic conventions from within to reveal the limitations of literary realism. Thus, for instance, *Money* "strives to record the meticulous facts of outward appearances, yet it simultaneously asserts the instability and illusion of that reality" (Keulks 2003: 192). Keulks's position that *Money*, by blending mimesis with fabulation and realism with metafiction, creates "a hybrid form of experimental postmodern realism" (2003: 197) is indebted, as he admits, to two earlier essays by Amy Elias and Catherine Bernard, both published in *British Postmodern Fiction* (1993).

Elias places *Money* with works like Graham Swift's *Waterland* (1983) and Julian Barnes's *Flaubert's Parrot* (1984) that "blur the boundaries between post-modern 'experiment' and 'Realism.'" She goes on to ask, "Can one define in these novels a British 'postmodern Realism' that is not a contradiction in terms?" (Elias 1993: 9). Relying on Brian McHale's distinction in *Postmodernist Fiction* (1987) between the reliance on epistemology (the study of knowledge) in modernist fiction and on ontology (the study of being) in postmodernist fiction, she reinterprets this differentiation to suggest: "Traditional Realism attempts to duplicate the world [. . .] On the other hand, postmodern Realism might be understood as *mimesis* with an ontological dominant. In postmodern Realism the world has become textualized." In other words, she argues, both traditional and postmodernist texts are realist, the latter because they are "true to the new definitions of self and society in a postmodern culture" (Elias 1993: 12). Using this definition, she sees Amis's novels as postmodern because they problematize reality itself, in particular the "blurring of boundaries between the experiential 'real' and media representation or recreation" (Elias 1993: 20). Focusing on the way in which Self's tinnitus in *Money* leaves him unable to distinguish between foreground and background sounds (*M* 7), she reads his condition as metaphorical: "it is the condition of contemporary British culture, which also cannot sort and rank the various versions of the real that bombard it through media representation" (Elias 1993: 21). One of the book's many ironies is the fact that Self is taken in by "a con—staged reality—which is itself about producing a film" (Elias 1993: 21). Nevertheless, Amis's novels "try to come to terms with a reality in which the referent [reality, the modern world] 'seems to have slipped more or less totally out of control'"—she is quoting from Scott Lash's *Sociology of Postmodernism* (1990) (Elias 1993: 22).

Catherine Bernard comes to a similar conclusion by a different route. Comparing Amis's *Money, London Fields*, and *Time's Arrow* to Swift's *Waterland* and *Out of this World*, Bernard argues that if these metafictional novels "question and foreground the way we make sense of the world, they also [. . .] reaffirm the necessity for fiction to shoulder reality." She claims that these novels are a reworking of the mimetic tradition of fiction "in which only the degradation of literary codes may measure up to the degradation of the world" (Bernard 1993: 122). Like Swift, Amis uses excess and the subversion of mimetic conventions to represent the modern world's self-alienation and sense of loss. "If hackneyed mimetic stratagems prove unable to account for an insane world, the same stratagems, carried to their limits, may recover a contradictory relevance to the referent" (Bernard 1993: 123). Amis undercuts truth, causality, motivation, and representation itself to show the provisional nature of certainty in a world where uncertainty is the more common experience. "*Waterland* and *London Fields*, as mock-detective stories, tend to highlight certain mimetic realistic principles in order to subvert them from within. Instead of ultimately reinstating order, Tom Crick's and Sam's tales emphasize the conventionality of such notions as cause and effect" (Bernard 1993: 132). As for excess, Bernard argues that *Money* and *London Fields* "rely on a rhetoric of excess, on the systematization of a mode of representation the distortion of which ultimately proves to bear a new and disconcerting relevance" (Bernard 1993: 137). She sees the characters in both these novels as representative modern figures of their time, "products of a diseased world hurtling to its end" (Bernard 1993: 138). This is why, like Nicola, who plans her own eclipse just after the eclipse of the sun, they all "identify with the planet" (*LF* 259). For Bernard, Marmaduke's inch-high eczema acts as "a sadly burlesque equivalent of the impending apocalypse" (1993: 141). Representation using this kind of excess "thus appears but make-believe, a masquerade intending to conceal the frightening eclipse of meaning" (Bernard 1993: 142). Amis's make-believe draws attention to the make-believe harbored by his protagonists in these novels: "In [. . .] *Money*, and *London Fields* illusion seems to have consumed reality, just as John Self or Keith Talent are consumed by make-believe, by the vapid rhetoric of television" (Bernard 1993: 143). As Amis told Will Self, "What people are up to now is Post-Modernist, in the sense that they are loose beings in search of a form. And the art that they bring to this now, to shape their lives, is TV" (Self 1993a: 151).

My own essay on *Time's Arrow* (Finney 2006) uses a specific postmodernist concept—the postmodern sublime—to show that *London Fields* and *Time's Arrow* belong to the mode of the postmodern. According to Lyotard, the sublime entails a "combination of pleasure and pain, the pleasure that reason should exceed all presentation, the pain that imagination or sensibility should not be equal to the concept" (Lyotard 1984: 81). This leads modern art to stage a permanent crisis of representation. If modern art is distinguished by its presentation of "the unpresentable in presentation itself" (Lyotard 1984: 81), then the postmodern mode is distinguished—and leant its jubilatory connotation—by its "invention of new rules" (Lyotard 1984: 80), of "allusions to the conceivable which cannot be presented" (Lyotard 1984: 81). Both of Amis's novels, I argue, are postmodern in that they "offer critiques of representation, of what Lyotard calls 'the "lack of reality" of reality'" (Finney 2006: 103). Concentrating on *Time's Arrow*, I argue that

> the first mode [the melancholic], like the chronological account of Odilo Unverdorben's life in *Time's Arrow*, induces feelings of regret (albeit extreme), whereas the second mode [celebratory], like the chronologically reversed account of his life, produces feelings of jubilation—ones that derive from the radical critique of conventional representation inherent in the postmodern sublime.
>
> (Finney 2006: 103)

In 1979, Amis wrote an essay, "The Sublime and the Ridiculous: Nabokov's Black Farces," in which he declared: "Sublimity replaces the ideas of motivation and plot with those of obsession and destiny [. . .] The sublime is a perverse mode, by definition. But there is art in its madness" (Amis 1980a: 76) (see Criticism, **p. 91**). So, I suggest, "Lyotard does offer a useful definition of the way modern art critiques representational realism, a critique that assumes its most radical form through the postmodern sublime, which simultaneously evokes pleasure and pain in the reader" (Finney 2006: 104). Accordingly, in *Time's Arrow*, Amis offers the reader "both a literal [and pleasurable] fantasy (a journey to innocence) and a figurative [and painful] dismissal of that fantasy (an impossible return to childhood or to pre-Holocaust history)" (Finney 2006: 113). As Dermot McCarthy puts it, "the normative convention of realistic fiction—the inability to see the future—becomes the [postmodern] inability to recall the past" (McCarthy 1999: 294).

Looking ahead to his next novel, *The Information*, Amis told an interviewer, "This will be a way of getting at the humorous end of self-conscious postmodern fiction" (Morrison 1990: 99). In 2006, Catherine Bernard returned to the subject of Amis's use of postmodernism—this time in *The Information*. To the extent, she begins, that *The Information* taps "the anxiety fuelled by the postlapsarian narratives of endings and disintegration," it can, like *Yellow Dog*, "'be called distinctively postmodernist,' 'disjointed and fragmentary, disunified and mediated, entropic and dynamic' [Keulks 2003: 193]" (Bernard 2006: 117). Bernard still sees Amis as attempting to combine in the novel the chaos of the postmodern world and the order that a realist work of fiction attempts to impose on this postmodern material. "Confronted with ontological collapse, Amis both wallows in chaos [in postmodern fashion] and struggles to uphold the hermeneutic agenda of fiction [as a realist medium] precisely by making sense of—and out of—pain and *agon*" (Bernard 2006: 117). The risks are obvious: How can literature "anatomize the current sense of loss, while resisting the lures" of "a counterproductive reintegration within the orbit of affirmative culture," and while "preserving its force of impact?" (Bernard 2006: 118). Bernard proceeds to trace the way in which the novel shows the main characters suffering from a loss of identity: "Ever more transient, insubstantial, and alienated, identity is caught in a whirlwind of information [. . .] in depthless self-love, in media-produced images of interchangeable selves" (Bernard 2006: 119–20). One of the supporting passages from the novel that she cites is the New York literary agent's explanation of how she represents writers: "Writers need definition. The public can only keep in mind one thing per writer. Like a signature. Drunk, young, mad, fat, sick: you know" (*I* 94). Bernard comments: "Trapped in the entropic circulation of empty signs, man has become but a figment" (2006: 120). She concludes by speculating that Amis would probably argue that "neither realism nor experimentation is up to the task of coming to terms with our dark present if they are not pitted against each other" (Bernard 2006: 134).

Gavin Keulks sees *Night Train* and *Yellow Dog* as responses to antirealist novelists' dilemma at the turn of the millennium: "what to do when the techniques which animated such [postmodern] writing—reflexivity, metafiction, irrealism, temporal inversion, and problematized subjectivity—became themselves conventionalized and clichéd?" (2006: 158). After summarizing the backlash against postmodern indeterminacy and alleged nihilism that set in late in the 1990s and consolidated in the new century, Keulks lists the numerous ways in which recent literary scholars have stipulated in its stead a "wistful return to realism [. . .] 'dirty realism,' 'postmodern realism,' 'neorealism,' 'deep realism,'" and so on (2006: 159). Keulks seems at first to be repeating his assertion in his 2003 book that Amis is steering a course between "postmodern perseverance and a realist accommodation." Where *Night Train* seemed to signal "a patent retreat to psychological realism," *Yellow Dog* "invalidated such hypotheses" (2006: 160). However he proceeds to postulate a new position that Amis has moved on to: the reconciliation of humanist realism with a post-postmodernism. "Believing omniscient narration to be discredited yet recognizing that metafictional games-manship has failed to preserve humanist value, Amis has begun [. . .] to map an emergent form of late-phase postmodernism," which Keulks calls "sanitized postmodernism" (2006: 160). By this last term, Keulks means, "a striving to *sanitize* postmodernism of its nihilist excess while restoring a degree of *sanity*, of emotional value and sincerity, to its fictional worlds" (2006: 161). Within this perspective, he sees *Night Train* and *Yellow Dog* as "Amis's attempts to reshape postmodernism to validate the competing claims of representation and self-representation, reality and the grotesque, rationalism and contingency. It is an artistry that endeavors to revive and rehumanize [. . .] the dehumanized subject while preserving epistemological indeterminacy" (Keulks 2006: 161).

Keulks discerns in *Night Train* many of the hallmarks of radical postmod-ernism. Its backdrop remains textualized, absurdist, and bleak; it exhibits an absent center and shifting margins; and it acts as a revaluation of two earlier postmodern novels concerned with murder/suicide, *London Fields* and *Other People*. Yet, it "reveals the challenges Amis continues to face as he struggles to recuperate humanism, subjectivity, and agency in a world that seemed convinc-ingly postmodern in 1997" (Keulks 2006: 162). In particular, it diverges from his previous fiction in "its un-ironic, non-aesthetic treatment of human suffering. (Keulks 2006: 162)" (see Works, p. 60). So, it simultaneously embraces humanist sentiments while employing "postmodern indeterminacy and metafictional insta-bility (Keulks 2006: 162)." What distinguishes *Night Train* from its predecessors is the use of Mike's voice as a reliable source for the reader. "*Night Train* vacil-lates between surface and depth, contesting the hyper-textualized, multi-medi-ated world of postmodernism with the emotional sincerity of Mike's moral, humanist, reconstituted subjectivity" (Keulks 2006: 163). At the same time, post-modern indeterminacy intrudes in the form of the numerous interpretations that Jennifer's death inspires: "deconstructive as well as destructive," her death "acti-vates a familiar postmodern crisis of legitimacy [. . .] and destroys the ordered moral worlds of other characters" (Keulks 2006: 163). Keulks sees Mike as a realist trying to come to terms with radical postmodernism epitomized by the apparent senselessness of Jennifer's suicide. Mike might fail to restore order to her world, but she remains sincere and caring to the end. "In short," Keulks concludes, "*Night Train* depicts a crisis of signification within postmodernism itself—not realism—a crisis torn between a suffering humanist subject and its structural and thematic fidelity to postmodernism" (2006: 165).

Where Keulks feels that as a realist Mike puzzles over and fails to negate Jennifer's postmodern act of motiveless suicide, "*Yellow Dog* dramatizes the humanizing (and sentimentalizing) of the postmodern" (Keulks 2006: 168). For Keulks, *Yellow Dog* represents a bad misstep. "It retreats to an ancillary post-modernism; commences with a relativist and ironic assault; progresses through amnesia and comic rage; and culminates in heavy-handed moralizing, as Amis proceeds to resensitize not only Xan Meo but the reader as well" (Keulks 2006: 169). As he sees it, "the novel originates in a politicized form of first-phase post-modernism [. . .] before over-correcting to an aggressive pietism grounded upon love, family, and children" (Keulks 2006: 170). "Xan's assault migrates from postmodern amnesia, relativism, and absurdity to realist linearity, positivism, and causality, and in the process he becomes rationalized and humanized" (Keulks 2006: 171). Keulks's argument depends on reading the novel as primarily focused on Xan Meo. But this only forms one of four strands in the narrative. If one considers the other plot strands (Diedrick calls them "baroque narratives" [2004: 226]), all remain firmly in the postmodern to the end: Clint discovering that "k8" is transgendered; Joseph Andrews meeting a death as violent as his life and his world was; Clint being blinded when he could never see straight with his eyesight intact; King Henry IX abdicating and offering as his reason a playful intertextual response to Dryden's play: "All for love and the world well lost" (*YD* 325); and Flight CigAir 101 making its crash landing on Interstate 95, a comic reminder of the tragic plane crashes on September 11, 2001. Even Xan's memory in the last chapter of the tied-up yellow dog in his childhood which stands for female victimization (also appropriately the title of Clint's sexist column in the *Morning Lark*) establishes a connection to the postmodern world of pornography and violence that is countered in the book by Amis's use of postmodern comedy (see Works, p. 65). Maybe the strand concerning Xan "swerves into mannered didacticism" (Keulks 2006: 175). But the other comically handled strands place this novel firmly in a comic postmodern context.

While Keulks offers a negative response to *Yellow Dog*, which he thinks betrays Amis's discomfort with sanitized postmodernism, and prefers *Night Train*, he ends up finding a number of similarities between *Night Train* and *Yellow Dog*. Both novels "exhibit his efforts to assimilate realist humanism and depth within metafictional and reflexive postmodern frameworks [. . .] Both attempt to sanitize extremist postmodernism, whether radical (*Night Train*) or vulgar (*Yellow Dog*)" (Keulks 2006: 175). Keulks ends up suggesting that, rather than representing a decline in Amis's powers, both novels "exhibit his efforts to assimilate realist humanism and depth within metafictional and reflexive postmodern frameworks" (Keulks 2006: 176). Less thoroughly postmodern than *Money* or *London Fields*, they nevertheless retain many of the features associated with postmodernism: indeterminacy, contingency, self-reflexivity, hyperreality, intertextuality, and polyphonic discourse. Yet, "both works resolve their epistemological crises through a resurrected moralism that struggles to cleanse and redeem. Their swerve into sanctimoniousness may reveal Amis's latest attempt to shock readers out of postmodern irony, detachment, and complacency" (Keulks 2006: 176). Keulks concludes by attributing their relative weakness to their attempt to reach a new accommodation with the conventions of postmodernism. "That these novels do not rank as masterpieces only confirms the difficulty of evolving a voice that can articulate realist, post-ironic constructs of identity, love, agency, and family while preserving subjectivist postmodernist critiques of media, textuality, contingency, and motivation" (Keulks 2006: 176).

## Author, reader, narrator, and narration

Raised in a household of writers, writing has always been a topic of major interest to Amis throughout his working lifetime. Literature, as David Thomson points out, "is a prominent feature of every novel" by Amis. He continues, "His first character, Charles Highway, is a self-conscious narrator, and every novel since, with the exception of *Time's Arrow*, has featured a narrator fully aware of the manipulative power of storytelling" (Thomson 1998: 16). Amis has admitted to a fascination with the varieties of narrative perspectives that can be used to throw fresh light on the subjects that he handles in his fiction:

> I rather like these impositions of difficulty. In *Other People* I used the localized third person [. . .] In *Money*, I had a semiliterate alcoholic. In *Time's Arrow*, I have a kind of super-innocent narrator living in a world where time runs backwards. You're always looking for a way to see the world as if you've never seen it before.
>
> (Riviere 1998: 121)

His narrators may stand outside the narrative (what Genette calls extradiegetic) or—more often—are themselves major characters within the narrative (intradiegetic) (Genette 1972: 227–34). In either case, they are usually highly intrusive narrators offering observations to the reader on the action or commenting metafictionally on the narrative act in which they are involved. To add to this use of a self-conscious intrusive voice, Amis sometimes introduces what is called "narrative involution," which involves the entry into the fictional world of the author—or, rather, of the fictionalized quasi-author who provides one more persona distancing the author from his creation. This use of narrators and authorial stand-ins creates multiple levels of narrative, with the author-character occupying the privileged position concerned with the narration of the narrative. Beneath the "author's" narration stands that of the narrator (what Genette calls the metadiegetic level), and beneath his or hers stands that of the characters, who often produce their own written narratives that provide a fourth level of narration. Amis plays endless sophisticated games with the way these different levels of narration connect with one another.

Amis's first novel, *The Rachel Papers*, already shows his preoccupation with the act of writing and narrating a life—so much so that the writing comes to preempt the life. "The novel enacts the process of its own creation, as the young narrator shapes the countless diaries, files, notebooks, letters, and sketches he has amassed to form the story we are reading" (Maczynska 2004: 193). Charles Highway, the first-person narrator, in effect attempts to escape from the vagaries of real life by substituting in their place the controllable certainties of writing

> In the spirit of modern semiotics, he edits not only his notes and letters, but also his looks, his accent, his clothes. 'What clothes would I wear? . . . What persona would I wear?' [*RP* 42] he asks himself [. . .] Such attempts at controlling reality parallel Charles's authorial practices, demonstrating his awareness of the artifice invariably involved in the process of constructing a narrative, but also in all verbal and non-verbal social interaction.
>
> (Maczynska 2004: 194–5)

Late on in the novel, Charles's rapacious use of literature to realize his adolescent goals in life meets with its one external rebuke from his Oxford tutor, Charles

Knowd: "Literature has a life of its own, you know. You can't just use it [. . .] ruthlessly, for your own ends" (*RP* 215) (see Life and Contexts and Works, **pp. 5, 37**). Here, Amis is asserting his view of the nonmimetic way in which fiction functions. But he is also introducing an authorial stand-in who reduces the whole of Charles's narration to a metadiegetic level of narration, that is, to one of subordination to that of the author's fictional representative. Amis told John Haffenden that Charles "is a nascent literary critic, with all the worst faults of the literary critic—that comfortable distance from life [. . .] Reading the book again after five years I saw with pleased surprise that the tutor was an author figure, because all my other books have author figures" (Haffenden 1985: 10) (see Works, **pp. 36–7**). Yet, this author figure has more authority and is less subject to the relativity of fictional characterization than any of Amis's succeeding author figures.

In his next two novels, both the extradiegetic narrator of *Dead Babies* and the two intradiegetic narrators(-cum-protagonists) of *Success* become more intrusive in their metafictional comments on the way in which they are narrating their stories. According to Magdalena Maczynska, whose 2004 essay on "Writing the Writer" is drawn on throughout this section, "Amis's partiality to metafictional commentary is apparent in *Dead Babies*' intrusive narrator, who offers numerous remarks concerning the development of the novel's plot and characterization" (Maczynska 2004: 195). She offers as an instance of such remarks the narrator's direct address to the reader near the beginning, concerning the reality status of his characters: "Are we presenting characters and scenes that are somehow fanciful, tendentious, supererogatory? Not at all" (*DB* 16). At the same time, Amis's narrator makes certain that we do not mistake his grotesque characters for other than what they are—caricatures of 1960s culture: "These are the six that answer to our purposes," he announces, reducing them to *actants,* that is, characters who are subordinated to the narrative functions that they fulfill (*DB* 19). In particular, the narrator contrasts the freedom of choice he has with Keith's lack of determination over his actions. The narrator can fulfill Keith's longing to have different forms of sex with Diana, Celia, or Roxeanne—"we can bring this about any time we like—but Keith can't, oh no" (*DB* 61). Later, the narrator apologetically addresses Keith directly: "we're afraid that you simply *had* to be that way [. . .] merely in order to serve the designs of this particular fiction," and warns him, "things get much, much worse for you later on" (*DB* 146–7).

In my essay of 1995, I address the narrative act itself in Amis's work, asking,

> Why does death, murder and victimization appear so frequently in Amis's fiction? The answer lies not just in the murderous nature of contemporary civilization. It also has to do with the nature of the narrative act. In his later novels beginning with *Other People* this prevalence of violence against one or more of the characters is accompanied by the introduction into the narrative of the narrator in person (rather than as a disguised author-figure, such as the tutor near the end of *The Rachel Papers*). This typically postmodern device draws attention to the highly ambiguous role played by any narrator in fiction. Whoever narrates a story both creates and annihilates characters.
>
> (Finney 1995: 3)

By inserting the writer's substitute self, the narrator, into the action, the author is inviting his readers to share with him his unease at the role he is asked to play as novelist. In effect he is problematizing the act of narration and implicating his wanton readers in the way they—we—encourage him to play god and kill his characters for his and our sport. Amis wants his readers, like a theatre audience, to recognize their simultaneous immersion in and exteriority to the action.

(Finney 1995: 4)

Already in *Success* he has both alternating narrators draw their reader into the narrative with remarks such as, "you might pass me one of these days; you wouldn't know it" (*S* 32), or, of Ursula, "You'd fancy her, I reckon" (*S* 54). As he told one interviewer, "I'm all for this intense relationship with the reader. I really want the reader in there [. . .] I really want him close" (Morrison 1990: 98). But, in *Other People*, Amis involves the reader in a more serious and sinister way.

As I point out, in *Other People*, the "narrator simultaneously expresses his sense of guilt and immediately proceeds to spread the responsibility for what he has done and is about to do to the novel's protagonist" (Finney 1995: 4). The responsibility becomes as much the reader's as the narrator's. "As readers we are invited to enjoy a story about a woman who gets murdered by participating ourselves in her literary murder. We are both spectators of the action and aiders and abetters of the murdering author/narrator" (Finney 1995: 5). Prince, the narrator, is simultaneously Mary/Amy's savior as her policeman-lover, her Prince Charming, and her destroyer as her repeat murderer, her Prince of Darkness (see Works and Criticism, **pp. 45, 86**). Amis explained that "as narrator and as murderous demon-lover he has equal power to knock her off; they are exactly analogous" (Haffenden 1985: 18). Like the narrator of this fiction, "Prince could go anywhere. Everywhere had to let Prince in" (*OP* 123). This ambiguous narrator and participant in the action constantly addresses, appeals to, and lectures the reader: (of the "fallen women" in the Church Army Hostel) "Who did this to them? How would *you* feel?" (*OP* 70); (of Alan and Mary) "Well, how would *you* rate their chances?" (*OP* 128); (of Alan) "He thinks that other stuff was as bad as stuff could get. He's wrong. You wait" (*OP* 129). Not only does Amis target, by italicizing "*you*," the reader, but he also involves the reader in the narrative by placing him or her in a position of superior knowledge to that of the characters (apart from Prince as narrator). Yet, even Prince loses his privileged vantage point at the end. In the Epilogue, he confesses, "I'm not in control any more, not this time" (*OP* 224). Amis

appears to be suggesting that by the end of the narrative the near omniscient narrator is as much in the power of the character he has been victimizing as she was in his power earlier. Her power to make feel bad has finally worked on the conscience of her murderous creator/narrator. He is a prisoner of his own fiction and is returned to the hellish cycle from which only a reformed Amy can set him free. Both the narrator and the reader (who has been encouraged throughout to identify with him) end up caught in the web of the fictional construct

they have been conspiring together to weave around the hapless Mary
[. . .] This is a refusal of narrative closure with a vengeance.

(Finney 1995: 8) (see Works, p. 45)

With his next novel, *Money*, Amis introduces, in addition to a narrator/protago-
nist, an author stand-in, "Martin Amis." As he has said more than once, "The
writer is in a god-like situation to what he creates" (Bragg 1989a). Amis explains
that in *Money* his authorial stand-in is "a foil to the main character," and continues, "in *Money*, the narrator [. . .] is being controlled and used by everyone, and he
doesn't know it because he has no sort of cultural references [. . .] And of course the
person who's duping and buggering him about the most is the author" (Smith
1985: 79) (see Works, p. 47). The presence of a fallible narrator who is the butt of
the narrative's humor forces the reader to identify with the author—or at least the
author-in-the-text, which is a technique Amis says that he acquired from Nabokov:
"Nabokov said, 'Never identify with a character, identify with the author'—see
what the author is thinking or trying to do" (Fuller 1995). As Magdalena
Maczynska suggests, "If Self suspects that he is controlled by an external agency
[*M* 305], he also nurtures a suspicion that the readers are involved in the joke, that
they are on the enemy's side: 'And you're in on it too, aren't you. You are, aren't
you,' he accuses" [*M* 264] (Maczynska 2004: 198). Yet, she continues,

> as Elie A. Edmondson observed, the author's descent into the narrative
> is 'an acknowledgement that he, as writer-creator, is also constituted by
> a larger narrative line, a player on the stage' [Edmondson 2001: 149],
> thus confirming the postmodern intuition that all subjectivity, even that
> of the author, is a discursive construct.

(Maczynska 2004: 199)

Maczynska argues that Amis "avails himself of a series of alter egos who aid him
in his authorial task": Fielding Goodney, his lover, Doris Arthur, and Martina
Twain; "all these auxiliary quasi-authorial characters present John Self with
narratives that serve as analogues to his own story." She cites Fielding's film,
*Prehistoric*, the title story of Doris's volume, and the opera, *Otello*, to which
Martina takes Self. "Only at the end of the book does John free himself from all
influences and achieve a tentative control over his life, ending up, as Martin Amis
put it in an interview, 'outside the novel, outside money and *Money*, in endless
and ordinary life' [Haffenden 1985: 24]", much like Amy at the end of *Other
People* (Maczynska 2004: 200).

Amis has frequently stressed how important he considers the author's voice. "I
think that novels are about the author's voice [. . .] It has to do with what is inim-
itable about the writer." What makes a writer unique is "a tone, it's a way of
looking at things. It's a rhythm" (Riviere 1998: 124–5). Richard Todd has
contended that the voice Self adopts in *Money* is one that, "stylistically speaking, is
explicitly virtuoso, yet whose owner is at pains to tell us that he has read little and
absorbed less." The problem Todd confronts is "the extent to which the novel's
various voices both are and are not claiming to be aspects of a single consciousness" (Todd 1990: 133) (see Criticism, p. 118). His solution to this seeming

dilemma is to assume that all the apparently disparate voices in the novel are recognizably that of their author: "in devising a voice for John Self, the extra-fictional Martin Amis has [. . .] quite explicitly chosen to use his own voice that is clearly recognizable from his own published fiction" (Todd 1990: 135). Todd goes on to cite instances of where "Martin Amis" airs his views on contemporary literature, views that are virtually identical to Amis's expressed in interviews, such as his view that, "The distance between author and narrator corresponds to the degree to which the author finds the narrator wicked, deluded, pitiful or ridiculous" (M 229). What Todd ignores is the tone Amis employs to distance the opinions of "Martin Amis" from those of himself, a tone that is both sententious and inappropriate in this context. Amis has more than one literary voice at his disposal (see Criticism, p. 152). Even when employing involution, he is careful to distinguish his quasi-author "Martin Amis" from himself. The way he arranges for Self to escape from his creator's and manipulator's hold at the end of the novel is intended to emphasize the distance between real and quasi-author. As Amis explained, "Self has escaped the novel. He has escaped control of the author figure, me. The last section is in italics because it is, in a way, outside the novel" (Alexander 1994: 586–7). But, while it is beyond the control of "Martin Amis," it is still the creation of Martin Amis (see Criticism, pp. 93, 113).

Elie Edmondson offers a different account of how, in *Money*, Amis establishes sufficient distance to detach the reader from the identifying with the narrator-protagonist (see Criticism, p. 89). He claims that Amis employs two narrative methods to achieve this end: "First, he introduces a protagonist who is so obsessed with an illusion that he cannot function in his world, cannot even recognize his real environment when it is encountered." Through this device Amis distances "the reader from the text by inserting layers of narrative between the narrator and the reader" (Edmondson 2001: 145). In other words, Self's repeated misinterpretations of what is happening involve the reader in a reinter-pretative activity that detaches the reader from Self. "That the narrative is somehow essentially larger than the characters who inhabit [*sic*] is Amis's second formal point, one he makes by distancing the reader from anything resembling authority within the text" (Edmondson 2001: 146). This brings us back to the entrance of the quasi-author in the text. Edmondson claims that Amis "shows that the concept of a fully refined and omnipotent consciousness is, by definition, deluded," because the "individual's reality is constituted by a larger narrative," what Foucault would call the discourse of knowledge/power (Edmondson 2001: 146). Amis's inclusion in the narrative of his authorial stand-in is, Edmondson writes, a "tacit admission of the author's lack of control over himself. His presence in the text is an acknowledgement that he, as writer-creator, is also constituted by a larger narrative line" (2001: 149). This brings Edmondson via a different route to a similar conclusion to that reached by Maczynska: "At the end of the novel the narrator is still alive, and the intent of the author [to have Self commit suicide] has been frustrated" (Edmondson 2001: 154). One has to conclude from these arguments that when Amis asks that the reader identify with the author, he means the author outside the text and not his substitute persona within it subject to the indeterminacy of textuality. Such an identification requires much work which takes the form of multiple acts of interpretation on the reader's part.

Catherine Bernard argues that both *Money* and *London Fields* feature "narrators whose unreliable voices and ambiguous identities should be seen as structural clues to the ontological precariousness of discourse" (Bernard 1993: 124). These narrators are "the prismatic and defracting lenses of the world's mad farce, of its loss of meaning, the subversion of the status of the narrator being an index of the questioning of representation at large" (Bernard 1993: 126). Both Frederick Holmes and Peter Stokes make use of Roland Barthes' essay, "The Death of the Author," to analyze Amis's unusual use of narrators in *London Fields*. In his essay, Barthes argues that furnishing a text with an author has the deleterious effect of limiting a text's polysemic potentiality, that is, of preventing it from proliferating multiple meanings and thereby giving maximum pleasure to the reader. Barthes writes, "a text is made of multiple writings, [. . .] but there is one place where this multiplicity is focused and that place is the reader [. . .] a text's unity lies not in its origin but in its destination" (Barthes 1977: 148). Holmes claims, "Amis's *London Fields* both comically illustrates Roland Barthes's thesis about the death of the author and parodies it by rendering it literal" (1996: 53). He sees the novel as self-consciously dramatizing "a contest for authorship; all of the characters are 'authors' of one sort or another who are vying with each other to shape events into the form of a story that will count as authoritative" (Holmes 1996: 53). Yet, their assumption of authorial control is illusory. None of the characters "is the real originator of the plots, which issue from the intertextual web formed by the various codes operative in the culture at large" (Holmes 1996: 53). In the plan of one of these aspiring authors, Nicola, "the death of the author becomes a paradoxical assertion of the power of the author." "But," Holmes asks, "is Nicola actually in control, and is her death really an exit from the labyrinth of the text?" (Holmes 1996: 54). Similarly, he asks whether Sam, the ostensible author of the text, like Nicola, "might be the fictional creation of the writer Mark Asprey." Yet, in the final analysis, "Asprey, too, is just another character, behind whom is Amis" (see Criticism, p. 53). In this way, Amis "performs the paradoxical feat of nihilistically denying the possibility of meaningful creation while simultaneously creating a memorably corrosive, if somewhat compromised, satire of contemporary society" (Holmes 1996: 54).

Focusing on both *Money* and *London Fields*, Peter Stokes makes two claims for Amis's fiction: "first, that it problematizes, relativizes, and disseminates the univocal authority over text and meaning that is commonly assigned to the author. Amis's work figures authorial voices as necessarily composite" (1997: 301) Second, "Amis's fiction positions literature as anything but an exhausted activity by mining a critical recursive agency in the loss of truth and the production of truth-effects: an agency that Amis characterizes as being marked by a rearticulation of the function of the author and authority in general" (Stokes 1997: 301). Agreeing with most other critics that Amis wants to free literature from the circumscription of the author, Stokes argues that he manages this, "not by killing the author, but by relativizing the power of the author's authority over the text and by questioning the kinds of truths that authority gives form to" (1997: 302). By staging Asprey's theft of the novel from Sam, Amis "attempts to problematize the credibility of narrative authority en route to suggesting that such authority is essentially formless, insubstantial" (Stokes 1997: 306). Yet, like Barthes, Stokes sees this killing off of the author in positive, not negative terms:

in *London Fields* that formlessness is once again valued positively. The text is free to travel, surviving even its author's suicide. Because the author function is transfigured here as a composite author, the text is offered other means of finding its way into circulation, into print. Amis's novel thus plays with the notion of text-theft in such a way as to suggest that disconnecting a text from its author is the best way to keep it moving, to get it read.

(Stokes 1997: 306)

His post-structural conclusion is that Amis's fiction endorses "the power of discourse, rather than the power of the author" (Stokes 1997: 310).

*Time's Arrow* employs a variant of the duped narrator, splitting Odilo Unverdorben into, on the one hand, the protagonist who had committed atrocities as an Auschwitz doctor and then escaped to America and, on the other hand, the innocent narrator who represents Odilo's soul. Adam Glaz offers an interesting insight into this split by first concentrating on the use of first and third person in the text. For the first long part of the novel, "the story is told in the third person. The narrator, the protagonist's *alter ego*, an inner voice or conscience, refers to himself as *me* and to the protagonist as *him*" (Glaz 2006: 111). However, he observes, once the narrator-protagonist arrives in Auschwitz "the two personas are united and third-person narration changes into first-person narration: 'I' is the narrator-Odilo Unverdorben" (Glaz 2006: 113). Of course, in normal chronological time, the Auschwitz period was the moment in his life when Odilo underwent a classic split in personality, the doubling which Lifton diagnosed (see Works and Criticism, **pp. 54, 103**). In what McCarthy wittily calls the "chronillogical" world of *Time's Arrow*, once we reach the Auschwitz period, "Amis *unites* the protagonist and the narrator—in *Time's Arrow* this is a state as abnormal as a personality split in the real world [. . .] What in the real world requires a personality split, in this novel requires a merger" (Glaz 2006: 113). Glaz then distinguishes the thermodynamic time's arrow (everything progresses from order to disorder) from the psychological time's arrow (which controls the way in which memory works). Whereas before Auschwitz the thermodynamic time's arrow was reversed (Odilo recovers his health) while the psychological time's arrow proceeded normally (enabling the narrator to discern that time was running in a reverse direction), once they arrive at the camp, "both the thermodynamic and the psychological time's arrows point in the same direction, opposite to the one found in the real world" (Glaz 2006: 113). However, when they approach the beginning of the war (in reverse), "the integrated Odilo becomes two selves and minds again. Everything returns to the initial abnormality: again there is a split not only between the narrator and the protagonist but also within the narrator himself," who once again knows that time is running in reverse (Glaz 2006: 114). Glaz ends, then, by suggesting that not only is there a split between protagonist and narrator, but within the narrator. But he offers no narrative reason why the pair return to their initial state.

Although the third-person narrator makes only one appearance as "MA" in *The Information* (*I* 43), the authorial narrator in this novel, as Maczynska observes, "is still intrusive, commenting extensively on such problems of contemporary fiction as the confusion of genres, the bankruptcy of motivation, or the decline of literary heroes—all of which are enacted by the novel itself" (2004: 204). Amis has commented on the way in which the first-person narrator disappears halfway through the book. This, according to him, is meant to reflect the fact that it "is a book about mid-life, and for me the mid-crisis came in the form of blanket ignorance" (Laurence and McGee 1995). As the narrator exclaims, "I have no words" (*I* 89) (see Works, **p. 59**). Nevertheless, the narrator continues to offer metanarrative comments right up to the last paragraph, employing a generalized "we" and addressing the reader as "you." As Catherine Bernard points out, "the novel is fraught with self-awareness." Yet, the narrator's pose as puppetmaster "may be a mere posture to mask his lack of control and self-identity. No longer that of the omniscient mastermind, the voice has become estranged, ghostly, disembodied" (Bernard 2006: 132). Joe Moran suggests one ingenious reason for this ambiguous positioning of the author's narrative voice. He singles out the contradiction between the cult of the author as personality in the marketplace (of which Amis is a prime example) and academia's assumption that the author is either dead, a function of the text, or a skillful recycler of earlier texts.

> If the author becomes merely an image to attach to interchangeable literary products to boost the profits of the major publishers, then he or she is deprived of agency and intention [. . .] Barry's inexorable rise and Tull's decline in *The Information* seem to touch on these anxieties about the survival of authorship as a meaningful activity in an age of the corporate ownership of ideas and images.
>
> (Moran 2000: 314)

Luc Verrier offers a more nuanced interpretation of the role of the narrator in *The Information*. On the one hand, he claims that "the narrator flaunts his dominance" over the puppetlike characters. He argues that the narrator's dominance is exemplified "by the generic presentation to which his characters are subjected. They are but puppets in what is a tragicomedy, as he recalls: 'Never fear. You are in safe hands. Decorum will be respected' [*I* 362]." Such intrusions, he continues, "when the narrator buttonholes the narratee, tend to blur the distinction between the fictional world of characters and the actual world of readers" (Verrier 2005: 279). Citing Patricia Waugh's contention that characters are paraded as fictions to suggest "that we are all, *metaphorically*, fictions," Verrier concludes that such violations of the levels separating narrator and narratee "imply that readers themselves are depersonalized, mere paper readers" (2005: 279–80). Nevertheless, he cautions, the narrator's persistent use of intertexts undermines his omnipotence: "the 'I' printed on the front cover of the novel is a personal pronoun which, although it theoretically refers to one individual, incorporated in reality so many other voices that it becomes, if not a universal, at least a collective pronoun" (Verrier 2005: 280). This brings him back to an understanding of the narrator's voice, which is similar to Bernard's description of his "ghostly, disembodied" voice, when Verrier concludes, "the text has reached what Foucault calls 'the anonymity of a murmur'" ("What Is an Author?") (Verrier 2005: 281).

The role of the narrator in Amis's recent fiction has not yet received much critical attention. But in both *Night Train* and *House of Meetings* he employs a first-person narrator to very different ends. Both narrators are flawed yet relatively honest about themselves. Despite their flaws (major in the case of the narrator of *House of Meetings*), both invite our sympathy. Both have a metaphysical dimension in their discussion of major issues of life and death. Both novels also make unusual use of narrative closure or, rather, its absence. As Diedrick observes, *Night Train* enacts the mystery of death, especially suicide, "at the most basic level of plot and structure, purposefully frustrating the reader's desire for a satisfactory ending," which "drives the reader back to its beginning in search of clues" that may account for its refusal of conventional closure (2004: 161–2). In the closing letter that the narrator of *House of Meetings* writes to his stepdaughter, Venus, he excoriates her suggestion that he seek "closure" for his ill-spent life. "Closure *is a greasy little word which, moreover, describes a nonexistent condition. The truth, Venus, is that* nobody ever gets over anything" (*HM* 236). Amis is still devising narrative strategies, forms of narration that better accommodate the themes and preoccupations of each narrative. And he is still using his narrator to manipulate his reader, in this case by exposing the status of closure as a psychological and narrative fantasy.

## Genre

From the beginning of his career, Amis has seen himself as a comic novelist. His initial inspiration was his father. To John Haffenden, he cited the ending of *Lucky Jim* where Dixon is about to denounce the Welch family but instead erupts in laughter at the fact that they're wearing each other's hats. Amis explains, "his laughter—not his denunciation—is the deliverance of comedy. You don't punish, you laugh" (Haffenden 1985: 11). Seven years later, he was still claiming that he and his father used a similar tone, "humorous, slightly mock epic, describing low things in a high voice, and a bit the other way round" (Bigsby 1992: 170). Yet, the way he developed comedy owed more to Nabokov, whom his father detested. Like Nabokov, Amis believes that the comic genre has undergone a disconcerting change in the later part of the twentieth century. Because the tragic, heroic, and epic genres do not resonate in a postmodern world, the modern novelist is forced to resort to comedy, which approximates most nearly to the contemporary condition. Consequently, "comedy is full of things that shouldn't really be there, like rape and murder and child abuse, real sin and evil" (Bigsby 1992: 172). As a result, the "comic novel now seems to have gone into spaces formerly occupied by other sorts of writing, such as the melodrama; and nasty types are just laughed at" (McGrath 1987: 191). Amis derived the idea of laughing villainy off stage rather than punishing it from Nabokov's lectures in which, as Amis reports, he said, "You use ridicule, not an obsolescent machinery of punishment and conversion because that just doesn't convince anymore" (Wachtel 1996: 53). The comedy that Amis, like Nabokov, employs, is darkened by the new, potentially tragic subject matter it is forced to handle: "What I'm interested in is heavy comedy, rather than light comedy. It's a wincing laughter, or a sort of funky laughter, rather than tee-hee-hee. Sort of a hung-over laughter, where it hurts"

(Morrison 1990: 96) (see Life and Contexts and Criticism, **pp. 22, 88**). He sees writing as "black fun, not the expression of deep miseries or dissatisfaction" (Ross 1987: 24).

From his first novel, Amis has constantly experimented with different genres, not just appropriating them but also bending them to his unique comic vision. *The Rachel Papers*, which Amis called a variant of the adolescent novel (Haffenden 1985: 9), is, as Diedrick and Keulks have argued, not simply a parody of the coming-of-age novel but "a parody of a specific instance of that genre, *Lucky Jim*" (Diedrick 2004: 38), which initiated "a literary battle over genre and mode" (Keulks 2003: 119) (see Life and Contexts and Works, **pp. 9, 35–6**). Amis called his next novel, *Dead Babies*, a "weekend-house-party novel, dressed down for the voracious Seventies" (Michener 1986: 138). Diedrick notes that the country-house-weekend novel was made famous by P. G. Wodehouse (2004: 40) (see Life and Contexts, **p. 40**). But Amis, convinced that 1970s England had lost its moral bearings, uses the genre to parody the earlier idealization of the English countryside that it embodied. Quentin explains that when he got married he determined to live somewhere "where there was still some England" (*DB* 50). But this pastoral Eden turns into a hell for everyone presided over by the nihilistic, murderous "Johnny" of the finale. Amis called *Other People* "an 'unconventional' thriller" (Michener 1986: 138). Prince explains why it is unconventional: "Usually we find a body and have to look for a murderer. With Amy Hide we find a murderer and have to look for a body" (*OP* 121).

One can see both *Success* (which the blurb described enigmatically as "a modern-day Jacobean revenge comedy") and *Money* (also stories like "Heavy Water," "State of England," (see Works, **p. 71**) and "The Coincidence of the Arts") as variants on the condition-of-England novel (now dominated by yob culture), just as *London Fields*, a prequel to *Other People*, returns to the genre of the unconventional thriller. Equally, *Money* and *Time's Arrow* have each been termed an inverted *Bildungsroman*—*Money* because in it "the self gains no insight through growth and experience" (Keulks 2003: 195), and *Time's Arrow* because it details "the *de*volution of the protagonist" (McCarthy 1999: 294). McCarthy also sees *Time's Arrow* as belonging to the detective or mystery novel, a genre to which Amis returns in his first departure from the comic mode, *Night Train*. *Night Train* parodies the police procedural not just by making its protagonist a woman detective who is so masculine as to seem in some ways ungendered but also by turning the conventional who-did-it into an unconventional why-do-it (see Life and Contexts, **p. 27**). *Experience* is a unique variant of the contemporary memoir, omitting large sections of his life and subordinating chronological to thematic organization (see Life and Contexts and Works, **pp. 28–9, 71–2**). *Yellow Dog* is modeled on Dickens's melodramas. *House of Meetings*, his latest novel to date, also departs from the comic mode. Using tragedy, which felt like new territory to him, Amis draws on the subgenre describing the experience of concentration-camp life especially associated with the USSR. The tragedy is not confined to the novel's three protagonists. "The deeper grief," Amis has said, "is the loss of Russia's soul" (Goring 2006: 6).

Amis, then, makes revisionist use of genre to give him a new and different purchase on the substance of his fiction. An interesting instance of this practice is Amis's forays into science fiction, a genre that he was reviewing (under a pseudonym) from his earliest days with the *Observer* (see Life and Contexts and Works, **pp. 7, 67**). As Diedrick observes, all of Amis's fiction tends to undercut distinctions between "high" and popular literature, which is what much science fiction does (2006: 180). While Diedrick, in his first edition of *Understanding Martin Amis* (1994), and subsequent critics saw Amis as consciously employing the conventions of science fiction from *Einstein's Monsters* (1987) onwards, Diedrick revised this opinion in his 2006 essay for Keulks' anthology. There, he argued that Amis's reading of Ballard's science-fiction works of the 1960s and 1970s helped shape his earlier two novels, *Dead Babies* and *Other People*. Quoting Amis's later admission that he lifted a whole paragraph of Ballard's *The Drowned World* (1962) to use in *Dead Babies* (cf. *DB* 163), Diedrick claims that the characters in *Dead Babies* are stranded in a futuristic cultural landscape "where narcissism is doing the work of the future floods that nearly drown Ballard's protagonists." These characters show the same "death of affect" which Ballard discerned as "the century's most terrifying casualty" (Diedrick 2006: 188). He concludes: "It is as if Amis set out in *Dead Babies* to marry the comedy of manners [. . .] to the 'apocalyptic-epiphanic' mode of science fiction" pioneered by Ballard (Diedrick 2006: 186–7). What drew Amis to Ballard's work was Ballard's conviction that "it is inner space, not outer, that needs to be explored" in future uses of the genre (Diedrick 2006: 184). Diedrick next turns to Ballard's *Crash* (1973), a novel that Amis reviewed and returned to obsessively in his subsequent reviews of Ballard's work. In reviewing the film adaptation, Amis wrote that *Crash* "emerged from a background of surrealism, cultural activism, hyper-permissiveness and lysergic acid" (*WAC* 110)—"the same milieu Amis savages in *Dead Babies*," Diedrick comments (2006: 189). Diedrick proceeds to call *Other People* "his most Ballardian novel" (2006: 191). Mary, its protagonist, is "a radical embodiment of the 'death of affect' Ballard associates with the postmodern condition" (Diedrick 2006: 192). In reviewing *Other People*, Ballard praised it for its exploration of "inner space," its portrayal of everyday reality as "that ambiguous conspiracy between the universe and our psyches," and gave it the generic label of a "metaphysical thriller" (Diedrick 2006: 193).

In his earlier book, Diedrick saw the three postapocalyptic stories in *Einstein's Monsters* as examples of Amis's undisguised use of science fiction, a genre he had already made use of in his film script, *Saturn 3* (1980), and in *Invasion of the Space Invaders* (1982) (see Works, **p. 67**). David Moyle suggests that after Amis "snapped into cold war reality, his fiction [. . .] began to break the laws of commonly understood reality" (1995: 306). In the first story, "Bujak and the Strong Force," the narrator says, "we live in a shameful shadowland" in which "our idea of the human has changed, thinned out" (*EM* 48). Moyle writes that this "'shameful shadowland,' while technologically advancing, is spiritually / emotionally regressing" (Moyle 1995: 307). It is around this paradox that Amis constructs his futuristic stories. The first postapocalyptic story, "The Time Disease," offers a variant on science fiction's play with the idea of time travel. Diedrick thinks that the next story, "The Little Puppy That Could" employs the genre of the mythic fable, in this case the myth of Andromeda. The last story, "The Immortals," is set in 2045 and has a protagonist who is deluded by the effects of solar radiation into thinking of himself as immortal. These futuristic visions of a world transformed by nuclear warfare equally inform *London Fields*. Moyle compares Nicola to Dr. Frankenstein in her hubristic attempt to control the course of human life. "Nicola, endowed by Amis with the science-fictionesque ability of prescience, of foresight, stands as a symbol of our nuclear death wish" (1995: 311). In the case of *Time's Arrow*, Moyle suggests that Amis reverts to the idea he makes use of in "Bujak and the Strong Force" which derives from Stephen Hawking's speculation as to whether, if the universe began to contract, time's thermodynamic arrow would reverse and disorder begin to decrease. The backward-flowing universe which in Auschwitz turns chaos into order satirically comments on the reverse actuality of our post-Holocaust world. Moyle concludes that when Amis turned to science fiction, he did so "because it suddenly seemed necessary to break earth-bound rules in order to express adequately his perception of the world, a world in which horror has moved beyond the black hole" (1995: 314–15).

In *The English Novel in History, 1950–1995* Steven Connor describes the rise in the nineteenth century of what came to be called the condition-of-England novel, which involved both "an enactment of the problem of imagining the whole of a nation and a utopian prefiguring of such a vision of healing unity" (1996: 44). In an aside, he remarks that *Money* addresses the condition of England "via flagrant violation of every requirement of the condition of England novel" (Connor 1996: 92). Jon Begley takes Connor's aside as his starting point for an examination of just how *Money* flouts this genre's conventions. Begley sees *Money* as questioning the ability of this narrative genre to embrace the complexities of a global economy that helps determine nationstates while undermining their powers of self-determination: "Amis's departure from generic convention implies an acute recognition of the contemporary inadequacy of narratives premised upon national circumscription and social organicism" (Begley 2004: 80). While still concerning itself with the genre's traditional conflict between humanist values and materialism, Amis broadens his canvas with his chapters alternating between London and New York to register "the condition of a declining, postimperial Britain within an international framework of deregulated finance capitalism, economic globalization, and cultural democratization" (Begley 2004: 80). To add force to his diagnosis of the new globalized condition of England, Amis deliberately marginalizes the importance of national governments, "the scarcity of references to Reagan and Thatcher affirming the subordination of political power to the exigencies of global economic conditions" (Begley 2004: 81). Simultaneously, Amis registers the condition-of-England novel "against the backdrop of a transatlantic shift in cultural and economic influence" (Begley 2004: 82). Far from offering a narrative that provides an imagined organic community, Amis's "transatlantic variation on the condition-of-England novel" represents "a nation increasingly excluded from the determining forces of the zeitgeist [. . .] incapable of self-determination, [. . .] and seemingly destined to adopt the commodified culture emanating from America's frontier of global consumerism" (Begley 2004: 83).

Amis is clearly fascinated by the conventions of the detective/murder/mystery novel. He first (mis)uses the genre in *Other People*, returns to it in *London Fields*, employs it again in *Time's Arrow*, and comes closest to a straight parody of it in *Night Train*. Viewed in the light of this genre, *London Fields* "opens as a perverted murder mystery," as Wendy Nakanishi puts it, "and ends rather as a 'why-dunnit' than a 'who-dunnit'" (Nakanishi 2006). *London Fields* portrays Sam as a deluded detective attempting to write a traditional murder story in which he, as detective, remains in control of events and restores order at the end. As I observe, however, "What Sam fails to see is that he too is writing within a narrative genre, the thriller, which he is simultaneously subverting by turning it into a 'whydoit.'" (Finney 1995: 12). Finally, Sam discovers that he has been set up to become the murderer by an author who remains absent from the narrative.

Dermot McCarthy argues that *Time's Arrow* also follows "the conventions of the detective or mystery novel." Like that genre, the novel reverts to the past as it advances in its attempt to reconstruct the original scene of the crime. "To use a video metaphor, the narrative structure of the novel is the 'reverse scan' implicit in the detective's quest: *Time's Arrow* is a 'replay' of an action that has already happened." McCarthy sees the "I/him" split within the narrator's consciousness as the perfect expression of "the gap between amnesia [loss of memory] and anamnesis [a recollection of past events] which the narrative closes when the narrator as amnesiac detective discovers that he is the criminal he has been seeking." McCarthy links the narrator's schizophrenic state with that of the contemporary generation which has equally forgotten the horrors of Auschwitz: "His narrator's condition may be Amis's comment on contemporary historical sensibility, the woeful historical ignorance amongst contemporary youth, or the ignorance/indifference of their educators, but the narrator-detective's belatedness is also the necessary precondition for his ironic knowledge" (McCarthy 1999: 306). As was the case with Samson Young, this narrator ultimately finds himself the object of his search: "once we recognize how the template of the detective mystery underlies the narrative structure, it is possible to see behind Amis's construction of the narrator the figure of the interrogator." However, what McCarthy calls the chronillogical method "inverts the paradigm and its conventions: the interrogator interrogates himself and undergoes his own torture." He is both criminal and victim. Finally, McCarthy compares the interrogative narrative of the mystery to the psychoanalytic genre. Once again, the reversal of chronology "makes *Time's Arrow* an ironic form of the 'talking cure' because it produces narration that mimics as it understands the therapeutic norm—moving as it does from the articulate to the pre-articulate. The end is terrible silence, the muted significance of smoke above a crematorium" (McCarthy 1999: 307). Actually, the end may be silent, but it is the silent, traumatic experience of rebirth that now again awaits the narrator (see Works, **p. 57**).

Beata Piatek's intertextual interpretation of *Night Train* has already been referred to (see Criticism, **p. 94**). She reads this metatextual novel as one in which "Amis is playing with the genre, the medium and with his own literary reputation" (Piatek 2004: 158–9). In her view, *Night Train* is a "provocation," a "parody of the detective story in all its manifestations from literature, through film to television" (Piatek 2004: 161, 162). Clues to this interpretation within the novel include the name of the Indonesian expert in dissection (Dr. No; cf. Ian Fleming's Bond novels), and of Trader Faulkner (cf. William Faulkner's co-writing of the screenplay for *The Big Sleep*). "As a parody, the novel does not imitate reality, but other texts and genres," making it supremely metatextual in its focus on the literary nature of its composition (Piatek 2004: 171). Daniel

Oertel thinks that *Night Train* explores two subgenres of the detective story, the hard-boiled detective story and the police procedural (Oertel 2001: 132). The text initially presents itself as a crime novel in which "we are instantly led into the world of the Chandleresque 'tough guy'-story with its typical mode of straightforward and self-conscious narration" (Oertel 2001: 133). Mike, the narrator, pursues a series of leads, which we expect in this genre, only for us to realize by the end that "none of the clues and suspects lead anywhere." The story is "[n]ot a whodunit, but a whydunit—yet one whose question remains unanswered. A hard-boiled police procedural with no dénouement, no closure, no murderer, no revelation" (Oertel 2001: 134). The novel turns out to be not a detective story but a psychological study. Yet, in manipulating the genre, Oertel claims, Amis makes us aware of the unreal nature of our generic expectations. "In real life, there isn't always a showdown, a satisfactory closure, a 'motive' that explains what people are like and what life is about" (Oertel 2001: 135) (see Works, p. 62). Oertel thinks that the overall effect of Amis's refusal to observe the conventions of the genre is to turn his readers into active partici-pants in the construction of meaning. In effect, Amis's rejection of the closure demanded by the detective story can be seen as a gesture in the direction of greater narrative realism.

Peter Childs calls *The Information* "a kind of a revenger's tragedy" (2005: 52), in that Richard sees his task as "a literary endeavor, a quest, an exaltation—one to which he could sternly commit all his passion and his power. He was going to fuck Gwyn up" (*I* 25). Magdalena Maczynska views this novel as the successor to a line of novels of literary rivalry and doppelgangers originating in George Gissing's *New Grub Street* (1891) and continuing in the work of Borges and Nabokov. Either way, Richard's attempt to take his revenge on his literary rival turns into a form of comedy—an anti-comedy, or a revenge anti-comedy (Amis called its prototype, "Career Move," "a revenge fantasy" [Bauer 1999]) (see Works, pp. 58, 70). *The Information* is a novel that shows the effect that misplaced seasons of the year have on the four principal literary genres identified by Northrop Frye in *Anatomy of Criticism: Four Essays* (1957). In his third essay, titled "Archetypal Criticism: The Theory of Myths," Frye associates the four archetypal genres or pregeneric *mythoi* (plots) of literature with the four seasons: comedy with spring, romance with summer, tragedy with autumn, and irony or satire with winter (see Life and Contexts, p. 6). *The Information* cites this schema in order to show how what has acted as a norm to date no longer holds true (*I* 35). In the novel's late-twentieth-century world in which human intervention has caused mutations of the seasons, literary genres find themselves correspondingly out of sync: "They have bled into one another. Decorum is no longer observed" (*I* 35). The abandonment of literary decorum complements the abandonment of social and moral decorum in the modern world. Genre plays a major narrative role in *The Information*. Even a minor character like Steve is portrayed as a modern anti-hero, "the hero of a novel from the future" (*I* 350). The deterioration in literary protagonists accompanies a deterioration in literary genre. Like Steve's, Richard's life is shaped by literary genre. "What *was* Richard? He was a revenger, in what was probably intended to be a comedy" (*I* 96) (see Works, p. 59). Richard's life is not just a life devoted to literature. It is described as a literary construct. "His life, his whole life, was approaching its third-act climax [. . .] What genre did his life belong to? [. . .] In fact, it was comedy. Or anti-comedy, which is [. . .] a more modern kind of comedy" (*I* 131). This displaced genre invades the narrative, determining its structure and skewed outcome. As the narrator informs us, "We did satire in summer, and comedy in autumn, and romance in winter" (*I* 362). As the novel ends in spring, it ought to be comedy, which was used up in autumn. But "comedy has two opposites; and tragedy, fortunately, is only one of them" (*I* 362). John Nash concludes that Amis recounts the ending of the novel in the generic conventions of anti-comedy, or a comedy that "is not tragic but melancholic" (1996: 217). While the melancholic offers an appropriate mode for the information about death that reaches Richard, Nash concludes that through its use "some other world, an after life, is envisaged as at least conceptually possible," both a material and a literary one (1996: 218). Amis again internalizes Frye's taxonomy of genres in *Koba the Dread*, where he asks:

> Russia, 1917–53: what is its genre? It is not a tragedy, like *Lear*, nor an anti-comedy, like *Troilus and Cressida*, nor yet a problem comedy, like *Measure for Measure*. It is a black farce, like *Titus Andronicus*. And black farce is very Russian, from *Dead Souls* to *Laughter in the Dark*.
>
> (*KD* 258).

*Yellow Dog* belongs to the same comic or burlesque genre Amis used for *Money*, *London Fields*, and *The Information* (see Works, **p. 59**). Its poor reception illustrates the truth of Amis's earlier admission that comedy is "a risky area—what we find funny or amusing or endearing. The novel as it's evolved, the comic novel, has taken in riskier characters increasingly" (Bragg 1989a). These novels employ a wide range of comic subgenres that make them hard to define precisely in generic terms. To instance *London Fields*, it has been called by Diedrick "an unstable mixture of millennial murder mystery, urban satire, apocalyptic jeremiad, and domestic farce" (2004: 119); by Jack Kroll "an upside-down murder mystery, morality tale, nuclear science fiction and postmodern love story" (1990: 62); by Magdalena Maczynska a mixture of "the mystery story and medieval romance" (Maczynska 2004: 201); and by Susan Brook "a postmodern detective novel" the end of which is "a glorious rewriting of Agatha Christie's *The Murder of Roger Ackroyd*" (Brook 2006: 94, 93). The status of *Yellow Dog* is made problematical by the fact that in it Amis tried to combine the tragic ("this'll be a post-September 11 novel") with the comic ("it'll be a comic novel") (Doshi 2002) (see Works, **p. 62**). Jean-Michel Ganteau attempts to explain this generic contradiction by placing the novel within the transgressive tradition of novels of the contemporary extreme. Not content with staging extreme violence, the novel displays such violence "in dialectical relation with [. . .] [its] tonal opposite, i.e. humor" (Ganteau 2006: 137). It "evinces both fascination for and condemnation of violence" (Ganteau 2006: 140). Ganteau, therefore, thinks that *Yellow Dog* is "less a realistic novel than a romance of the dark type" (2006: 133). To justify calling it a romance, even if "what *Yellow Dog* promotes is some romance of the dark, apocalyptic, violent type," Ganteau cites the fact that the final Chapter 10 takes place on February 14, St. Valentine's Day, the day dedicated to the martyr of love. "This I see as a way of asserting *in extemis* the resilience of human love as antidote in an age that, despite its addiction to violence, eschews the menaces of post-humanism and clings to a romantic vision" (Ganteau 2006: 140). While this may be seen as a possible interpretation of the episodes in the novel concerning Xan Meo and the King, it hardly seems applicable to the episodes focused on Clint Smoker or Flight CigAir 101.

## Gendered readings

In most of his fiction, Amis writes as a male, mainly about male characters, addressing an implied male reader, and largely drawing on male literary sources. It is hardly surprising that his work has attracted considerable feminist criticism—varying between angry accusations of misogyny, pornography, and sexism to sophisticated readings detecting unconscious gender bias. Amis attributes his treatment of sexual relations to the age in which he lives. Citing Bellow's pronouncement that "ours is a sclerotic Eros"—an Eros that has grown unresponsively hardened over time—he still believes that romantic love "will always be there, but it's harder for it to flourish" (Stout 1990: 48). He is also convinced that in our media-saturated culture "authentic experience is much harder to find." Consequently, even when we are in the sack, he claims, "we're thinking, 'How does this measure up? How will this look?' We've all got this idea of what it should look like—from movies, from pornography" (Morrison 1990: 101). In addition, he believes that sex offers him as a writer a vehicle "for revealing characters 'when they're not just going through the motions.' It's an area where need and greed converge, and where tenderness is accidental, a rare thrill" (Stout 1990: 36). Like drink, sex is an "area where people behave very strangely and yet go on being themselves" (Haffenden 1985: 6). But even his defense of his writer's need and right to employ sex for its psychological revelations can be and has been interpreted as idiomatic of the male writer's use of the pen (which Amis still uses in the age of computers) as a phallic weapon.

Never intimidated by the forces of political correctness, Amis recognized from early on the powerful role that male fantasies played in sexual interaction and the extent to which those fantasies can be manipulated by the porn industry. In 1973, the year his first novel was published, he wrote two articles for the *New Statesman* under the pseudonym of "Bruno Holbrook" on the contemporary commercialization of sex. "Fleshpots," the first article, is about London's sex industry, and "Coming in Handy" is a survey of sex magazines of the time. M. Hunter Hayes describes Amis's satiric strategy: The Holbrook persona operates "by first adopting a pose of awkward sympathy and then subverting the performative medium to out-burlesque the burlesque" (Hayes 2006: 207). In "Fleshpots" Amis comments on nude girl shows: "Certainly one could be stirred neither to desire nor distaste by something so unlike life" (quoted in Hayes 2006: 208). Here, he detaches himself from the pornographic intention of arousing (male) sexual desire while assuming that his readership ("one") is exclusively male. His ethical response to porn magazines is equally measured: "The only moralistic line one can take against these magazines is that they are *malum per se*: they cheapen and dehumanize; although they may not be corrupting, they are corrupt" (Amis 1973a: 923). According to Hayes, these pieces "critique pornography as escapist, banal fantasy, trash entertainment for the imaginatively impoverished that exacerbates a disengagement from society and relationships" (2006: 209). Almost three decades later, Amis wrote an essay on "Sex in America" for *Talk* magazine (see Life and Contexts and Works, **pp. 12, 32, 64**). By the millennium, pornography had become a multibillion-dollar industry in which anal sex (graphically symbolic of male domination in the sex act) has supplanted heterosexual intercourse as the most saleable form of sex. Watching a porn movie being shot in Los Angeles, Amis, now a twice-married man with children, remarks that "the instinct being aroused in me was not sexual but protective"—of the female porn stars (Amis 2001b: 134). His summary reveals his considered take on pornography: "porno, it seems, is a parody of love. It therefore addresses itself to love's opposites, which are hate and death. 'Choke her!'" "porno is littered— porno is heaped—with the deaths of feelings" (Amis 2001b: 135). The consequences of the displacement of feelings by disembodied desire is a recurring theme in his fiction. "Pornography," Amis has said, "isn't really erotic, it's carnal" (Haffenden 1985: 21).

Amis is quite clear-sighted about the appeal that porn has for men. "Pornography works on men because the whore relationship is exciting, because it involves money and money drives out feeling, because you can manipulate it, because you can have it your way" (Bragg 1989a). But he also came to realize that for his children's generation pornography has become a "sort of sex instruction for the young" (Elias 2003). Pornography has become an inescapable part of contemporary life, and he believes that any worthwhile writer has to accept this fact and incorporate its effects in his writing. Pornography is rarely absent from his novels. Many of his characters are addicted to it or influenced by it, especially John Self in *Money*, Keith Talent in *London Fields*, Steve Cousins in *The Information*, and Xan Meo in *Yellow Dog*. Where critics differ is in their assessment of how successfully Amis's narrators or implied authors have distanced themselves from the pornography-obsessed protagonists. This becomes especially problematical when the protagonist is also the narrator, as is the case with *Money*. Even Amis's earliest novels were attacked for a lack of narrative distance. The crude and simplistic response of Shanti Padhi to *The Rachel Papers* and *Dead Babies* illustrates what happens when readers fail to appreciate the tone of irony that Amis dexterously employs in his first novel and that of savage satire he uses in his second novel. Or, rather, Padhi claims, Amis "had assumed the stance of a satirist only to wallow in descriptions of marathon events and double-turns in bed" (Padhi 1982: 37). Assuming the mantle of a critic who understands irony and satire, he reveals an underlying moral puritanism: "despite the literary astuteness of both these novels, the culture reflected in them is shameless, ruthless, nasty" (Padhi 1982: 38). Yet, a more sophisticated critic like Neil Powell also accuses Amis in his first three novels of failing to consistently distinguish between pornography and literature that requires a more complicated response, claiming that these books contain "passages where the ironist's or satirist's distancing fails entirely" (1981: 44).

A parallel charge leveled at Amis has been that from the start his fiction shows a barely concealed streak of misogyny in its treatment of female characters. While admitting that when he looks back at *The Rachel Papers* "there is some misogyny there," because his readers used to be predominantly men (Weich 2003), Amis has called his first three novels "not antifeminist but prefeminist" (Morrison 1990: 101). He has also pointed out that a positive female role model has no place in his fictive world: "There'd be nothing for her to do, given that the guys in my novels are either victims or predators [. . .] I'm writing comedies. Vamps and ballbreakers and golddiggers are the sort of women who belong in comedy" (Bellante and Bellante 1992: 5). As I observe, "Such women are types, the subjects of fictional narratives, genre-specific" (Finney 1995: 13). This has not prevented reviewers and critics from accusing Amis of showing an animus against women. Reviewing *Success* for the *New York Times Book Review*, Jay Parini wrote, "Misanthropy becomes misogyny in *Success* [. . .] The novel's two narrators, Gregory Riding and Terry Service, hate women almost as much as they hate themselves, though it remains unclear where Mr. Amis stands on all this" (Parini 1987: 8). A similar charge can be made against such passages in *The Rachel Papers* as Charles's discovery that the inside of Rachel's discarded panties contain pubic hair and "a stripe of suede-brown shit, as big as my finger" (*RP* 181), or, in *Success*, such references as Gregory makes to his girlfriend Miranda's "ghostly smells" and the "underworld effluvia she leaves glistening on your sheets" (*S* 17) and his description of Jan's breasts as "[g]reat plates of blancmange the size of knapsacks, topped by curlicued sausage stubs" (*S* 90). Yet, in both cases, Amis is implicitly criticizing the male protagonists for their misogynistic response (see Works, p. 36). Amis indignantly rejects the charge of misogyny: "I don't think I've ever written about a woman with any hatred. I love my women characters, even the most scheming and tricksy [. . .] I know there's no hatred there" (Bragg 1989a).

*Money* became something of a cause célèbre in this critical debate. Even some of the reviewers who praised the novel still found "the vice enticing" (Korn 1984: 1119). "It is," Karl Miller explains, "as if [Self's] bad habits are being made endlessly delightful" (1985: 414). When asked by John Haffenden whether in *Money* he had not become something of a male apologist for pornography, Amis responded: "There are certainly one or two pornographic scenes in *Money*, and they're there for the effect they have on the narrator: he has no resistance to pornography" (Haffenden 1985: 21). For *Money* to qualify as pornography, Amis said, he, as its creator, would have to be excited by it, "and I'm not excited by anything except by how I'm going to arrange the words" (Haffenden 1985: 21). Amis has gone so far as to claim that he considers *Money* his "feminist book." "The hero does start to see the light, and being the kind of person he is, he fails to move into the light" (Morrison 1990: 101). Nevertheless, in a less defensive mood, Amis has confessed, "Sexism is like racism: we all feel such impulses. Our parents feel them more strongly than we feel them. Our children, we hope, will feel them less strongly than we feel them. People don't change or improve much, but they do evolve. It is very slow" (*WAC* 9). This would appear to justify Adam Mars-Jones's charge that Amis "defends the sexual status quo" (Mars-Jones 1990: 8). At the same time, the novel shows Self as the victim of his own taste for pornography. As Tamás Bényei remarks, Self's "pursuit of pleasure amounts to a quest for deferral, an avoidance of jouissance, the traumatic pleasure that threatens the consistency of his desire. His fetishism also isolates him from human relationships" (Bényei 2006: 42–3).

In 1990, *Money* featured as the representative text in a full-length feminist essay on sexism in Amis's fiction. In "Sexy Greedy Is the Late Eighties," an essay on *Money* and Churchill's *Serious Money*, Laura Doan charges that Amis fails to extend his critique of 1980s Western capitalism to gender, race, and class. As a result, his "restricted focus hinders a critique of the gender system which is, instead, upheld and reified (i.e. maintained)" (Doan 1990: 70). Doan points, for instance, to a passage in which the first thing Self asks himself when he meets a woman is "will I fuck it?" (*M* 222). She comments: "By substituting 'it' for 'her', Self, like the pornography he devours, denies woman personhood, placing her in the ultimate state of disempowerment and disembodiment" (Doan 1990: 74). Repeatedly, Doan indicts Self with sexism and assumes that this proves that Amis is sexist. "Self affirms Selina's assertion that 'men use money to dominate women' [*M* 88], and complacently recognizes women's greater potential for victimization but, rather than register concern, the thought fuels his suspicion that women somehow deserve it" (Doan 1990: 75). Near the end of her essay, she makes this unconscious equation between narrator/protagonist and author: "Amis elects to stay within the patriarchal gender boundaries by upholding the pattern of dominance and submission" (Doan 1990: 78). Gavin Keulks counters, "underneath John Self's sexist veneer [. . .] the novel's thematic grammar is declaratively feminist" (Keulks 2003: 179). Feminist or not, the novel offers a series of authorial stand-ins to prevent the reader from thinking that its narrator's attitudes and behavior are endorsed by his creator.

James Miracky offers a more nuanced critique of *Money*'s alleged sexist bias. He argues that, "although *Money* lampoons the masculinist desires of the consumerist 1980s to a disparaging extreme, it never fully escapes its own critique. In making its protagonist a sympathetic character who apparently cannot help himself, the novel seems to revel in the greed and misogyny it mocks" (2003: 137). When Amis told John Haffenden, "I am fascinated by what I deplore, or I deplore what fascinates me: it's hard to get it the right way round," his last remark reveals just this ambivalence (Haffenden 1985: 3). Yet, if Self had been a totally unsympathetic character, the reader would have lost interest in him long before the end of the book. Amis's empathy for the character he victimizes is an essential part of his narrative strategy. Miracky reveals the selective nature of his reading when he criticizes the finale in which Amis, in interviews, claimed to present a reformed Self. In the last paragraph, Miracky writes, Self watches "Georgina moving toward him ticking on her heels which conjures up memories of the other women who have, to his mind, walked all over him [. . .] suggesting that he has not really escaped his attraction to [. . .] his abusive relations with women" (2003: 142). It might conjure up memories of other women for Miracky, but nothing in the text at this point refers back to earlier occasions on which women figuratively had walked over Self (as he sees it). If one is going to perform a detailed textual analysis of this last sentence, one would need to take notice of the fact that all of the epithets Self applies to Georgina concern her personality, not her erotic properties, a change that indicates a reformed and nonabusive attitude to women.

Emma Parker has offered the subtlest reading of this novel informed by queer theory. By focusing on what she perceives as "the unstable borders of identity and desire," she claims to demonstrate that *Money* "subverts the ideology of its bigoted protagonist by deconstructing the heteropatriarchal concepts 'woman' and 'man' and creating what Judith Butler terms 'gender trouble'" (2006: 55). She argues that it is through Self, whom she describes as a "racist, sexist homophobe," that Amis "most clearly subverts a patriarchal model of masculinity" (Parker 2006: 55, 58). Because pornography misrepresents female sexuality, it renders him impotent when he meets Martina Twain, a woman outside the world of pornography (see Works, p. 48). In pursuing this traditional feminist line of argument, Parker comes across the impasse of androcentric feminist criticism: "attempts to recoup *Money* by reading it as a critique of masculinity are limited if the novel simply inverts the positions of men and women in the gender hierarchy" (2006: 60). Instead, she argues, "*Money* challenges male hegemony [. . .] By destabilizing the binary categories of gender and sexuality, the novel privileges a queer perspective" (Parker 2006: 61). Citing numerous instances from the text, Parker shows how Self's clothes and behavior are camp and how he desperately attempts to suppress his feminine characteristics. Further, he reveals an underlying homosexuality. "While Self submerges same-sex desire in the struggle to establish heteronormative masculinity, his repressed homosexuality finds expression at the level of subtext" (Parker 2006: 63). As instances of this proclivity, Parker cites Self's relations with his homosexual dentist and with the cross-dressing Fielding Goodney with whom he spends a steamy, drunken evening at Zelda's. Where Self previously addressed a gendered reader, Parker focuses on his address in the penultimate paragraph ("*Humans, I honour you*" [M 363]) to argue that in the book's conclusion Amis "suggests the possibility—or indeed the necessity—of transcending gender altogether" (Parker 2006: 68). Rejecting Doan's charge that *Money* is a sexist text that reinforces patriarchy, Parker claims that a queer reading of the novel shows it deconstructing "man" and "woman," thereby escaping "the binary structures that its critique of masculinity appears to uphold" (2006: 69).

The publication of his next novel, *London Fields*, brought into the public eye the animosity that by this stage some feminists directed at any work Amis produced. Two women on the judging panel for the Booker Prize and one woman judge for the Whitbread Prize refused to shortlist it for its "supposed sexist offensiveness" (Bragg 1989b: C1). Maggie Gee, a novelist and one of the two female Booker judges, attempted to justify her resistance to the novel by arguing that there is confusion in the function of the narrator, Samson (sometimes he is a norm, other times he is a participating character), ignoring the deliberate confusion that Amis creates by opening the book with a note from "M.A." who, as Sam's literary executor, is responsible for the text as it appears and who may, as Sam suspects, have set him up and have been in control all along. At the same time, Gee confesses that "matters discounted by most of the critical establishment—sexual politics, for one [. . .] have an inevitable place in judgements of taste" (Tredell 2000: 98) (see Life and Contexts and Criticism, pp. 22, 97). Even some female critics who admired the novel criticized it for its alleged misogyny. Penny Smith writes that Nicola's depiction "invites accusations of misogyny, even though Amis's apparent intention is for his female character to be read as a symbol of her age rather than a sign of her gender. Nicola is self-destructive, compelled not just to cancel love but to murder it." She claims that it is also sexist in engineering Nicola's murder at a man's hands (Smith 1995: 123).

Similarly, Betty Pesetsky writes that the novel makes its readers entertain "the sneaking suspicion that a misogynist lingers here somewhere" (Pesetsky 1990: 1). Susie Thomas offers a more extensive attack of this kind on *London Fields*. She finds it staggering that this book should have been greeted as an important, metropolitan novel when it is "anti-working class" and "riddled with racist stereotypes." Its implied reader is "white, male and middle class." As Amis's sexism has been frequently exposed, her treatment of gender is only treated "in so far as it affects Amis's representation of race and class." She maintains that all the novel's characters are "flat because he has no depth to give them." Accordingly, "Nicola's insistence that she knows she is a 'male fantasy figure' ([*LF*] 260) does not stop her being one." The same accusation is leveled at the book's working-class female characters. Trish is reduced to "a titmag pin-up with a speech bubble." Kath "never manages to be more than a bundle of contradictions." (Cannot this be equally the definition of a three-dimensional character?) Thomas refuses to grant Amis any significant distance between author and not just narrator(s) but also characters. "Amis hides behind his narrator, who in turn hides behind Keith, who is made to spout racist [and sexist] babble." "Amis seems to enjoy hiding behind his ventriloquist's dummy and getting him to make comments that neither he nor his educated narrator could get away with" (Thomas 2003: 25). To treat an author's characters as his ventriloquist dummies is to respond to fiction, especially self-reflexive fiction, with extreme naivety. Defending himself, Amis insists that a primary purpose of the novel is to satirize "certain male illusions" (Naughtie 2001).

In 1995, *London Fields* was used by Sara Mills as the test case for a feminist essay titled "Working with Sexism: What Can Feminist Text Analysis Do?" Dissatisfied with analyses of sexism that concentrate exclusively on either language or ideology, she argues, "there are structures which mediate between the ideology of sexism and particular words or grammatical choices" (Mills 1995: 208). She calls these structures "narrative schemata" and claims that they "lead to particular representations of women" (Mills 1995: 214). Narrative schemata tend to be deterministic, predisposing readers to think about women, for instance, in certain ways. In the narrative schemata Amis employs in *London Fields*, Mills writes, Nicola "wishes to be acted upon and paradoxically strives to bring that about" (1995: 216). The narrative schemata of sexism are so familiar that they invite the reader to accept them as common-sense knowledge. The role of the feminist critic is to expose their constructed nature. "Rather than simply dismissing the plot out of hand, it is necessary to map out in detail its constructed nature, so that these building blocks of thought are shown to be only one choice amongst many others" (Mills 1995: 217). Mills' aim is to move feminist critics "forward from blanket accusations of political incorrectness" to a demonstration of "the way that certain texts offer us constructions which are retrograde" (1995: 218). Gavin Keulks responds that the reader's choice whether to accept sexist schemata or to react against them is a choice already offered in both *Money* and *London Fields*. Using *Money* as his example, Keulks claims that Amis "embeds such ideological dualism within *Money* by establishing an oppositional tension among its three major characters, John Self, Martina Twain, and Selina Street." In particular, Amis "polarizes the novel's two main female characters." Martina is "the embodiment of [Amis's] feminized and feminizing viewpoints [. . .] Selina is an houri, a lamia, a succubus to Self." He concludes that "Self's choice of Selina over Martina toward the end of the novel represents the melancholy triumph of misogyny, and Self loses everything as a result" (Keulks 2003: 180). So, the novel is self-correcting in rejecting its sexist schemata at the end. One could equally apply this argument to *London Fields* in which Nicola outplots the masculinist agendas (or schemata) of all three male protagonists. Her choice to become a victim/murderee does not represent a surrender to patriarchy; it acts as a gesture of rejection of a patriarchal world from which love has absented itself.

Frederick Holmes selects *London Fields* to focus on Keith's inability to recognize the moral crassness of what he values. On the one hand, the novel "does not really seem to allow for the existence of a base outside mass culture from which it could be repudiated." On the other hand, an application of Fredric Jameson's conception of postmodern culture ("the consumption of sheer commodification as a process") "cannot account for what readers sense to be the novel's intention to lament the very cultural sickness in which it participates" (Holmes 1996: 59). Instead, Holmes attempts to make sense of this ambiguous quality in *London Fields* by employing Linda Hutcheon who "argues that postmodernism's complicity in the capitalist process of commodification does not negate, although it does compromise, its political critique of that same process" (1996: 60). Holmes uses Hutcheon's definition to explain the ambiguous responses to Amis's parodic yet sexist representations of the images of mass culture (such as those of women):

> [Nicola] has more power and freedom than any of the other characters in manipulating and revising the ready-made scripts of society, but paradoxically the exercise of this freedom entails her own oppression [. . .] the plots that she orchestrates necessitate that she enact and parody the very roles which feminists have rejected as limiting and destructive: those of Madonna and whore, which she plays for Guy and Keith respectively. Her detached awareness that these roles do not express her essential identity [. . .] do not [. . .] liberate her from them.
>
> (Holmes 1996: 61)

Consequently, her only escape is through death. While Amis leaves himself open to criticism for the limited options he offers Nicola, "the bleakness of *London Fields* subserves a carnivalesque comic and satiric energy which, however, is implicated in the culture which it ridicules and attacks" (Holmes 1996: 61).

Most recently, Susan Brook has responded to Sara Mills' criticism and Susie Thomas's diatribe by arguing, "it is precisely the 'lifeless' quality of Amis's characters that helps to destabilize gender identity by revealing it as both fictional and unstable." Drawing on Butler's *Gender Trouble*, she continues, "gender identity is the effect of a series of physical performances and linguistic iterations, with the result that it can be exaggerated and manipulated." She shows how Guy's and Keith's masculinity are constructs, just as "Nicola's femininity is linguistic and performative." Next, she turns to Amis's argument against charges of sexism—that Nicola has power and control—an argument that she finds problematical, as "powerful women can be aligned with the castrating phallic mother, who is both fetishized and devalued" (Brook 2006: 89). Drawing a distinction between the text of the novel and his defense of it, she claims that Amis's novels unsettle the distinction between power and powerlessness, in contrast to his facile comments in interviews. "Amis's apparently powerful characters are in fact powerless, because their actions are controlled by the author [. . .] However, the power of author figures is also undermined," as both author stand-ins, Sam and Nicola, die (Brook 2006: 89–90). Brook concludes by arguing that the novel deconstructs notions of authorial power and control. "Amis satirizes the abuse of power, and the plight of his manipulative author figures might be seen as self-punishment for his own authorial abuses. This interpretation further complicates the notion of power by suggesting that moral power might be gained through weakness or self-punishment" (2006: 90). This leaves Martin Amis (or "Martin Amis") occupying the ambiguous role of both sadist and masochist, each of which exerts power in opposing ways.

From his first novel on, Amis has made masculinity a central preoccupation of his writing. He devoted the first section of *The War on Cliché* to "Masculinity and Related Questions." He has explained that writing about it is disquieting because "the fear of impotence whips the carpet out from underneath you in a way that it is hard to think of a female equivalent" (Elias 2003). Seen in a wider historical perspective, masculinity is particularly problematical, he thinks, after the feminist revolution of the 1970s. "I think men and women are living a slight political fiction right now, in the sense that we've announced that there's equality, but men have been in power for five million years, and you can't pretend that the past has no weight" (Cutter 2003: 4). As a consequence, in England, "maleness has become an embarrassment" (*WAC* 5). If anything, Amis has come to elevate women to a higher position than men, referring to the "more mystical life that they have" (Haffenden 1985: 20) and declaring, "I am profeminist" (Morrison 1990: 102). In *Venus Envy*, Adam Mars-Jones claims to detect in Amis a hidden desire to "align himself with qualities traditionally associated with women, with a certain tender-mindedness." This "bears witness to the tidal pull of feminist thinking, and to a nagging doubt about the authenticity of male experience" (Mars-Jones 1990: 33). Reviewing *The Information*, Mars-Jones suggests that, nevertheless, Amis's "Venus envy" causes him to construct female characters who are generic, never individualized. "Amis's satire operates a discriminatory cartooniness, making men huge and absurd, women absurdly diminished [. . .] Gina may be the hero's wife, but everything she does is generic and labelled as such" (Mars-Jones 1995: 19). Julian Loose made a similar observation about this novel: "the women in the novel remain mere objects of desire and disappointment. They may know all about tears [. . .] but they don't get to read Proust, write books or take any decisions: Amis frankly gives up on the attempt to make them more than two-dimensional" (Loose 1995: 9). These criticisms predate the appearance of *Night Train*, which was seen by many reviewers as proof that Amis could depict women in their particularity. In the *Guardian*, Natasha Walter enthused that in Hoolihan, his female protagonist/narrator, and in Jennifer Rockwell, "Amis turns a corner; for the first time he has created heroines who are defined not by their underwear and the size of their breasts, but by their work and relationships and human disappointments" (Walter 1997: 29). This wide disagreement on the ways in which Amis portrays women in his fiction continues to the present day.

## Linguistic inventiveness

Virtually everyone agrees that Amis is a virtuoso when it comes to the way in which he uses language. Reviewers and critics claim either that "he writes like a fallen angel" (Brown 2001: 19), or that he is "the poet of profligacy, the expert on excess" (Loose 1995: 9). His style is so identifiable that it has been imitated by a number of his contemporaries, most notably by Will Self (and Zadie Smith in *White Teeth*), most notoriously by Jacob Epstein. His father disapproved of a style that draws attention to itself and told him there should be more sentences in his books that read: "He finished his drink and left." Amis strongly disagreed, telling an interviewer, "I think there should be fewer sentences like that in his books [. . .] There should be no dead areas." He insisted, "Style is not an icing but an ingredient, perhaps the main ingredient of your way of perceiving things [. . .] If it's a complicated perception it will need a complicated sentence." Amis is strongly opposed to what he calls "this clear-as-a-mountain-creek kind of writing, this vow-of-poverty prose" (Bigsby 1992: 179). Amis makes his reader sit up and attend from the opening lines of his novels. Think of *Success*:

"Terry speaking," I said.
The receiver cleared its throat.

(*S* 7)

It takes a moment to appreciate that so far the caller is unknown to Terry, who is simply listening to the receiver of his telephone. Or, consider Sam's opening line in *London Fields*: "This is a true story but I can't believe it's really happening" (*LF* 1). The entire ontological status of the fictional narrative is put into question from the moment it opens. Then there is Mike Hoolihan's deliberately mannered, because degendered, opening introduction in *Night Train*: "I am a police" (*NT* 11). Earlier an analysis was offered of Amis's use of neologism in the opening paragraph of *Money* (see Criticism, **p. 92**), and the way the opening paragraph of *Yellow Dog* parodies that of Dickens's *A Tale of Two Cities* (see Works, **p. 63**). Within the opening page of any of his novels or stories, Amis puts his readers on notice that they are going to have to pay more than customary attention to the way his fictions are written.

Amis's insistence on the importance of style is partly a consequence of his rejection of mimetic realism in his narratives. As he writes, "the more superbly an author throws away the crutches of verisimilitude, the more heavily he must lean on his own style and wit" (*WAC* 95). But, he insists, "Style is not neutral; it gives moral directions" (Haffenden 1985: 23). Nonrealist fiction might mean something different by morality than does realist fiction, but it does not necessarily enter a world of postmodern indeterminacy. As he sees it, style and content are inseparable. "It is not that, as is commonly supposed, you get your content and soup it up with style: style is absolutely embedded in the way you perceive" (Haffenden 1985: 4). In *Experience*, he elaborates, "I would argue that style is morality: morality detailed, configured, intensified. It's not in the mere narrative arrangement of good and bad that morality makes itself felt. It can be there in every sentence" (*E* 122n) (see Works, **p. 82**). Style reflects the kind of perception that the writer employs, especially by its freshness and accuracy. Even the sound of a sentence matters. Amis offers a revealing instance of the connection between style (in terms of internal rhymes) and moral perception when reviewing a collection of essays by V. S. Pritchett, whose prose, he writes, "has little time for the guidelines of elegance." It might be "full of [. . .] jangles—'Sitting behind the screen of the machine' is a random example—but the effect is entirely appropriate to his way of looking at life. Life *does* rhyme: it rhymes all the time. Life can often be pure doggerel" (*WAC* 69). Amis places style within a wider social context when he writes about his friend, James Fenton's Trotskyist acceptance of social realism: "I wondered how he, qua poet, could align himself with a system that saw literature as a servant of the state; and, I thought, he must hate the *language*, the metallic clichés, the formulas and euphemisms, the supposedly futuristic and time-thrifty acronyms and condensations" (*KD* 24). Although in *Koba the Dread* Amis criticizes at length the immorality of the murderous history of Soviet Communist rule, he finds its dishonesty equally in evidence in its murderous misuse of language. Above all else, he sees the unconscious use of cliché as a key giveaway, a glaring sign that the user is unconscious of the moral effect of what he or she is writing. In this he is again indebted to Nabokov, who "regarded cliché as the key to bad art" (*WAC* 245). Among other things, he has written that "prejudices are clichés: they are second-hand hatreds" (*WAC* 444). Reviewing Iris Murdoch's *The Philosopher's Pupil*, Amis notes how the narrator "uses quotation marks for such vulgarisms as 'sulks,' 'commuters' and 'worthwhile activities,' as well as for phrases like 'too good to be true,' 'the wrong end of the stick' and 'keep in touch.' The reader reflects that a cliché or an approximation, wedged between inverted commas, is still a cliché or an approximation." Amis next turns Murdoch's clichés against her: "Besides, you see how it would 'get on your nerves' if I were to 'go on' like this 'the whole time'" (*WAC* 92). As he writes in his Foreword, he has fought a lifelong campaign against not "just clichés of the pen but clichés of the mind and clichés of the heart" (*WAC* xv) (see Life and Contexts and Works, **pp. 29, 81**).

Gavin Keulks argues that Martin Amis countered his father's use of Henry Fielding's burlesque form of comedy with his own more ludic sense of comedy derived in particular from Nabokov. Martin's refusal to judge or punish his characters, Keulks writes, means that he "cannot easily be considered a moral satirist, as are Kingsley Amis and Henry Fielding" (Keulks 2003: 148). Yet, he admits that, like Fielding, both father and son "treat low things in a high style" (Keulks 2003: 49). Amis told John Haffenden the same thing, that he had inherited from his father "the English tradition of writing about low events in a high style, which is the tradition of Henry Fielding" (Haffenden 1985: 24). It has been shown how Amis has Charles reject Fielding's mock-heroic form of comedy in his first novel, only in his third book to employ Fielding's *Tom Jones* as a model (see Works and Criticism, **pp. 36, 102**). It is easy to see instances of Amis's use of Fieldingesque burlesque. In *The Information*, Richard and his son Marco are described taking one of their daily walks in the local Dogshit Park: "Hand in hand they did their tour of the urban pastoral, the sward beneath the heavenly luminary, its human figures brightly half-clad at rest and play" (*I* 99). In stark contrast to this deliberate use of archaisms like "sward," "luminary," and "half-clad," the following paragraph ends with deliberate banality: "the cleanest patch of grass in all Dogshit, the showpiece of the park [. . .] of course, was the dog toilet, where the dogs were meant to shit, and never did" (*I* 100). But Amis's verbal humor cannot be confined to such mock-heroic use of the burlesque. Sometimes he will employ allusion to reveal the distance separating his characters and the demotic language they employ from their heroic antecedents. In *Success*, for example, Terry unknowingly parodies the opening line of T. S. Eliot's *The Waste Land* by confiding to the reader: "April is the coolest month for people like myself" (*S* 92). Here, Amis is using the low style to bring attention to its debasement from its former glory (which of course originates in the opening line to Chaucer's *The Canterbury Tales* that Eliot was parodying with "April is the cruellest month"). In the above instance, Amis appeals to his readers' sense of stylistic appropriateness by assuming a knowledge of the classical canon that his characters do not possess. But when Terry informs us, "It's Jan's last day here (she's moving on. Temps do that—they move on. Temps *fugunt*)" (*S* 106), there is the suggestion that the character knowingly puns on the Latin aphorism *tempus fugit* (Time flies). The appeal is still to an educated implied reader. On another occasion, Terry seems unaware of the joke he is making at his own expense when he remarks, "I expect I drink so much simply because I'm losing my bottle" (*S* 30). By using the metaphor ("losing my bottle") purely figuratively, Terry employs rhyming slang (bottle and glass: arse; losing my arse: bowel movement: losing my courage). But unaware of its literal meaning (bottled: drunk) Terry robs language of its complexity and leaves the reader laughing at him.

A number of critics have investigated other aspects of Amis's style. Focusing on *Money*, Tamás Bényei points to Amis's frequent use of lists in his work. "Excessive, Rabelaisian, carnivalistic enumerations occur frequently, including the items in Self's modest library [*M* 67]; the purchases acquired during a shopping binge [*M* 178]; the endless list of Selina's unsavory suitors [*M* 18–19]; Lorne Guyland's previous roles [*M* 107]; or the smells of Self's tuxedo [*M* 277–8]" (Bényei 2006: 45). When applied to Selina (Bényei cites *M* 72 and 226) they reinforce the way "Selina, for Self, acts as an object of detail: we are never allowed to glimpse her face, and her body is revealed in glimpses" (Bényei 2006: 44). Bényei also pays attention to Amis's penchant for proliferating triptychs (as in *M* 109–10): "These series function as miniature replications of the repetitive plot: congeries, accumulations without progress, blatantly simulated for rhetorical effect" (Bényei 2006: 45) (see Works, **pp. 80, 83**). He suggests that Amis tries to revitalize clichés through the use of repetition. "Sometimes, repetition leads to the enfolding of meaning, an allegorical rift within similar words, as in the perfectly succinct phrase 'painful, like pain' [*M* 268]" (Bényei 2006: 45). He notes: "Diedrick contends that repetition is 'Self's favorite rhetorical strategy' (77), but it also forms the basis of the novel's (non)narrative logic, its compulsion to repeat." Repetition can result in loss and excess, and Bényei argues that in *Money* it paradoxically performs in both these ways (Bényei 2006: 47). A brief example of repetition occurs in the opening of Amis's short story, "The Time Disease": "We all think about *time*, catching *time*, coming down with *time*. *I'm* still okay, I think, for the time being" (*EM* 80). The last appearance of "time" without italics contradicts the assertion that we all think about time, showing how excess can produce its opposite.

Leonard Ashley has written a long analysis of Amis's use of onomastics in *Money*. Onomastics is the study of the origin and formation of proper names. The connotations of the names of many of Amis's characters have already been discussed. Concentrating on *Money*, Ashley shows how "parodic names [. . .] underline, undercut, understand the 'reality' [. . .] in which the hero is immersed" (Ashley 1987: 32). Ashley explores the comic ingenuity that Amis employs in inventing, for instance, the names of the novel's numerous moneymen (who turn out to be hired actors):

> Ossie Twain (the joke is in the story), Steward Cowrie (suggesting shells as money [some cowries or marine gastropods are used as currency in the South Pacific and Africa]), Bob Cambist (derived from *cambio*, Spanish for money), Ricardo Fisc (from *fiscal*), Tab Penmen (suggesting an accountant), Bill Levy (a Jew, with the added suggestion of levying a tax, etc.), and Gresham Tanner (where *tanner* is slang for a British penny [actually a sixpenny piece] and Gresham's Law concerns bad money driving out good money).
>
> (Ashley 1987: 9)

Fielding Goodney is "both upperclass and playing some game," someone "who turns out to be up to no good" (Ashley 1987: 11, 12). There is also Lorne Guyland, which, pronounced in a thick Long Island accent, sounds the same as Long Island. Ashley also comments on Amis's lists of invented car names, including "Boomerangs (because they are so often recalled to the factory? Or repossessed?)," book titles, minor characters' names (such as "one or another of Selina's forerunners, some model or stylist, some Cindy or Lindy or Judy or Trudy") where the rhymes denigrate the holders of these names, just as the repetition of "Burger" makes indistinguishable such invented fast-food chains as "Burger Den, Burger Hatch, Burger Shack, and Burger Bower" (Ashley 1987: 15–18). Ashley also points out the way in which Amis uses lists to deliberately confuse the important with the trivial in Self's mind, as in "Monet or Manet or Money or some such guy" (Ashley 1987: 19).

Amis frequently says that he enjoys impositions of difficulty. He appears to agree with the Russian Formalists, who asserted that the aim of creative writers is to renew readers' perceptions by defamiliarizing language that has become automatized by overuse. Discussing *Other People* and *Time's Arrow*, he says, "You're always looking for a way to see the world as if you've never seen it before. As if you'd never really got used to living here on this planet" (Riviere 1998: 121). For the contemporary novelist, he admits, "[i]t becomes harder and harder to be original, to see things with an innocent eye [. . .] As the planet gets progressively less innocent, you need a more innocent eye to see it" (Riviere 1998: 122). In a discussion of *The Information*, Catherine Bernard claims that Amis stretches pathetic fallacy to such a limit that Richard's attempts to anthropomorphize the universe only result in humiliation and loss. "The history of fiction does not only chronicle the slow degradation of the protagonist. It is coincidental with the 'progress of literature (downward) [... ] forced in that direction by the progress of cosmology [... ] From geocentric to heliocentric to galactocentric to plain *eccentric* [*I* 328–9]'" (Bernard 2006: 127). Amis's use of italics emphasizes the failure of Richard's and literature's use of pathetic fallacy to find a comforting place in an expanding universe. Another instance of the way in which Amis uses pathetic fallacy for specific effect concerns the spurious magazine for which Richard works. "The paper had been put to bed. To put to bed was what you did with children—whereas grownups *took* each other there. Crooned at and lullabied, given snacks and glasses of water, its fears assuaged, *The Little Magazine* had been put to bed" (*I* 120). In treating *The Little Magazine* as a child, the trope simultaneously relegates all it stands for to the realm of childishness.

Phil Joffe also devotes an essay to naming in *Time's Arrow*. His argument centers on how Amis capitalized on the way the Nazis, in designating Jews as vermin, literalized metaphors. "Germans were habituated to thinking of Jews, not as human beings, but as *üntermenschen*, as lice, as vermin, as diseases such as typhus against which Germans needed to be inoculated." He cites Theodor Adorno's declaration that "language itself [was] damaged, possibly beyond creative repair, by the politics of terror and mass murder." Joffe suggests that the Nazis employed a wide vocabulary of euphemisms to avoid confronting the reality of their murderous activities. "By renaming, they sought to make verbally manageable the atrocious [. . .] And so, the Jews were singled out for 'special handling,' they were 'resettled,' then 'liquidated,' never merely murdered" (Joffe 1995: 3). Turning to *Time's Arrow*, Joffe shows how "Amis reveals the linguistic duplicities of the Nazis in some of the 'revealing examples of camp argo' [*TA* 124], which the narrator provides." One such instance that he offers is the cynical contempt with which "the Nazis suggest that [those prisoners who are bent over from starvation and hopelessness] are Jews who will soon be converted (St. Paul's conversion of the Jews), but into ash, only." In conclusion, he analyses the fact that Odilo Unverdorben "prides himself on the precision with which he uses language and on his superb vocabulary, his excellent English." This, he argues, "is Amis's way of drawing to our notice our assumption that those who insist on precision and accuracy in language are less inclined to delude themselves about the consequences of their actions, which then makes Odilo more fully culpable in his crimes against humanity" (Joffe 1995: 7).

In my own essay on *Time's Arrow*, I show the effects of Robert Jay Lifton's *The Nazi Doctors* on Amis's depiction of the misuse of language by Unverdorben. Lifton, it is pointed out, reveals how the Nazis' practice of misnaming was firmly established at Auschwitz where "'Outpatient centers' were a 'place for selections' and hospital areas, 'waiting rooms' before death" (Lifton 2000: 186). Amis undermines this Nazi distortion of terminology by employing irony to assert an opposing ethic. Unverdorben's successive name changes present a further instance of the way in which Amis uses irony to upend Nazi doctrine.

> When the novel's chronology is reversed, Tod Friendly becomes John Young: despite Tod's association with death (in German), he becomes a younger Jack-of-all-trades. John then transforms into the gold-rich Hamilton de Souza, who assumes his birth name of Odilo Unverdorben. His last name means "un-depraved" or "un-corrupt" in

German. Thus he moves from death to innocence. The reader simultaneously transposes the narrative inversion, of course, which shifts Unverdorben's journey: he becomes a bearer of death, mirroring the change in his ideology.

(Finney 2006: 113)

I parallel Diedrick's observation that Unverdorben's name "contains both himself and his double" (2004: 138) with Amis's use of irony, which "offers both a literal fantasy (a journey to innocence) and a figurative dismissal of that fantasy (an impossible return to childhood or to pre-Holocaust history)." I conclude by showing how, for Amis, style and morality are indissolubly linked: "The dual use of language parallels the dual time scheme and the dual codes of ethics" (Finney 2006: 113).

Amis has repeatedly stressed the importance of voice in his writing: "Style is serving something else, which is I suppose a voice. When you're writing you run it through your mind until your tuning-fork is still, as it were" (Haffenden 1985: 15–16). He is acutely aware of the metrical element in prose. "Under Nabokov's prose, under Burgess's prose [. . .] the English sentence is like a poetic meter. It's a basic rhythm from which the writer is free to glance off in unexpected directions. But the sentence is still there" (Riviere 1998: 120). Convinced that most of his contemporaries write with rhythms of thought that are thirty years out of date, he wants to "suggest the new rhythms of thought which change all the time." The principal way in which modern rhythms of thought are changing is that they are "heading away from innocence" (Laurence and McGee 1995). Amis searches for these modern rhythms, starting with his first novel, which, Diedrick asserts, "possesses a ferocious verbal energy" (2004: 29). In *Money*, Self describes four different voices competing within him (*M* 104–5). Yet, Amis has talked about the gamble he took in this novel, putting all his eggs "in the basket of voice"—one unifying voice that incorporates its rival sub-voices (Weich 2003). As Diedrick explains, "Taken together, all four voices constitute a fragmented, decentered self" (2004: 75–6). Bényei, however, calls Self's voice dialogic; it is split between the voices of money and pornography and "another voice—an educated, poetic one." He calls this double-voicedness "irony, which has been nominated as the supreme trope of fetishism" (Bényei 2006: 46). Mars-Jones offers an interesting overview of Amis's use of voice: "Amis's originality as a stylist has been to separate verbal beauty from the cause it has traditionally served, to detach lyrical language from the lyrical impulse." He concludes, "Only in satire [. . .] could [Amis] write so many pages [. . .] full of commandingly vivid detail, none of it sensuous. Not a sensation enjoyed, hardly even a tune heard with pleasure, no food taken into the body without latent or patent disgust" (Mars-Jones 1995: 19).

Many reviewers have considered Amis's inventive use of language his principal asset, something they praised even as they were savaging his later work. But it was also attacked, first and notably by his father. Amis told John Haffenden, "what he dislikes about my prose is overkill." He went on to make a declaration that has been frequently used as evidence by critics charging that his work is spoiled by unnecessary stylistic embellishments. "I would certainly sacrifice any psychological or realistic truth for a phrase, for a paragraph that has a spin on it: that sounds whorish, but I think it's the higher consideration [. . .] I would sooner let the words prompt me, rather than what I am actually representing" (Haffenden 1985: 16). The most perceptive critic of his style has been Adam Mars-Jones, who voiced his reservations most clearly in two assessments of *Einstein's Monsters*. In a review of the book he wrote, "No one works harder on a sentence than Martin Amis, and no one stores up more pleasure for the reader with his phrasing. But sometimes it seems that the need to stamp each sentence with his literary personality defeats his ambition as a literary artist" (Mars-Jones 1987: 457). Three years later, in *Venus Envy*, he articulated his criticism more explicitly. "Martin Amis' progress has not been so much a career as an escalation, the persona increasingly truculent, the style ever more bristling. His very method is overkill" (Mars-Jones 1990: 12). It seems no coincidence that Mars-Jones employs Kingsley's term, "overkill."

> A style like Martin Amis' represents [. . .] a radical doubt about the business of writing, an authorial identity crisis that can be postponed by having each sentence declare the presence of the author [. . .] It is this absence of a neutral register from Martin Amis' work [. . .] that his father Kingsley complains of, the lack of workaday sentences not hell-bent on shock or charm.
>
> (Mars-Jones 1990: 14)

He charges Amis with a "desire to make a mark at all costs." As an example, he cites from "Thinkability" "the warped atoms, the groveling dead" (*EM* 4). Mars-Jones comments, "this is a holocaust with a monogram, almost a copyright logo" (Mars-Jones 1990: 17). But, *Einstein's Monsters*, especially "Thinkability," its polemical opening essay, is not representative of Amis at his best. David Thomson offers a fairer assessment of Amis's "energetic wordplay" when offering an overview of Amis's achievement: "his chief virtue as a novelist is his inventive and wickedly comic language" (Thomson 1998: 17).

## Further reading

There are three studies of Amis's work that offer advanced analyses. John A. Dern's *Martians, Monsters and Madonna: Fiction and Form in the World of Martin Amis* (2000) concentrates on the combination of postmodern elements combined with Amis's original style to examine all his work up to *Heavy Water and Other Stories*. Gavin Keulks's *Father and Son: Kingsley Amis, Martin Amis, and the British Novel since 1950* (2003) focuses on the relationship between father and son through intertextual readings of selected works by both writers. *Martin Amis: Postmodernism and Beyond*, edited by Gavin Keulks (2006) is an anthology of essays employing critical theory that covers most of Amis's work up to *Yellow Dog*. In addition, there are many essays published in scholarly journals, to which this section of the book refers.

# 4

# Chronology

Bullet points are used to denote events in Amis's life and career, and asterisks to denote literary contexts and historical events.

1949
- Martin Louis Amis born (25 August) in Oxford, second son of Kingsley Amis and Hilary Bardwell (Philip, the first son was born in 1948); family moves to Swansea where Kingsley obtains a position as Assistant Lecturer at University College

1954
- Sally, sister, born
* Kingsley publishes *Lucky Jim*, a bestseller

1956
* Suez Canal Crisis signals Britain's diminished role in world affairs

1959
- Family spends academic year in Princeton, New Jersey

1960
* D. H. Lawrence's *Lady Chatterley's Lover* is cleared in court of charges of obscenity

1961
- Family moves from Swansea to Cambridge

1962
* Cuban Missile Crisis brings the world close to nuclear war

1963
- Family leaves Cambridge; children in Soller, Majorca for the school year; Kingsley leaves Hilary to live with Elizabeth Jane Howard
* Release of Beatles' first album, *Please, Please Me*, marks arrival of new era; President Kennedy assassinated

1964
- After returning to London, goes with mother to West Indies to play part in *High Wind in Jamaica*; spends next three years in numerous schools and crammers

1967
- Attends a crammer, Sussex Tutors, in Brighton

1968
- To Exeter College, Oxford University on a scholarship

1969
* Beginning of the "Troubles" in Northern Ireland

1970
* Publication of Germaine Greer's *The Female Eunuch* signals start of era of militant feminism in Britain

1971
- Obtains a formal first; leaves home; spends four months in a Mayfair art gallery; begins writing *The Rachel Papers*; November: reviewing for the *Observer*

1972
- Appointed Editorial Assistant for the *Times Literary Supplement*

1973
- *The Rachel Papers* published; awarded Somerset Maugham Award; widening circle of friends includes Craig Raine, Julian Barnes, Clive James, and Christopher Hitchens
* After a referendum, Britain enters the European Economic Community; Oil Crisis leads to inflation in the West

1974
- Spends three months with mother in Ronda, Spain; quits the *Times Literary Supplement* to become Deputy Literary Editor of the *New Statesman*, working with Christopher Hitchens and James Fenton; has brief affair with Lamorna Seale who gives birth to their daughter, Delilah.
* Miners' strike and consequent three-day working week cause downfall of Edward Heath's Conservative government

1975
- *Dead Babies* published
* First works of fiction, *First Love, Last Rites* by Ian McEwan, and *Grimus* by Salman Rushdie, published

1977
- Becomes Literary Editor of the *New Statesman*

1978
- *Success* published.

1979
- Leaves the *New Statesman* to become a full-time writer; to Paris for seven months where he writes *Other People*
* Margaret Thatcher becomes Conservative Prime Minister for next eleven years; Craig Raine publishes *A Martian Sends a Postcard Home*

1980
- *Saturn 3* (film for which he wrote the screenplay) released; meets Antonia Phillips; start of frequent visits to the USA
- * Ronald Reagan elected President (1980–88); first novels, *Metroland* by Julian Barnes, and *The Sweet Shop Owner* by Graham Swift, published

1981
- *Other People: A Mystery Story* published
- * Scientists identify a new sexually transmitted virus, AIDS

1982
- *Invasion of the Space Invaders: An Addict's Guide* published
- * Britain repels Argentine invasion of the Falkland Islands; Kazuo Ishiguro publishes first novel, *A Pale View of the Hills*

1984
- *Money: A Suicide Note* published; marries Antonia Phillips; birth of son, Louis

1986
- *The Moronic Inferno and Other Visits to America* (twenty-seven essays and reviews on American subjects) published; spends summer vacations on Cape Cod; birth of son, Jacob
- * Kingsley Amis wins the Booker-McConnell Prize for *The Old Devils*

1987
- *Einstein's Monsters* (five stories and a polemical introduction) published

1988
- Begins work on *The Information*

1989
- *London Fields* published; fall: puts aside *The Information* to write *Time's Arrow*
- * The fall of the Berlin Wall, constructed in 1961, heralds the end of the Cold War

1991
- *Time's Arrow, or, The Nature of the Offence* published; shortlisted for the Booker Prize
- * Iraq's invasion of Kuwait leads to the Gulf War in which the USA and allies drive Iraq's occupying forces out of Kuwait

1992
- In Hollywood writing script (subsequently rejected) for film, *Mars Attacks*; begins affair with Isabel Fonseca
- * Bill Clinton elected US President (1992–2000)

1993
- Moves out of family home; visit to Antonia in Cape Cod fails to result in reconciliation; learns that cousin Lucy Partington had been murdered back in 1973; *Visiting Mrs. Nabokov and Other Excursions* (collection of occasional journalism) published

1994
- Undergoes reconstructive surgery on teeth and lower jaw in New York

1995
- Replaces Pat Kavanagh with an American agent, Andrew Wylie, to obtain large new advance; Julian Barnes breaks off friendship; *The Information* published; reunited with daughter, Delilah Seale; father dies

1996
- Birth of daughter, Fernanda

1997
- *Night Train* published
* Tony Blair becomes Prime Minister after his New Labour Party wins a landslide victory; Diana, Princess of Wales is killed in a car accident in Paris

1998
- Marries Isabel Fonseca in London; *Heavy Water and Other Stories* (nine stories dating from the 1970s to the 1990s) published

1999
- Birth of daughter, Clio; puts *Yellow Dog* aside to write two nonfiction books

2000
- *Experience: A Memoir* published; awarded the James Tait Black Memorial Prize
* George W. Bush elected President of the USA (2000–8)

2001
- *The War Against Cliché: Essays and Reviews, 1971–2000* published; wins the 2002 National Book Critics Circle Award; film of *Dead Babies* released; sister Sally dies; responds to terrorist attack of September 11 with first of many newspaper articles on Islamism, "Fear and Loathing"
* September 11: Islamic terrorist attacks on the World Trade Center, the Pentagon and a fourth plane hijacking in which, in addition to the nineteen hijackers, 2,974 people died; the beginning of the war in Afghanistan begins on 7 October with an aerial bombing campaign

2002
- *Koba the Dread: Laughter and the Twenty Million* (political memoir) published

2003
- *Yellow Dog* published
* On March 20, the USA and its allies launch the invasion and occupation of Iraq and the overthrow of Saddam Hussein (Second Gulf War)

2004
- *Vintage Amis* (a selection from his fiction and nonfiction) published; settles in beach house in Jose Ignacio, Uruguay for next two and a half years; "In the Palace of the End," story, published
* The terrorist bombings of the Madrid railways system occur on 11 March, resulting in 191 people killed and 2,050 wounded

2005
* Islamic terrorist bombings of London's transport system on 7 July result in fifty-two people losing their lives

2006
● "The Last Days of Mohammad Atta" (story) published. *House of Meetings* published; summer: returns to London

2007
● September: Takes up appointment as Professor of Creative Writing at the University of Manchester
* Tony Blair steps down and Gordon Brown becomes new Prime Minister of the Labour government

2008
* *The Second Plane: September 11: Terror and Boredom* (essays and two stories) published

# Bibliography

Ableman, Paul (1978) "Sub-Texts," *Spectator*, April 15, pp. 23–4.

—— (1981) "Fairies and Violence," *Spectator*, March 21, p. 22.

Acocella, Joan (2000) "Family Romance," *New Yorker*, June 19–26, p. 182.

—— (2007) "Prisoners: Russian Terrors Old and New," *New Yorker*, January 15, pp. 83–5.

Alexander, Victoria N. (1994) "Martin Amis: Between the Influences of Bellow and Nabokov," *Antioch Review*, 52 (4): pp. 580–90.

Althusser, Louis (1971) *Lenin and Philosophy and Other Essays*, trans. Ben Brewster, New York: Monthly Review Press.

Amidon, Stephen (1989) "Manipulation of Love and Death," *Financial Times*, September 23, p. 17.

Amis, Kingsley (1970) "He Was a Child and I Was a Child," *What Became of Jane Austen? And Other Questions*, London: Cape, 1070, pp. 77–85.

—— (1976) *Lucky Jim*, London and New York: Penguin.

—— (1991) *Memoirs*, New York: Summit/Simon & Schuster.

—— (2001) *The Letters of Kingsley Amis*, ed. Zachary Leader, New York: Hyperion.

Amis, Martin (1973a) "Coming in Handy" *New Statesman*, December 14, pp. 922–3.

—— [as "Henry Tilney"] (1973b) "Science Fiction," *Observer*, December 23, p. 23.

—— (1976) *It's Disgusting at Your Age, New Review*, September, pp. 19–24.

—— (1977) "My Oxford," in Ann Thwaite (ed.) *My Oxford*, London: Robson, pp. 203–13.

—— (1978) "Martin Amis," *New Review*, summer, p. 18.

—— (1980a) "The Sublime and the Ridiculous: Nabokov's Black Farces," in Peter Quennell (ed.), *Vladimir Nabokov: A Tribute*, New York: William Morrow, pp. 73–87.

—— (1980b) "A Tale of Two Novels," *Observer*, October 19, p. 26.

—— (1986) *Money: A Suicide Note*, London and New York: Penguin. First published 1984.

—— (1987) *The Moronic Inferno and Other Visits to America*, London and New York: Penguin. First published 1986.

—— (1990a) "Creepier than Thou," *Spectator*, October 5, p. 25.

—— (1990b) *Einstein's Monsters*, New York: Vintage International. First published 1987.

—— (1991a) *Dead Babies*, New York: Vintage International. First published 1975.

—— (1991b) *London Fields*, New York: Vintage International. First published 1989.

—— (1991c) *Success*, New York: Vintage International. First published 1978.

—— (1992a) "The Coming of the Signature," *Times Literary Supplement*, January 17, p. 18.

—— (1992b) *The Rachel Papers*, New York: Vintage International. First published 1973.

—— (1992c) *Time's Arrow, or, The Nature of the Offense*, New York: Vintage International. First published 1991.

—— (1994) *Other People: A Mystery Story*, New York: Vintage International. First published 1981.

—— (1995) *Visiting Mrs. Nabokov and Other Excursions*, New York: Vintage International. First published 1993.

—— (1996) *The Information*, New York: Vintage International. First published 1995.

—— (1997) "I Wish I'd Written," *Guardian*, October 2, p. T18.

—— (1998) *Night Train*, New York: Vintage International. First published 1997.

—— (2000a) *Experience: A Memoir*, New York: Hyperion/Talk Miramax.

—— (2000b) *Heavy Water and Other Stories*, New York: Vintage International. First published 1998.

—— (2001a) "Fear and Loathing," *Guardian*, September 18. Online. Available <http //www.guardian.co.uk/g2/story/0,3604,553584,00.html> (accessed July 13, 2007).

—— (2001b) "Sex in America," *Talk*, February, pp. 98–103, 133–5.

—— (2002a) "The Voice of the Lonely Crowd," *Guardian*, June 1, pp. 4–6.

—— (2002b) *The War Against Cliché: Essays and Reviews, 1971–2000*, New York: Vintage International. First published 2001.

—— (2003a) *Koba the Dread: Laughter and the Twenty Million*, New York: Vintage International. First published 2002.

—— (2003b) "The World: An Explanation," *Daily Telegraph*, March 8, p. 29.

—— (2004) *Yellow Dog*, New York: Vintage. First published 2003.

—— (2006a) "The Age of Horrorism: Faith and the Dependent Mind," *Observer*, September 10, pp. 4–10.

—— (2006b) *House of Meetings*, New York: Knopf.

—— (2006c) "The Last Days of Muhammad Atta," *New Yorker*, April 24, pp. 152–63.

—— (2007a) "Martin Amis: You Ask the Questions," *Independent*, January 15. Online. Available: <http://news.independent.co.uk/people/profiles/article 2154795.ece> (accessed July 12, 2007).

—— (2007b) "9/11 and the Cult of Death," *Times*, September 11. Online. Available <http://www.martinamisweb.com/commentary_files/911_ cultof death.pdf> (accessed October 15, 2007).

—— (2007c) "Why I'm Headed North," *Manchester Evening News*, February 16. Online. Available <http://www.manchestereveningnews.co.uk/news/ education/s/236/236441_martin_a_mis_why_im_headed_north.html> (accessed February 17, 2008).

—— (2008) *The Second Plane: September 11: Terror and Boredom*, London: Cape
Amis, Martin and Amis, Kingsley (1989) "Relative Values: Deux Amis," *Sunday Times Magazine*, December 3, pp. 11, 14.
Ashley, Leonard R. N. (1987) "'Names Are Awfully Important': The Onomastics of Satirical Comment in Martin Amis's *Money: A Suicide Note*," *Literary Onomastics Studies* 14: 1–48.
Baker, Robert S. (2005) "Kingsley Amis and Martin Amis: The Ironic Inferno of British Satire," *Contemporary Literature* 46 (3): pp. 544–54.
Baker, Simon (2006) "Back to Top Form," *Spectator*, September 30, pp. 51–2.
Banville, John (2006) "Books Of," *Irish Independent*, December 23, p. 1.
—— (2007) "Executioner Songs," *New York Review of Books*, March 1, pp. 14–17.
Barthes, Roland (1977) *Image—Music—Text*, trans. Stephen Heath, New York: Hill & Wang.
Basel, Marilyn K. (1989) "Amis, Martin (Louis)," *Contemporary Authors (New Revision Series)*, Vol. XXVII, pp. 19–22.
Battersby, Eileen (2006) "Eloquently Outraged Sorrow," *Irish Times*, October 14, p. 10.
Bauer, Justin (1999) "Interview," Philadelphia citypapernet. Online. Available: <http://www.citypaper.net/articles/021199/20q.shtml> (accessed July 19, 2007).
Bawer, Bruce (1987) "Martin Amis on America," *New Criterion*, 5 (2): pp. 20–6.
Begley, Jon (2004) "Satirizing the Carnival of Postmodern Capitalism: The Transatlantic and Dialogic Structure of Martin Amis's *Money*," *Contemporary Literature* 45 (1): pp. 79–105.
Bellante, Carl and Bellante, John (1992) "Unlike Father, Like Son," *Bloomsbury Review*, March 4–5, p. 16.
Bellow, Janis Freedman (1995) "Necropolis of the Heart," *Partisan Review*, 62 (4): pp. 699–718.
Bényei, Tamás (2006) "The Passion of John Self: Allegory, Economy, and Expenditure in Martin Amis's *Money*," in Gavin Keulks (ed.), *Martin Amis: Postmodernism and Beyond*, London and New York: Palgrave Macmillan, pp. 36–54.
Berman, Paul (2002) "A Million Deaths Is Not Just a Statistic," *New York Times Book Review*, July 28, p. 7.
Bernard, Catherine (1993) "Dismembering/Remembering Mimesis: Martin Amis, Graham Swift," in Theo D'Haen and Hans Bertens (eds), *British Postmodern Fiction*, Amsterdam and Atlanta, Ga.: Rodopi, pp. 121–44.
—— (2006) "Under the Dark Sun of Melancholia: Writing and Loss in *The Information*," in Gavin Keulks (ed.), *Martin Amis: Postmodernism and Beyond*, London and New York: Palgrave Macmillan, pp. 117–36.
Bigsby, Christopher (1992) "Martin Amis," in Malcolm Bradbury and Judy Cook (eds), *New Writing*, London: Minerva, pp. 169–84.
Bilmes, Alex (2006) "30 Things I've Learned About Terror," *Independent on Sunday*, October 8, p. 39.
Birnbaum, Robert (2003) "Martin Amis: Author of *Yellow Dog* Talks with Robert Birnbaum," identitytheory.com. Online. Available <http://www.identitytheory.com/interviews/birnbaum135.html> (accessed May 10, 2007).

Blades, John (1987) "A Literary Counterattack on Einstein's 'Monsters'," *Chicago Tribune*, June 11, p. 3.

Bloom, Harold (1975) *A Map of Misreading*, New York: Oxford University Press.

Brady, Thomas (1999) "'The Janitor on Mars' and Other Stories," *Philadelphia Inquirer*, February 14, p. H2.

Bragg, Melvyn (1989a) "Martin Amis," television broadcast, *South Bank Show*, London Weekend Television, September 17.

—— (1989b) "A Novel Experience," *Sunday Times*, December 17, p. C1.

Brockes, Emma (2003) "Even the Praise Is Bad for You," *Guardian*, August 29, Features, p. 2.

Brook, Susan (2006) "The Female Form, Sublimation, and Nicola Six," in Gavin Keulks (ed.), *Martin Amis: Postmodernism and Beyond*, London and New York: Palgrave Macmillan, pp. 87–100.

Brooks, Neil (2006) "'My Heart Really Goes Out to Me': The Self-Indulgent Highway to Adulthood in *The Rachel Papers*," in Gavin Keulks (ed.), *Martin Amis: Postmodernism and Beyond*, London and New York: Palgrave Macmillan, pp. 9–21.

Brown, Allan (2001) "Martin Amis: The Sunday Encounter: Laughter and Lost Daughters," *Scotland on Sunday*, October 28, p. 19.

Brown, Richard (1994) "Postmodern Americas in the Fiction of Angela Carter, Martin Amis and Ian McEwan," in Ann Massa and Alistair Stead (eds), *Forked Tongues? Comparing Twentieth Century British and American Literature*, London and New York: Longman, pp. 92–110.

Buchan, James (1991) "The Return of Dr Death," *Spectator*, September 28, pp. 37–8.

Buford, Bill (1980) "Introduction," *Granta*, March 1, pp. 7–16.

Butler, Judith (1993) *Bodies that Matter: On the Discursive Limits of "Sex,"* London and New York: Routledge.

—— (1997) *The Psychic Life of Power: Theories in Subjection*, London and New York: Routledge.

Byrne, Ciar (2007) "Eagleton Stirs Up the Campus with Attack on 'Racist' Amis and Son," *Independent*, October 4. Online. Available <http://news.independent.co.uk/uk/this_britain/article3024729.ece> (accessed October 15, 2007).

Byrne, Kevin (1974) "The Two Amises," *The Listener*, August 15, pp. 219–20.

Cash, William (1992) "Martian Amis," *Times Saturday Review*, August 1, pp. 4–5.

Charyn, Jerome (1976) Review of *Dead Babies*, *New York Times Book Review*, February 8, p. 3.

Childs, Peter (2005) *Contemporary Novelists: British Fiction since 1970*, London and New York: Palgrave Macmillan.

Connor, Steven (1996) *The English Novel in History 1950–1995*, London and New York: Routledge.

Cowley, Jason (2002) "Catastrophe Theories," *Observer*, September 8. Online. Available <http://observer.guardian.co.uk/review/story/0,6903,787928,00.html article_continue> (accessed July 19, 2007).

Curiel, Jonathan (2001) "Working with Words on All Fronts," *San Francisco Chronicle*, November 4, Sunday Review, p. 2.

Curtis, Nick (1995) "Cold Tones of Literary Retribution," *Financial Times*, March 25, Books, p. 8.

Cutter, Kimberley (2003) "Amis Amiss," *Women's Wear Daily*, October 21, p. 4.

Davis, Duane (2003) "Martin Amis Bares His Teeth in *Yellow Dog*," *Rocky Mountain News* (Denver), November 21, p. 27D.

De Curtis, Anthony (1991) "Britain's Mavericks," *Harper's Bazaar*, November, pp. 146–7.

Dern, John A. (2000) *Martians, Monsters and Madonna: Fiction and Form in the World of Martin Amis*, New York: Peter Lang.

Diedrick, James (1997) "From the Ridiculous to the Sublime: The Early Reception of *Night Train*," *Authors Review of Books*, November 16. Online. Available <http://www.martinamisweb.com/reviews.shtml#night_train> (accessed April 30, 2007).

—— (2004) *Understanding Martin Amis*, 2nd edn, Columbia, S.C.: University of South Carolina Press.

—— (2006) "J. G. Ballard's 'Inner Space" and the Early Fiction of Martin Amis," in Gavin Keulks (ed.), *Martin Amis: Postmodernism and Beyond*, London and New York: Palgrave Macmillan, pp. 180–96.

Doan, Laura L. (1990) "'Sexy Greedy Is the Late Eighties': Power Systems in Amis's *Money* and Churchill's *Serious Money*," *Minnesota Review*, 34–5: 69–80.

Doshi, Tishani (2002) "Laughter in the Dark," *Hindu Literary Review*, October 6. Online. Available <http://www.hinduonnet.com/thehindu/thscrip/print.pl?file= 2002100600090100.htm&date=2002/10/06/&prd=lr&> (accessed May 10, 2007).

Dougary, Jinny (2006) "The Voice of Experience," *Times Online*, September 17. Online. Available <http://www.ginnydougary.co.uk/2006/09/17/the-voice-of-experience/> (accessed July 13, 2007).

Douglas-Fairhurst, Robert (2003) "Dickens with a Snarl," *Observer*, August 24, Review, p. 15.

Drabble, Margaret (1976) Review of *Dead Babies*, *New York Times Book Review*, February 8, p. 2.

Dyer, Geoff (1993) "Down to the Serious Fun of Writing," *Manchester Guardian Weekly*, November 14, p. 28.

—— (2001) "Critical Velocity," *Guardian*, April 14, p. 10.

Edmondson, Elie A. (2001) "Martin Amis Writes Postmodern Man," *Critique: Studies in Contemporary Fiction*, 42 (2): 145–54.

Elias, Amy J. (1993) "Meta-*mimesis*? The Problem of British Postmodern Fiction," in Theo D'Haen and Hans Bertens (eds) *British Postmodern Fiction*, Amsterdam and Atlanta, Ga.: Rodopi, pp. 9–31.

Elias, Justine (2003) "Dirty Little Secrets," *Newsweek*, December 4. Online. Available <http://www.msnbc.msn.com/id/3637080/site/newsweek> (accessed July 2, 2007).

Ellison, Jane (1989) "Battle Fields," *Guardian*, October 12, p. 21.

Falconer, Rachel and Peter Hitchcock (1998) "Bakhtin's Chronotope and the Contemporary Short Story," *South Atlantic Quarterly*, 97 (3/4): pp. 699–732.

Finney, Brian (1995) "Narrative and Narrated Homicides in Martin Amis's *Other People* and *London Fields*," *Critique: Studies in Contemporary Fiction*, 37 (1): pp. 3–15.

—— (2006) "Martin Amis's *Time's Arrow* and the Postmodern Sublime," in Gavin Keulks (ed.), *Martin Amis: Postmodernism and Beyond*, London and New York: Palgrave Macmillan, pp. 101–16.

Fischer, Tibor (2003) "Someone Needs to Have a Word with Amis," *Daily Telegraph*, August 4, p. 18.

—— (2006) "It Is Time Martin Amis Wrote a Bona Fide Novel Again," *Sunday Telegraph*, October 1, p. 55.

Fremont-Smith, Eliot (1974) Review of *The Rachel Papers*, *New York Magazine*, April 29, p. 76.

Fuller, Graham (1987) "Yob Action," *Village Voice*, December 1, p. 66.

—— (1990) "Murder He Wrote: Martin Amis's *Killing Fields*," *Village Voice*, April 24, p. 75.

—— (1995) "The Pros and Cons of Martin Amis," Interview, May 5. Online. Available <http://findarticles.com/p/articles/mi_m1285/is_n5_v25/ai_ 16869725 > (accessed July 18, 2007).

Galef, David (2002) "The Importance of Being Amis, Revisited," *Southwest Review*, 87 (4): 554–64.

Ganteau, Jean-Michel (2006) "Violence Biting Its Own Tail: Martin Amis's *Yellow Dog*," in Alain-Philippe Durand and Naomi Mandel (eds), *Novels of the Contemporary Extreme*, London and New York: Continuum, pp. 132–42.

Genette, Gérard (1972) *Narrative Discourse: An Essay in Method*, trans. Jane E. Lewin, Ithaca, N.Y.: Cornell University Press.

Gerard, Jasper (2001) "Is There Still a Masterpiece in the Boy?" *Sunday Times*, April 15. Online. Available <http://www.lexisnexis.com/academic> (accessed March 26, 2007).

Gessen, Keith (2003) "Growing Up All Wrong," *Nation*, December 8, pp. 50–4.

Getlin, Josh (2007) "For Martin Amis, It's OK to Lose his Cool," *Los Angeles Times*, February 3, pp. E1, 16.

Glass, Charles (1995) "It's Best to Roll with the Big Cats," *Guardian*, January 10, p. 18.

Glaz, Adam (2006) "The Self in Time: Reversing the Irreversible in Martin Amis's *Time's Arrow*," *Journal of Literary Semantics*, 35 (2): 105–22.

Glendinning, Victoria (1981) "Lamb's Tale from Amis," *Listener*, March 5, pp. 319–20.

Goring, Rosemary (2006) "Still Life in the Old Dog," *Herald* (Glasgow), September 30, The Guide, p. 6.

Gross, John (1985) Review of *Money*, *New York Times*, March 15, p. C25.

Grossman, Lev (2007) "Q & A with Martin Amis," *Time*, February 5, p. 1.

Haffenden, John (1985) "Martin Amis," *Novelists in Interview*, London and New York: Methuen, pp. 1–24.

Hall, Stuart (1988) "The Toad in the Garden: Thatcherism among the Theorists," in Cary Nelson and Lawrence Grossberg (eds), *Marxism and the Interpretation of Culture*, Urbana and Chicago, Ill.: University of Illinois Press, pp. 35–57.

Hamilton, Ian (1984) "Martin and Martina," *London Review of Books*, September 20, October 3, pp. 3–4.

Harris, Greg (1999) "Men Giving Birth to New World Orders: Martin Amis's *Time's Arrow*," *Studies in the Novel*, 31 (4): 489–505.

Harrison, M. John (1991) "Speeding to Cradle from Grave," *Times Literary Supplement*, September 20, p. 21.

Hawkes, David (1997) "Martin Amis," in G. Stade and C. Howard (eds), *British Writers, Supplement IV*, New York: Scribner's, pp. 25–44.

Hayes, M. Hunter (2006) "A Reluctant Leavisite: Martin Amis's 'Higher Journalism,'" in Gavin Keulks (ed.), *Martin Amis: Postmodernism and Beyond*, London and New York: Palgrave Macmillan, pp. 197–210.

Heawood, Jonathan (2002) "The Books Interview: Martin Amis," *Observer*, September 8, Review Pages, p. 18.

Hensher, Philip (2001) "Nothing Matters More than Prose," *Spectator*, April 21, pp. 33–4.

—— (2003) "Treasures Buried in the Mud," *Spectator*, September 6, pp. 37–8.

Hitchens, Christopher (2000) "What Kingsley Amis Really Thought About that 'Little Shit' Martin," *Evening Standard*, May 8, p. 10.

—— (2002) "Don't. Be. Silly.," *Guardian*, September 4, G2, p. 6.

Hoare, Philip (1991) "Martin Amis," *Details*, November, pp. 132–3.

Hollinghurst, Alan (2003) "Leader of the Pack," *Guardian*, September 6, Saturday Pages, p. 9.

Holmes, Frederick (1996) "The Death of the Author as Cultural Critique in *London Fields*," in Ricardo Miguel Alonso (ed.), *Powerless Fictions? Ethics, Cultural Critique, and American Fiction in the Age of Postmodernism*, Amsterdam and Atanta, Ga.: Rodopi, pp. 53–62.

Howard, Elizabeth Jane (2003) *Slipstream: A Memoir*, London: Pan Macmillan.

Hubbard, Kim (1990) "Novelist Martin Amis Carries on a Family Tradition," *People Weekly*, 33 (16): 117–18.

Hunter-Tilney, Ludovic (2003) "Gr8 Expectations Even When Off-Form," *Financial Times*, September 6, p. 26.

Joffe, Phil (1995) "Language Damage: Nazis and Naming in Martin Amis's *Time's Arrow*," *Nomina Africana: Journal of the Names Society of South Africa* 9 (2): 1–10.

Jones, Lewis (2001) "The Living V-Sign," *Telegraph* (London), January 26. Online. Available <http://www.telegraph.co.uk/health/main.jhtml?xml=/ health/ 2001/01/26/ tlamis26.xml> (accessed January 9, 2007).

—— (2003) "Surrounded by Broken Myths," *Daily Telegraph*, August 30, p. 8.

Jones, Russell Celyn (1998) "Not Such Light Reading," *Times*, September 24, p. 40.

Jones, Tony (2006) "Tony Jones Speaks to Martin Amis," *Lateline*, Australian Broadcasting Corporation, November 1. Online. Available <http://www.abc. net.au/lateline/content/2006/s1779157.htm> (accessed July 11, 2007).

Jordan, Clive (1974) "Review of *The Rachel Papers*," *Encounter*, February, pp. 61, 64.

Kakutani, Michiko (1995) "Raging Midlife Crisis as Contemporary Ethos," *New York Times*, May 2, p. C17.

—— (2000) "For Writers, Father and Son, Out of Conflict Grew Love," *New York Times*, May 23, p. E1.

—— (2002) "Recounting the Suffering of Russia Under Stalin," *New York Times*, June 26, p. E9.

—— (2003) "Women May Be from Venus, but Men Are from Hunger," *New York Times*, October 28, p. E1.

—— (2007) "Love, Bludgeoned and Bent by the Camps," *New York Times*, January 9, p. E1.

Kaveney, Roz (1995) "Energy and Entropy," *New Statesman and Society*, March 24, p. 24.

Kemp, Peter (2003) "A Burnt-Out Case," *Sunday Times*, August 31, p. 41.

Kennedy, Douglas (2006) "Past Troubles Bleed into Present Horrors," *Times*, September 30, Features, Books, p. 5.

Kermode, Frank (1991) "In Reverse," *London Review of Books*, September 12, p. 11.

—— (2001) "Nutmegged," *London Review of Books*, May 10, pp. 27–8.

Keulks, Gavin (2003) *Father and Son: Kingsley Amis, Martin Amis, and the British Novel since 1950*, Madison, Wisc.: University of Wisconsin Press.

—— (2006) "W(h)ither Postmodernism: Late Amis," in Gavin Keulks (ed.), *Martin Amis: Postmodernism and Beyond*, Houndmills: Palgrave Macmillan, pp. 158–79.

Korn, Eric (1984) "Frazzled Yob-Gene Lag-Jag," *Times Literary Supplement*, October 5, p. 1119.

Kristeva, Julia (1986) *The Kristeva Reader*, ed. Toril Moi, New York: Columbia University Press.

Kroll, Jack (1990) "London Town Is Falling Down," *Newsweek*, March 5, p. 62.

Lanchester, John (1987) "As a Returning Lord," *London Review of Books*, May 7, pp. 11–12.

—— (2000) "Be Interesting," *London Review of Books*, July 6, pp. 3, 5–6.

LaRose, Nicole (2005) "Reading *The Information* on Martin Amis's London," *Critique: Studies in Contemporary Fiction* 46 (2): 160–76.

Laurence, Alexander and McGee, Kathleen (1995) "Martin Amis Is Getting Old and Wants to Talk About It," *The Write Stuff (Interviews)*. Online. Available <http://www.altx.com/int2/martin.amis.html> (accessed February 12, 2007).

Lee, Hermione (1993) "Bad Habits in Good Company," *Independent*, October 3, Sunday Review, p. 40.

Lehman, David (1991) "From Death to Birth," *New York Times Book Review*, November 17, p. 15.

Lehmann, Chris (2007) "The Bard of Brash," *Radar*, February 16. Online. Available <http://radaronline.com/features/2007/02/martin_amis_1.php> (accessed July 16, 2007).

Levin, Bernard (1981) "Forgetfulness of Things Past," *Sunday Times*, March 8, p. 43.

Lifton, Robert Jay (2000) *The Nazi Doctors: Medical Killing and the Psychology of Genocide*, New York: Basic Books. First published 1986.

Lodge, David (1992) "The Novelist Today: Still at the Crossroads?" in Malcolm Bradbury and Judy Cooke (eds), *New Writing*, London: Minerva, pp. 203–15.

Loose, Julian (1995) "Satisfaction," *London Review of Books*, May 11, pp. 9–10.

Lyall, Sarah (2003) "For a British Novelist, Tornadoes in August," *New York Times*, August 26, p. E1.

Lyotard, Jean-François (1984) *The Postmodern Condition: A Report on Knowledge*, trans. Geoff Bennington and Brian Massumi. Minneapolis, Minn.: University of Minnesota Press.

McCarthy, Dermot (1999) "The Limits of Irony: The Chronillogical World of Martin Amis's *Time's Arrow*," *War, Literature and the Arts* 11 (1): 294–320.

McGrath, Patrick (1987) "Interview with Martin Amis," in Betty Sussler (ed.), *BOMB Interviews*, 1992, San Francisco, Calif.: City Light Books, pp. 187–97.

—— (1998) "Her Long Goodbye," *New York Times Book Review*, February 1, p. 6.

MacSweeney, Eve (1990) "Amis Behavin'," *Harper's Bazaar*, 123 (3340): pp. 200, 222.

Maczynska, Magdalena (2004) "Writing the Writer: The Question of Authorship in the Novels of Martin Amis," in Michael J. Meyer (ed.), *Literature and the Writer*, Amsterdam and Atlanta, Ga.: Rodopi, pp. 191–207.

Malvern, Jack (2002) "Amis Aims Below the Belt in Attack on Islam," *Times*, October 21, Home News, p. 3.

Marcus, James (2007) "History Made Him Do It," *Los Angeles Times*, January 14, p. R3.

Mars-Jones, Adam (1987) "Fireworks at the Funeral," *Times Literary Supplement*, May 1, p. 457.

—— (1990) *Venus Envy*, London: Chatto and Windus.

—— (1995) "Looking on the Blight Side," *Times Literary Supplement*, March 24, pp. 19–20.

—— (1998) "Books—What Big Boys are Made of," *Observer*, October 11, p. 14.

Matthews, David (2003) "Beyond the Porn, Amis Goes Slack," *Weekend Australian*, September 6, p. B27.

Mellors, John (1976) "Raw Breakfast," *Listener*, October 30, p. 582.

Menke, Richard (1998) "Narrative Reversals and the Thermodynamics of History in Martin Amis's *Time's Arrow*," *Modern Fiction Studies* 44 (4): 959–80.

—— (2006) "Mimesis and Informatics in *The Information*," in Gavin Keulks (ed.), *Martin Amis: Postmodernism and Beyond*, London and New York: Palgrave Macmillan, pp. 137–57.

Michener, Charles (1986) "Britain's Brat of Letters," *Esquire*, January, pp. 108–11.

Miller, Karl (1985) *Doubles: Studies in Literary History*, Oxford and New York: Oxford University Press.

—— (2000) "A Feast at the Amis Table," *Herald* (Glasgow), May 25, p. 14.

Mills, Sara (1995) "Working with Sexism: What Can Feminist Text Analysis Do?' in Peter Verdonk and Jean Jacques Weer (eds), *Twentieth Century Fiction: From Text to Context*, London and New York: Routledge, pp. 206–19.

Miracky, James J. (2003) "Hope Lost or Hyped Lust? Gendered Representations in 1980s Britain in Margaret Drabble's *The Radiant Way* and Martin Amis's *Money*," *Critique*, 44 (2): 136–43.

Moore, Geoffrey (1986) "Amis Scores a Hit," *Financial Times*, July 26, p. 14.

Moran, Joe (2000) "Artists and Verbal Mechanics: Martin Amis's *The Information*," *Critique: Studies in Contemporary Fiction*, 41 (4): 307–17.

Morrison, Blake (1973) "Nice and Nasty," *Times Literary Supplement*, November 16, p. 1389.

Morrison, Susan (1990) "The Wit and Fury of Martin Amis," *Rolling Stone*, May 17, pp. 95–102.

Moseley, Merritt (2005) "Amis, Father and Son," in Brian W. Shaffer (ed.), *A Companion to the British and Irish Novel 1945–2000*, Oxford: Blackwell, pp. 302–13.

Moss, Stephen (1998) "After the Storm," *Guardian*, October 3, p. 22.

Motion, Andrew (1993) *Philip Larkin: A Writer's Life*, New York: Farrar, Straus, Giroux.

Moyle, David (1995) "Beyond the Black Hole: The Emergence of Science Fiction Themes in the Recent Work of Martin Amis," *Extrapolation*, 36 (4): 305–15.

Muir, Kate (2003) "After His Crucifixion over *Yellow Dog*," *Times Magazine*, September 13, p. 9.

Nakanishi, Wendy Jones (2006) "Nihilism or Nonsense? The Postmodern Fiction of Martin Amis and Haruki Murakami," *Electronic Journal of Contemporary Japanese Studies*, May 8. Online. Available <http://www.japanesestudies. org.uk/discussionpapers/2006/Nakanishi2.html> (accessed June 28, 2007).

Nash, John (1996) "Fiction May Be a Legal Paternity: Martin Amis's *The Information*," *English*, 45 (183): 213–24.

Naughtie, James (2001) *BBC Bookclub*, August 5. Online. Available <http://www.bbc.co.uk/radio4/arts/bookclub/bookclub_list.shtml> (accessed July 3, 2007).

Oertel, Daniel (2001) "Effects of Garden-Pathing in Martin Amis's Novels *Time's Arrow* and *Night Train*," *Miscelánea: A Journal of English and American Studies*, 22: 123–40.

Orr, Deborah (2000) "England is Great," *Independent*, May 19, p. 7.

Padhi, Shanti (1982) "Bed and Bedlam: The Hard-Core Extravaganzas of Martin Amis," *The Literary Half-Yearly*, 23 (1): 36–42.

Parini, Jay (1987) "Men Who Hate Women," *New York Times Book Review*, September 6, p. 8.

Parker, Emma (2006) "Money Makes the Man: Gender and Sexuality in Martin Amis's *Money*," in Gavin Keulks (ed.), *Martin Amis: Postmodernism and Beyond*, London and New York: Palgrave Macmillan, pp. 55–70.

Paulin, Tom (1978) "Fantastic Eschatologies," *Encounter*, September 3, pp. 73–8.

Pesetsky, Bette (1990) "Lust Among the Ruins," *New York Times Book Review*, March 4, pp. 1, 42.

Phillips, Adam (1997) "Cloud Cover," *London Review of Books*, October 16, pp. 3, 6–7.

Piatek, Beata (2004) "'Bullshit TV Conversations' or Intertextuality in *Night Train*," in Zygmunt Mazur and Richard Utz (eds), *Homo Narrans: Texts and Essays in Honor of Jerome Klinkowitz*, Kraków: Jagiellonian University Press, pp. 157–73.

Porlock, Harvey (1997) "Critical List," *Sunday Times* (London), September 28, 8 p.2.

Powell, Neil (1981) "What Life Is: The Novels of Martin Amis," *PN Review* 20, 7 (6): 42–5.

Power, Carla (2000) "Growing Up with Kingsley," *Newsweek*, June 26, p. 66.

Price, James (1976) Review of *Dead Babies*, *Encounter*, February, p. 68.

Profumo, David, (1987) "Interview: David Profumo Drops in on Martin Amis," *Literary Review*, 107: pp. 41–2.

Prose, Francine (1994) "Novelist at Large," *New York Times Book Review*, February 27, p. 17.

Publishers Weekly (2003) "Yellow Dog," *Publishers Weekly Reviews*, October 13, 55.

Pulver, Andrew (2001) "You Lying Hippies," *Guardian*, January 23, Features, p. 14.

Ratcliffe, Michael (1995) "What Little Boys Are Made Of," *Observer*, March 26, p. 17.

Rawson, Claude (1981) "Claude Rawson Considers the Behaviour of Reviewers," *London Review of Books*, May 7–20, pp. 19–22.

Reynolds, Margaret, and Jonathan Noakes (eds) (2003) *Martin Amis: The Essential Guide*, London: Vintage.

Richards, Linda (2000) "January Experiences Martin Amis," *January Magazine*. Online. Available <http://www.januarymagazine.com/profiles/amis.html> (accessed July 19, 2007).

Riviere, Francesca (1998) "Martin Amis," *Paris Review*, 40 (146): 108–35.

Ross, Jean W. (1989) "CA Interview," *Contemporary Authors, New Revision Series*, Vol. XXVII, Farmington Mills, Mich.: Thomson Gale, pp. 23–5.

Scott, A. O. (1999) "Trans-Atlantic Flights," *New York Times Book Review*, January 31, p. 5.

Scruton, Roger (1991) "International Books of the Year," *Times Literary Supplement*, December 13, p. 12.

Self, Will (1993a) "An Interview with Martin Amis," *Mississippi Review*, October, pp. 143–69.

—— (1993b) "Something Amiss in Amis Country," *Esquire: British Edition*, April, pp. 70–6.

Service, Robert (2002) "How Uncle Joe Hoodwinked the West," *Sunday Times* (London), August 25, Features, p. 33.

Sexton, David (1995) "Marty in His Middle Age," *Guardian*, March 28, p. T6.

Shnayerson, Michael (1995) "Famous Amis," *Vanity Fair*, May, pp. 133–40, 160–2.

Shriver, Lionel (2006) "When Boredom Is a Violent Emotion," *Daily Telegraph*, October 7, p. 26.

Silva-Campañón, Carlos (2004) "Through the Looking Glass: America in Martin Amis's *Money: A Suicide Note*," *Atlantis* (Salamanca, Spain), 26 (2): 87–96.

Silverblatt, Michael (2007) "Interview with Martin Amis," radio broadcast, *KCRW*, February 15.

Sissman, L. E. (1974) "Miss, Near Miss, Hit," *New Yorker*, June 24, p. 102.

Smith, Amanda (1985) "Martin Amis," *Publishers Weekly*, February 8, pp. 78–9.

Smith, Penny (1995) "Hell Innit: The Millennium in Alasdair Gray's *Lanark*, Martin Amis's *London Fields*, and Shena Mackay's *Dunedin*," *Essays and Studies*, 48: 115–28.

Soar, Daniel (2007) "Bile, Blood, Bilge, Mulch," *London Review of Books*, January 4, pp. 14–17.

Stead, Deborah (1990) "The Planet as Murder Victim," *New York Times Book Review*, March 4, p. 42.

Stokes, Peter (1997) "Martin Amis and the Postmodern Suicide: Tracing the Postnuclear Narrative at the Fin de Millénium," *Critique: Studies in Contemporary Fiction*, 38 (4): pp. 300–11.

Stout, Mira (1990) "Down London's Mean Streets," *New York Times Magazine*, February 4, pp. 32–6, 48.

Summerscale, Kate (2007) "Martin Amis Leaps Back into the Ring," *Telegraph*, October 15. Online. Available <http://www.telegraph.co.uk/news/main.jhtml?xml= /news/ 2007/10/13/namis113.xml> (accessed October 21, 2007).

Sutherland, John (2001) "Dead Babies, Sick Jokes," *Guardian*, May 2, Features, p. 6.

Szamuely, George (1990) "Something Amiss with Martin," *National Review*, May 28, pp. 46–8.

Thomas, Susie (2003) "Posing as a Postmodernist: Race and Class in Martin Amis's *London Fields*," *Literary London: Interdisciplinary Studies in the Representation of London*, 1 (2). Online. Available <http://www.literarylondon.org./londonjournal/september2003/thomas.html> (accessed December 10, 2007).

Thomson, David (1998) "Martin Amis," *Dictionary of Literary Biography*, Vol. 194, Asheville, N.C.: University of North Carolina Press/Gale Group, pp. 7–18.

Thubron, Colin (2002) "Martin Versus Stalin," *Times*, September 4, Features p. 11.

Todd, Richard (1990) "The Intrusive Author in British Postmodern Fiction: The Cases of Alasdair Gray and Martin Amis," in Matei Calinescu and Douwe Fokkema (eds), *Exploring Postmodernism*, Amsterdam and Philadelphia, Pa.: John Benjamins, pp. 123–37.

—— (2006) "Looking-Glass Worlds in Martin Amis's Early Fiction," in Gavin Keulks (ed.), *Martin Amis: Postmodernism and Beyond*, Basingstoke: Palgrave Macmillan, pp. 22–35.

Tredell, Nicholas (ed.) (2000) *The Fiction of Martin Amis*, Basingstoke: Palgrave Macmillan.

Trueheart, Charles (1991) "Through a Mirror Darkly," *Washington Post*, November 26, pp. B1–2.

Ungless, Janet (1995) "Viewpoints," *Newsday*, May 9, p. A35.

Verrier, Luc (2005) "Inevitable Yet Impossible Impersonality: Martin Amis's *The Information*," in Christine Reynier and Jean-Michel Ganteau (eds), *Impersonality and Emotion in Twentieth-Century British Literature*, Montpellier: Université Montpellier III, pp. 273–85.

Wachtel, Eleanor (1996) "Eleanor Wachtel with Martin Amis," *Malahat Review*, 114: 43–58.

Wagner, Erica (2003) "Tiring Old Tricks," *Times*, September 3, p. 18.

Walden, George (2003) "Back to Blighty," *New Statesman*, September 8, pp. 48–50.

Walsh, John (2003) "Twilight of the Idol? The Knives Are Out for Martin Amis," *Independent*, August 15, pp. 2–3.

—— (2006) "Go and Make Some Coffee, John," *Independent*, June 27, Features, p. 7.

Walter, Natasha (1997) "Dark Side of the Tracks," *Guardian Weekly*, September 28, p. 29.

Ward, David (1996) "A Black Comedy of Manners," *Virginia Quarterly Review*, 72(3): 561–4.

Weich, Dave (2003) "Old Martin Amis Is in Your Face Again," Powells.com. Online. Available <http://www.powells.com/aut hors/amis.html> (accessed February 19, 2007).

Wilson, Jonathan (1995) "A Very English Story," *New Yorker*, March 6, pp. 96–106.

Wood, James (2000) "Fearful Symmetry of Father and Son," *Guardian*, May 20, p. 8.

# Index